Moving Out, Moving On

Based on rich interview data drawn from a large-scale longitudinal study of homeless young people, this book examines the personal, familial and structural factors that impact on homeless young people's long-term outcomes. While telling the personal stories of young people's experiences, the book refers to the wider research and policy literature on youth homelessness, engaging with key debates about the causes and meanings of homelessness in western societies. The book addresses important issues such as employment and education, engagement with services, social support, connection to family and friends, as well as personal factors including physical and mental health, sexual practices and drug use.

Homeless young people are typically portrayed as leading chaotic, risky lives, trapped in a downward spiral of drug use, mental and other health problems, and long-term homelessness. By giving voice to young homeless people, the book challenges this stereotype and demonstrates young people's capacity to move out of homelessness and make satisfactory lives for themselves.

Research findings are positioned in the context of a broad, international literature on youth homelessness and this book is important reading for undergraduate and postgraduate students of psychology, sociology, youth and social work, as well as researchers, policymakers and service providers in all western cultures.

Shelley Mallett is an anthropologist. For the last decade her research has focused on the health, well-being and pathways to employment, education and training of young people experiencing disadvantage. She is currently the General Manager of Research and Social Policy at Melbourne Citymission. She is also an Honorary Senior Lecturer at the Key Centre for Women's Health at the University of Melbourne.

Doreen Rosenthal is a developmental psychologist. She was Founding Director of the Australian Research Centre in Sex, Health and Society and most recently Professor of Women's Health and Director, Key Centre for Women's Health in Society at the University of Melbourne. In 2003 she was made an Officer in the Order of Australia for her services to adolescent research and policy. She is now Professor Emeritus at the University of Melbourne.

Deborah Keys is a sociologist with extensive research experience in the field of youth homelessness, particularly motherhood and homelessness among young women. She is currently a Senior Research Officer at Melbourne Citymission.

Roger Averill is a freelance writer, researcher and editor. His PhD was on sociological interpretations of biography. He recently published a memoir, *Boy He Cry: An Island Odyssey* and has a novel scheduled for publication in 2010.

Adolescence and Society

Series editor: John C. Coleman

Department of Education, University of Oxford

This series has now been running for over 20 years, and during this time has published some of the key texts in the field of adolescent studies. The series has covered a very wide range of subjects, almost all of them being of central concern to students, researchers and practitioners. A mark of the success of the series is that a number of books have gone to second and third editions, illustrating the popularity and reputation of the series.

The primary aim of the series is to make accessible to the widest possible readership important and topical evidence relating to adolescent development. Much of this material is published in relatively inaccessible professional journals, and the objective of the books in this series has been to summarize, review and place in context current work in the field, so as to interest and engage both an undergraduate and a professional audience.

The intention of the authors has always been to raise the profile of adolescent studies among professionals and in institutions of higher education. By publishing relatively short, readable books on topics of current interest to do with youth and society, the series makes people more aware of the relevance of the subject of adolescence to a wide range of social concerns.

The books do not put forward any one theoretical viewpoint. The authors outline the most prominent theories in the field and include a balanced and critical assessment of each of these. Whilst some of the books may have a clinical or applied slant, the majority concentrate on normal development.

The readership rests primarily in two major areas: the undergraduate market, particularly in the fields of psychology, sociology and education; and the professional training market, with particular emphasis on social work, clinical and educational psychology, counselling, youth work, nursing and teacher training.

Also available in this series:

Moving Out, Moving On
Young People's Pathways In and
Through Homelessness

Shelley Mallett, Doreen Rosenthal,
Deborah Keys and Roger Averill

Routledge
Taylor & Francis Group

LONDON AND NEW YORK

Published in 2010
by Routledge
27 Church Road, Hove, East Sussex BN3 2FA

Simultaneously published in the USA and Canada
by Routledge
270 Madison Avenue, New York, NY 10016

*Routledge is an imprint of the Taylor & Francis Group, an Informa
business*

Copyright © 2010 Psychology Press

Typeset in Times by Garfield Morgan, Swansea, West Glamorgan
Printed and bound in Great Britain by TJ International Ltd, Padstow,
Cornwall
Cover design by Hybert Design

This publication has been produced with paper manufactured to strict
environmental standards and with pulp derived from sustainable
forests.

British Library Cataloguing in Publication Data
A catalogue record for this book is available from the British Library

Library of Congress Cataloging-in-Publication Data
Moving out, moving on: young people's pathways in and through
homelessness / Shelley Mallett . . . [*et al.*].
    p. cm.
    Includes bibliographical references and index.
    ISBN 978-0-415-47029-2 (hb) – ISBN 978-0-415-47030-8 (soft
cover) 1. Homeless youth. 2. Homelessness. I. Mallett, Shelley, 1960-
    HV4493.M68 2010
    362.7086'942–dc22
                                                    2009023304

ISBN: 978-0-415-47029-2 (Hbk)
ISBN: 978-0-415-47030-8 (Pbk)

We dedicate this book to the young people
whose stories it tells.

Contents

Acknowledgements

The research that led to this book involved the participation and support of many people and organizations. First, we thank the young people who enthusiastically participated in the study, often when their lives were in turmoil. Their life stories humble, challenge and inspire us.

Workers from services across metropolitan Melbourne referred young people to our study. Without their support and enthusiasm for the research we could not have undertaken this project. We thank them for their assistance and acknowledge their skill, dedication, passion and commitment to making a positive difference in young people's lives.

We had a committed research team working on this project. This included: Ben Rossiter, Paul Myers, Judy Edwards, Alina Turner, Rosie Finn, Colleen Hall, Tracey O'Hagan, Jen Hamilton, Jen Johnson, Liz Jones, Shon Klose, Jaquie Mayne, Annie Paliwal and Vicki Wells.

The Council to Homeless Persons (CHP) provided invaluable support for the research, particularly Deb Tsorbaris and David Wright-Howie. Peter Lake of the Victorian Office of Housing also provided great support to the project, as did Claire Nyblom at Melbourne Citymission. We are grateful for their insights and assistance.

The research for this book emerged from a collaboration between the Key Centre for Women's Health in Society at the University of Melbourne and the Center for Community Health at the University of California, Los Angeles (UCLA). Our collaborators at UCLA were Norweeta G. Milburn and Mary Jane Rotheram-Borus. We are particularly grateful for the support of Mary Jane Rotheram-Borus, whose knowledge of the field greatly enhanced our endeavours.

We are grateful to the National Institute of Mental Health (United States) who funded *Project i* (grant number MH61185).

1 Introduction

> I wouldn't change what's happened now, being honest, everything's
> happened to me for a reason, and I've learnt to deal with it now . . .
> learning to persevere has been the hardest thing to do, to keep my head
> held high and know that I am someone important and I have just as much
> to offer to everyone as a normal child who has come through a normal
> house with normal parents.
>
> (Imogen)

Homeless young people are typically portrayed as leading chaotic,
risky lives, trapped in a downward spiral of drug use, mental and
other health problems, and long-term homelessness. In this book,
based on a longitudinal study conducted in Melbourne, Australia,
called *Project i*, we challenge this stereotype through an examination
of young people's pathways into and through homelessness. We
describe the complexity of their pathways and identify the factors
that make a difference to their lives and especially their capacity to
exit homelessness. Remarkably, at the end of two years many young
people in our study had found a secure home base. However, others
were still grappling with structural, familial and personal impediments
that left them unable to shift from their marginalized circumstances.

In asking who becomes homeless and why, we recognize that
homelessness affects young people from many backgrounds and
diverse experiences. We look at the reasons why young people leave
home, their experiences while homeless, and their long-term outcomes. We take note of the structural factors that create environments
in which homelessness occurs and is accepted. The book focuses on
what happens to young people when they become homeless, what they
do to get by, who they relate to and how all these, together, impact
on their long-term outcomes. We take account of issues such as
employment and education, engagement with services, social support,

connection to family and friends, as well as personal factors including physical and mental health and drug use.

To answer our questions, we use extensive survey data but, importantly, give voice to young people through interviews that allow them to frame their experiences in their own words. Some young people told us stories that highlight escape from abusive or chaotic homes; others told positive stories about a journey towards a better understanding of themselves – and sometimes their families. The stories remind us that although many young people experiencing homelessness act in ways that put their health and well-being at risk, the vast majority of them survive. More than this, many discover a positive way forward for their lives. As Emma puts it at the end of her interview, 'I'm surprised I never died. I'm here. I'm off the drugs and my life's worth living.'

Who are homeless?

As we discuss in Chapter 2, multiple definitions of homelessness exist, ranging from a literal view that people are homeless only when they lack shelter, that is, 'rooflessness', to broader definitions that include those who have unstable or substandard forms of shelter. This latter approach may include, as a key criterion, a person's experience of the adequacy of their housing. One of the other key ways to understand homelessness is in relation to the meaning of home. For young people, home does not only mean a physical place; it is understood as a place where one feels connected, wanted and supported. Young people emphasized similar issues in their definitions of homelessness. Most understood it as much more than an absence of shelter; to be homeless is also the absence of caring, love or belonging (Crane and Brannock, 1996).

The way in which we define homelessness is important for many purposes, from specifying boundaries or criteria for development of policy and the provision of services to recruiting participants into research projects (Neil and Fopp, 1992; Crane and Brannock, 1996). Equally, definitions of homelessness impact directly on how we perceive the extent of this population.

How many homeless young people?

A range of data sources is used to estimate the number of homeless young people in any given location. These include point-in-time census data and survey data, and routinely collected service delivery data from services and agencies, such as homelessness services and government income providers. In Australia, service delivery data can provide alternative measures to census data by assessing the numbers of young people who receive assistance from relevant services and agencies and who are thus considered homeless. One issue with these types of data is that they only include those who received support from the service or agency and not those who were declined assistance or who did not seek support. Hence, there are likely to be underestimates.

Differences in data sources, together with differing definitions of homelessness and the dynamic nature of homelessness, mean that accurate numbers of young people experiencing homelessness cannot be determined and it is not possible to make meaningful comparisons of the prevalence of homelessness between countries. It is generally recognized that there exists a hidden population of youth experiencing, or at risk of, homelessness who do not access youth homelessness services and may not be captured in census data, a commonly used index of prevalence. Furthermore, in the USA, a distinction is made between homeless and runaway youth, although it is recognized that both groups of young people share similar experiences and vulnerabilities and indeed overlap.

The difficulties in precisely defining homelessness and thus obtaining accurate figures about the extent of this problem are highlighted by the conflicting data emerging from some western countries. A UK-wide review of youth homelessness found that the number of young people 'accepted as homeless' had remained constant over the last decade in Scotland and Northern Ireland; however, it had fallen in England and Wales (Quilgars *et al.*, 2008). Similar decreases have been shown in Dublin (Maycock *et al.*, 2008) and in Australia (Chamberlain and Mackenzie, 2008).

Leading risky lives?

Most of the research with homeless youth has concentrated on the difficulties and problems associated with homelessness. Key areas of concern include drug and alcohol use, physical and mental health, sexual practices and sexual health and violence and victimization. Young people who are homeless do have poorer health and well-being, higher levels of substance use and are at greater risk of contracting sexually transmitted infections (STIs) and experiencing victimization. Understanding these risks and dangers associated with homelessness is a fundamental step in supporting young people who find themselves without a home. However, as Zerger *et al.* (2008) acknowledge, the research tends to focus on individual-level risk and protective factors which 'detracts from the structural issues that have shaped these individuals' experiences in the first place and are key to resolving them' (Zerger *et al.*, 2008: 824). A focus on individual risk behaviours can not only preclude attention being directed to the structural factors that contribute to homelessness, but also result in youth being defined in terms of personal deficiencies (Bender *et al.*, 2007). Recent research on social supports is part of a wider shift of emphasis to a consideration of how young people survive and protect themselves on the street and how they move out of homelessness. It is important to note that most research is cross-sectional in nature, or at best follows young people's lives for short periods of time. Given the fluid nature of homelessness, even pathways approaches as currently employed can only illuminate relatively short periods in the lives of young people who experience homelessness. We cannot assume their situations at the close of the research periods will remain static, whether they are homeless or in homes.

Why leave home?

The many and diverse reasons given by young people for leaving home are usually couched in 'crisis' terms. Family environment is a major theme, generally described in terms of family conflict (see, for example, Ennett *et al.*, 1999; Ringwalt *et al.*, 1998), or sexual, physical or emotional abuse by family members (Ennett *et al.*, 1999; Lanyon *et al.*, 1999; Pears and Noller, 1995; Rew *et al.*, 2001; Rotheram-Borus *et al.*, 1996a; Whitbeck *et al.*, 1997a; Whitbeck and Simons, 1993).

Other reasons for leaving home appear less consistently. These include: personal drug use; school problems; sexual identity; neglect; drug or alcohol problems of a family member; family structure; family housing instability; and traumatic life events, for example, the death of a parent (de Man *et al.*, 1993; Rew *et al.*, 2001; Ringwalt *et al.*, 1998; Weiner and Pollack, 1997; Whitbeck and Simons, 1993). A handful of studies have reported personal drug use as a reason young people leave home, with the percentage of users citing this as a reason ranging from 9 per cent to 37 per cent (Rew *et al.*, 2001). This is interesting given the high rates of reported drug use among this population, estimated to be almost three to four times more prevalent than among non-homeless young people (Bailey *et al.*, 1998; Baron, 1999). These findings beg the question of which comes first, drug use or homelessness. We investigated this issue in a brief qualitative interview with more than 300 homeless young people who were part of our longitudinal study. We found some left home because of their own or parents' drug use, usually associated with conflict, whereas others initiated drug use after they became homeless. These findings highlight the importance of taking more than a single snapshot of young people's experiences, but rather following these experiences over time (Mallett *et al.*, 2005).

Some US researchers have described young people as 'running from' fractured and turbulent homes. This has been contrasted with reasons associated with 'running to', reported by a small minority of young people who initially leave home to assert independence, escape boredom, seek excitement or because of the allure of the street (Ennett *et al.*, 1999; Whitbeck and Simons, 1993). Whereas US studies emphasize the behaviour of the young people in family conflict, some British studies have gone beyond this to focus on family type and its impact on home leaving. For example, Smith *et al.* (1998) found that young people experiencing homelessness in London, came from two broad family types. Those who left stable families/stepfamilies were likely to have left because of their own practices – drugs, crime and/ or choice of boyfriends. In contrast, young people who had left disrupted families with a history of separation, family breakdown and recent stepparenting relationships were most likely to have left due to conflict.

Information about the reasons Australian young people leave home is based to a large extent on small-scale, service-initiated studies but is consistent with other literature in representing young people as 'running from' problematic family environments (see, for example, Lanyon *et al.*, 1999; Powers *et al.*, 1989; Robson, 1992). In our own work we have shown conflict with parents to be the most important reason for leaving, but a substantial number of young people nominated their desire for independence and/or adventure as the main impetus for leaving home (Rosenthal *et al.*, 2006).

Most studies – Australian and international – provide a list of the 'main' reasons why young people leave home. While this alerts us to the range of issues faced by this population, it does not allow us to assess possible relationships between the individual and structural factors that lead to homelessness. Most importantly, these studies are not framed within a broader understanding of the experiences which lead to homelessness among young people. Nor do they clarify how these experiences are implicated in young people's pathways through homelessness.

How the book is structured

In Chapter 2 we introduce debates about what is meant by homelessness and the causal factors, both structural and individual, that lead to homelessness. We describe the use of pathways analysis to depict young people's journeys into and through homelessness. Chapter 3 briefly describes the research and explains how we derived four pathways through homelessness, based on accommodation type and stability, through the use of stories told about the experiences of 40 young people interviewed 18 months after their recruitment into the study. Key characteristics of each pathway and its members are described. In Chapter 4 we focus on these young people's entry into homelessness, and examine key reasons given by members of the four pathways for leaving home, noting similarities and differences between these pathway members.

The next four chapters each provide an account of one of the four identified pathways through homelessness. In Chapter 5 we describe a group of highly vulnerable young people who predominantly came from troubled and abusive families and who remained in unstable, street-based circumstances. Chapter 6 tells of a group of young people whose pathway is characterized by sustained links with services. Unlike the first group, these young people had a clear and positive view of their futures, which included completing education and finding employment. The third group, described in Chapter 7, had moved in and out of home. Having left home at a time of intolerable stress and conflict, these young people nevertheless maintained their social networks and retained positive relationships with their parents. Chapter 8 tells of the group – the majority of our participants – who went 'home' after brief periods of homelessness. These young people came from homes that were relatively stable and had few drug-related or mental health problems themselves. The most distinctive feature of this group was their sense of agency, of personal direction and purpose.

Our final chapter gathers together this material and critically examines the impact of individual characteristics and structural features of young people's environments. We consider the implications of our findings for the conceptual underpinnings of homelessness policy and service delivery, taking account of the specific needs associated with each of the four pathways. In particular, we emphasize interdependence as a framing idea rather than the pursuit of independence and self-reliance commonly seen as a normative trajectory for adolescents.

2   Youth homelessness in context

> The main problem was just wondering why people didn't want me, just
> like, blaming myself for things that were happening in my life that were
> completely not under my control. I haven't done anything to cause this,
> it's just something that's happened. I'd been dealt a bad poker hand. Some
> get lucky and some don't and that's all there is to it.
>
> (Imogen)

Our understandings of the terms 'youth', 'young people', 'homelessness' and 'youth homelessness' are framed by the social context and
discourses in which they are employed. As such, they are contested
terms and our specific uses of them in this study need to be clearly
defined. What are the parameters of 'youth'? At what age does someone cease to be a 'young person'? If someone is living in medium-term
supervised accommodation can they be considered homeless? What
if they self-identify as such? What are the causes of youth homelessness? To what extent are these social or individual? These issues of
definition and cause are elaborated and clarified in the following
discussion.

Defining 'youth' and 'young people'

The demographic category of 'youth' and related terms such as
'young people' and 'adolescents' are historically and culturally constructed (Wyn and White, 1997; Bessant *et al.*, 1998; Moore, 2002;
Arnett, 2004). Thus how we think about young women and men, their
characteristics and abilities, their capacities to act on their own behalf
and on that of others, varies in any given time, place, culture and
social context. Two generations ago a young working-class male
might have attended a trade or technical school until he was age 14 or

15 and would then have entered the adult world of full-time employment (Brynner, 2001). At the same time, he would not have been granted the legal right to drink alcohol or to vote until he was 21. Now a male from a similar background might be expected to complete secondary school and then to undertake a vocational course at a tertiary training institution (e.g. in the Australian context a technical and further education, TAFE, college) before entering full-time employment. Yet he will have been granted full legal status as an adult citizen at the age of 18. Changes to expectations of and possibilities for females during the past half century have been even more extreme. Whereas two generations ago many young females considered their education and employment as a mere prelude to their main adult task of getting married and becoming a housewife and mother, now they typically stay in education as long or longer than their male counterparts and fully expect to remain in paid employment throughout their adult lives.

Age range definitions

As these changing expectations regarding education, employment, citizenship rights and legal status reveal, the boundaries between childhood and youth and youth and adulthood have been fluid over time. This is particularly evident when we consider the issue of age, one of the principal ways in which the youth sector, including educators and employers, defines young people. In both the academic and policy/service provision literature in Australia the term 'young people' may refer to people as young as 12 and as old as 25 (consistent with the World Health Organization's definition) or anyone in between. Each of the human service sectors works with different age ranges and develops policies and service responses that reflect differing definitions and perceptions of young people and their needs.

In this study we adopt an age range that begins and ends before and after the 'teen years', which have often been used as the markers of youth and adolescence. Hence, the young people who participated in our research were aged between 12 and 20 at the time of their recruitment. We adopt this broad demographic definition of 'young people' in order to reflect the wide range of ages targeted by youth policies and services. This, though, is done in the knowledge that the expectations and experiences of a young teen are very different from those of a 20 year old. As Arnett argues, people aged between 17 and 25 are no longer adolescents but are on the 'winding road' of 'emerging adulthood' (2004, 2006).

Transitions

As the age criteria for the category 'young people' remain fluid, so too does our understanding of the characteristics of people grouped in this category. In western contexts adolescence is commonly conceptualized as a transition from 'normal childhood' to 'normal adulthood', a stage of life between being a child and becoming an adult. Critiques of this definition of youth point out that it fails to value young people for who they are now, regarding them solely in terms of who they might become (Kelly, 2003), so that they exist merely as 'incomplete' adults, or adults in the making: 'citizens in pupae' (Bessant, 2002a: 34). Others criticize it for being an historically and culturally specific definition that claims universality; as if there are clearly identifiable, universal processes that all young people go through regardless of social context, that they all do share common experiences, or at least common characteristics and predispositions. Wyn and Woodman (2006) argue that the notion of youth transitions grew out of and is specific to the post-war 'Baby Boomer' generation and that subsequent generations of young people have been unfairly judged to have failed for not neatly fitting this mould:

> If we understand that the adulthood that was available to the Baby Boomer generation was a historical artefact, a product of a particular combination of economic realities, social policies and industrial settlements that have long since ceased to exist, it becomes possible to see what is missing from the conceptualisation of youth as simply transition.
>
> (Wyn and Woodman, 2006: 498)

The transitional model of adolescence is also predicated on a straightforward conception of psychological development (Cohen and Ainley, 2000), which implies that young people move from a state of immaturity, emotional and physical dependence and primary ties with family to maturity, autonomy and primary ties with others external to their family of origin, usually a partner and/or children. Thus conceived, adolescence represents a linear journey towards common desirable adult outcomes. With the journey and its destination so over-determined, if not pre-determined, it becomes easy to view young people who stray from it as somehow failing to transition into 'normal' adulthood. Because the nominated route to adulthood is often so narrowly defined, adolescence itself comes to be seen as problematic (Wyn and Dwyer, 2000). As a result, the history of youth studies is dominated by a focus on problems – problems typically understood to be located within the individual young person.

Adolescence is frequently portrayed as a stage when young people experiment, if not struggle with, identity issues. Conflict with parents, risk taking, 'storm and stress' and a loss of childhood innocence, instability and unpredictability are also commonly associated with this time-defined phase of life (Bessant, 2000; Bessant *et al.*, 2003; Moore, 2002). While this model has been and remains highly influential in western child rearing and child welfare practices and in popular cultural expression (Kelly, 2003; Moore, 2002; Wyn and White, 1997), it does not have the same currency or relevance in other cultural contexts or even among specific ethnic groups and/or generations within western societies such as Australia. In some cultures, places and times, adolescents are regarded as autonomous individuals (in the making), able to act on their own behalf. Others see them as remaining fundamentally and inextricably connected to family and kin (Mallett, 2003; Moore, 2002). These differing views alter how people (including policymakers and service providers) understand what young people can and should do, and to what extent they are responsible for, or answerable to, others, especially family and friends.

'At risk'

Our views of young people have also been affected by social research in this area. For example, early adolescence research focused on delinquency or deviance – deviance from some normative ideal behaviour. Sometimes this referred to deviance in a statistical sense, though more often it was about so-called bad or problematic behaviour. More recently, there has been a shift to a discourse of risk (Dryfoos, 1990; Dwyer and Wyn, 2001; Withers and Batten, 1995). In this discourse, young people risk jeopardizing desired and desirable futures through present behaviours. The problem with an all-embracing risk discourse is that it ignores the heterogeneity among young people, their individual realities, their gender, age, class, ethnicities and other differences, while constructing risk as a normative feature of all aspects of adolescent behaviour (see Bessant, 2000; Kelly, 2003). As many have noted, this discourse individualizes both the problem and the solution, inferring that the 'at risk' individual is solely responsible for changing his or her behaviour. Moreover, it allows for some classes of young people – usually the most vulnerable and marginalized – to be stigmatized as greater 'risk takers'. Thus we have a history of research into homeless young people framed in a risk discourse that focuses on problematic behaviours (e.g. drug use, unsafe sex, mental illness, etc.). Young people who engage in these behaviours are labelled in these terms (Bessant *et al.*, 2003), which often leads to greater stigmatization. What is lost or overlooked in this discourse are the positive aspects of young people's lived experience, the sense that risk also implies possibility, that young people are literally the embodiment of future hope (Arias, 1962).

While criticisms of the term 'at risk of homelessness' are justified and important, it must also be acknowledged that it has been employed by policymakers and practitioners to good effect, framing a plethora of effective preventative and early intervention programmes (e.g. parent/adolescent mediation, school focused youth services) for young people who threaten to leave or may be thrown out of home prematurely. While directed at individual young people and/or their families, in the Australian context these programmes are founded on an understanding of structural societal change regarding family, adolescents, employment and education. Moreover, as Chamberlain and MacKenzie (2004: 16) note, the practice discourse on risk articulated through these programmes emphasizes 'well-being, resilience, community involvement and young people's rights to assistance', rather than simply focusing on individual vulnerability.

The above discussion highlights some of the complexities that need to be considered in understanding adolescence as a normative stage of life. Clearly there are many perspectives on what defines a young person and how young people negotiate the period of life between childhood and adulthood. These perspectives are informed by the social context and by the developmental changes that occur as a result of biology and life experiences and interactions between these. By adopting a biographical approach to the qualitative component of our research (May, 2000), whereby the young people were encouraged to talk in an open-ended way about their experiences prior to, during and, where applicable, after their period of homelessness, we avoided framing our investigation through either a transitional or an 'at risk' definition of youth. However, elements of both these approaches to youth studies inform our organization and analysis of these accounts, so that, although not discussed as such, transitions from education to employment are emphasized, and issues that might be termed 'at risk behaviours' are given prominent attention. This is done knowingly, in full acknowledgement that while these frameworks remain contested and have significant conceptual limitations, they also continue to usefully inform both policy and practice and thereby have a social, lived reality that cannot be ignored. Perhaps unsurprisingly, given the influence of these discourses, they also resonate with young people as they attempt to describe and explain their experiences of homelessness.

Defining homelessness

As with the terms 'youth' and 'young people', definitions of 'homelessness' vary within and across research, policy and community contexts. They serve many functions, such as defining boundaries or criteria for the development of policy and the provision of services and the recruitment of participants into research projects like our own (Crane and Brannock, 1996; Neil and Fopp, 1992). These definitions range from a narrow conception of homelessness as a lack of shelter to one that encompasses the experiences of people who have unstable or substandard forms of shelter.

In the context of Australian homelessness research and policy, there are four discernible approaches to defining homelessness: literal/shelter; conventional or modified literal/shelter; person centred; and cultural (Chamberlain and MacKenzie, 1992; Crane and Brannock, 1996).

The *literal* approach defines homelessness as simply being without shelter or as 'rooflessness'. This is the most restricted and simplistic approach, as it ignores important related issues such as housing instability, recurring patterns of transience and the lived experience of the variety of people who claim to be homeless.

The *modified literal* approach expands the 'rooflessness' definition of homelessness to include people whose accommodation fails to meet a culturally relative minimum standard of housing (e.g. running water).

The *person-centred* approach asserts that an individual's experience of the adequacy of their housing is the key criterion in defining who and what constitutes homelessness. Under this most inclusive and subjective definition, a person would be considered homeless if they did not experience their current living arrangements as being a home (Chamberlain and MacKenzie, 1992; Crane and Brannock, 1996).

Arguably the most influential conceptualization of homelessness within Australian public debate and policy development is the '*cultural* definition' developed by Chamberlain and MacKenzie (1997, 2002). Adopted by agencies such as the Australian Bureau of Statistics, this approach defines homelessness (or inadequate housing) as a socially constructed concept that is historically and culturally contingent. In other words, as with our understandings of youth and young people, our conceptions of what constitutes home and homelessness vary over time and place. Chamberlain and MacKenzie assert that ideas about homelessness stem from shared community values regarding minimum standards of housing that are embedded in the housing practices of the day. Adequate housing is defined by the cheapest accommodation available in the private rental market. In Australia, they claim that this constitutes 'a small flat with a bedroom, living room, bathroom and kitchen secured by a lease arrangement' (Chamberlain and MacKenzie, 2002: 4).

In the current Australian cultural context, Chamberlain and MacKenzie identify three ordinal categories of homelessness: primary, secondary and tertiary. *Primary homelessness* refers to people without shelter and includes those living in public spaces such as streets, parks, derelict buildings and cars. *Secondary homelessness* refers to those in temporary living arrangements who do not have secure housing elsewhere. This category includes those living at a relative's or friend's home, as well as those accessing crisis accommodation services. *Tertiary homelessness* refers to those who live for long periods in single-room boarding houses. Chamberlain and MacKenzie acknowledge that this is a controversial category of homelessness but include it in their model as the majority of these residences do not meet their culturally and historically specific definition of adequate housing (Chamberlain and MacKenzie, 1997, 2002). These three categories of homelessness cover similar ground to the comprehensive and influential definition provided by Fitzpatrick *et al.* (2000) for Britain, which also includes intolerable conditions (e.g. overcrowding) and involuntary sharing (e.g. abusive relationships) as forms of homelessness (2000: 78).

Service delivery definitions

Other important definitions of youth homelessness emerge from and are enacted by government social services designed to assist young people experiencing homelessness or at risk of becoming homeless. In the Australian context, these are the targeted homelessness service, the Supported Accommodation Assistance Program (SAAP), and the more general youth allowance, administered through the welfare payments service, Centrelink.

The federal SAAP Act defines a person as being homeless 'if, and only if, he or she has inadequate access to safe and secure housing'. 'Inadequate access' is specified in a number of ways, including if the housing damages, or is likely to damage, the person's health, or threatens the person's safety. This service delivery definition of homelessness is broader than the cultural definition as it includes people at risk of homelessness.

The youth allowance is a federal government income support payment available to young people who are full-time students (aged 16–24) or unemployed (aged 16–21). If a young person is classified as 'independent' they can receive an 'away from home' rate which is not subject to parental income or asset tests. One way in which Centrelink classifies a young person as being 'independent' is if it is unreasonable for them to live at home. It is deemed unreasonable for a young person to live at home if they are unable to reside with either or both parents for reasons including extreme family breakdown, or serious risk to his or her physical or mental well-being due to violence, sexual abuse or other similar unreasonable circumstances.

While not intended as a definition of homelessness, these criteria nonetheless comprise an operational definition of young people who have a legitimate claim to homelessness status. In effect, young people are only deemed to be homeless, and therefore in need of additional income support, if their parents/guardians, Centrelink or significant third parties believe they are not capable of returning home, principally due to family violence, abuse, neglect or irreconcilable family conflict. Thus, young people are expected to remain or return home in all but the most exceptional or traumatic circumstances. Other reasons for young people leaving home and/or becoming homeless, such as a desire for independence or adventure, are excluded from these criteria. So too are young people's current living arrangements. Moreover, unlike other definitions of youth homelessness, these criteria draw on a range of people's subjective perceptions, including those of young people, parents, Centrelink officers and relevant third parties such as counsellors, to determine whether or not it is unreasonable for the young person to return home.

Operational research definitions

Beyond debates about policy formation, operational definitions of homelessness are also generated through research practice. The primary task of such definitions is to establish the parameters of the research being undertaken and thereby enable the recruitment of participants to the project. As with policy-focused definitions, operational research definitions range from restricted conceptions of homelessness, applicable only to people living on the streets or in shelters (Rotheram-Borus *et al.*, 1996b), to inclusive ones that confer homelessness on people who are 'couch surfing' at friends' places or staying in hotel rooms due to a lack of an alternative (Ennett *et al.*, 1999). These research definitions are also characterized by a temporal element which varies from study to study. While one research project might deem someone homeless if they have spent one night without shelter, another might extend that period to two nights or take a longer term view which defines someone as homeless only once they have experienced a series of unstable and/or inadequate accommodation outcomes.

Project i's definition

In the case of *Project i*, our operational definition of homelessness was largely derived from a combination of the person-centred and cultural approaches, in that the participants were recruited through their accessing of homelessness services. On the one hand, this meant that our research definition was implicitly subjective, as the participants had at that time thought of themselves as being in need of homelessness services, if not as being homeless. On the other, it was culturally and historically prescribed by the nature of the homelessness services available to the young people and the conditions of their access to them. Our own operational condition was that, at the time of their recruitment through these services, the young people had been living away from home for at least two nights.

Homelessness and the notion of home

On a more theoretical, even philosophical level, homelessness is considered to be an absence of home. Hence, to understand the former we must consider what we mean by the latter. Arguably, one of the key ways that homelessness is understood, experienced and defined by people is in relation to the notion of home. Research on the meaning and experience of home has proliferated over the past two decades, particularly within the disciplines of sociology, anthropology, psychology, human geography, history, architecture and philosophy (see Mallett, 2004). Many researchers now understand home as a multidimensional concept: home is variously described as, conflated with or related to, house, family, haven, self, gender and journeying. Many authors also consider notions of being-at-home, creating or making home and the 'ideal home'. However, with the exception of Després (1991) and Somerville (1997), few have translated this awareness into genuinely interdisciplinary studies of the meaning of home. The question then remains: How is home understood, defined and described? Is home a place(s), a space(s), a feeling(s), a set of practices, and/or an active state of being in the world? Is home always understood as a positive place, space, feeling and/or state?

Within the homelessness research field there has been increasing recognition of the interconnection between ideas of home and homelessness or the absence of home (e.g. Crane and Brannock, 1996; Somerville, 1992; Wardhaugh, 1999). For example, Wardhaugh (1999) asserts that home and homelessness exist in a dynamic relationship. They are not, as some suggest, fixed oppositional terms. Rather they refer to 'complex and shifting experiences and identities' (p. 93) that emerge and unfold in and through time. This recognition of the important relationship between ideas and experiences of home and homelessness has been reflected in an emerging Australian literature on homeless young people's understanding of home and homelessness. For example, the young people in Crane and Brannock's (1996) research typically thought of home as being less about a physical place, e.g. a family house, and more about the feelings and experiences they associated with living in such a place. Home was understood as a place where they were heard and supported, where they felt a sense of familiarity, connection and belonging. It was also a safe place, where they felt wanted and accepted. Interestingly, many of these same young people emphasized similar issues when defining and explaining homelessness. Most understood it as meaning much more than an absence of shelter. For them, to be homeless also meant the 'absence of qualities such as caring, love or belonging and/or the presence of negative feelings or circumstances' (Crane and Brannock, 1996: 65).

In our research, in the course of loosely structured interviews, 40 young people who were or had recently experienced homelessness were asked what home meant to them. Four themes emerged from their responses – safety, relationships, autonomy/control and physical place. While these themes do not cover the full range of their responses, they do capture the most frequently cited qualities that the young people associated with a notion of home.

Safety was seen as important to a sense of home in at least two ways. First, a home operates as a safe space or refuge from dangers and precarious experiences external to it. Second, this sense of safety is established by all those who share the space. For some this was defined as the absence of particular types of interaction, a place where there 'is no trouble, no violence, no yelling, no arguing, you know . . . just where you can be yourself'. For others it was the presence of people who were welcoming, loving, and who got along with one another. In this way, safety and the importance of *relationships* to home were intrinsically linked. For some, home-defining relationships referred exclusively to family, while for others they referred to friends or a partner, or more inclusively to anyone with whom they shared a dwelling and who made them feel comfortable, safe and secure.

Most of the young people needed to feel both a sense of *freedom and control* in and over their living situation for them to experience it as a home. These feelings were intimately connected to both their relationships within the place and the sense of safety or threat and insecurity that these created. The young people were not themselves seeking to control the household, rather they sought the freedom not to be controlled by someone else. Within the broader safety of a home, they wished to create and maintain a space or sanctuary of their own. On a more tangible, less relational level, many of the young people also understood home as being a house, a physical place – a defined space that provided shelter and basic amenities.

At home in homelessness services

Some young people spoke of the ways certain accommodation services had made them feel either at home or homeless. In most cases, the things that made the difference were small. The capacity to change or control their space was important to young people's sense of feeling at home in services. This included being allowed to put their things in the bathroom, choosing the furnishings in their room, being treated equally or given responsibility by workers. Their relationships with workers were also crucial to their experiences of services. Young people emphasized that they felt at home in services when workers cared about what they were doing, or made them feel as though they belonged by taking time to talk with them and by including them in activities and collective decision-making processes.

> When I was at the refuge . . . it was like two years ago or something, I felt like it was home because the workers were nice and it was that kind of environment where you felt like somebody actually cared about what you were doing and what – where you were going and whatever else. But, um, [name of different refuge deleted] has been more – basically it felt like an institution, where you have the workers and no control and they wanted to make you know that they were in control and basically, ultimately your life was in their hands. . . . I don't know what power trip they were on, but it was shocking.
>
> (Kirsty)

Having a measure of control over one's own space, a sense of safety and security, and the presence of caring, loving relationships with family members, partners and/or friends are, we found, critical features of young people's understandings of home. The young people who participated in *Project i* who lacked any or all of these features frequently characterized their living circumstances as a state of homelessness, making clear the connection between qualities of home, either idealized or experienced, and understandings of homelessness as the absence of these.

Understanding youth homelessness

Homelessness research has long attempted to understand the causes and experiences of homelessness, as well as how and why some people who experience homelessness are reaccommodated and/or are able to make a new home, while others become chronically homeless. Attempting to define the condition and/or experience of homelessness is merely the first task in this ongoing quest. Typically researchers want better to understand homelessness in order to inform and influence social policy, and ultimately to either reform or refine services designed to mitigate the experience, or to address its causes.

Causes and antecedents

Discussions of the causes of homelessness rarely escape the Gordian knot that ensnares so much social policy debate, the two strands of which are individual factors and social structures, agency and constraint (Fitzpatrick *et al.*, 2000). Do people become homeless as a result of their own dispositions, choices, actions and inactions, or are they victims of social and economic forces that limit, if not determine, the directions that their lives take? At times of high unemployment such as the Great Depression people readily accept a social explanation of the causes of homelessness. The conditions of homelessness during that period were well suited to a class analysis, in which it was argued that the fate of the working class was determined by the choices and actions of others – the owners of capital. What though is the case in good economic times, when work is easy to come by and housing stocks are high? Why do people become homeless then? And aren't people always, to some extent, able to alter their circumstances?

During the long economic boom that has recently ended, neoliberal economics (its most influential proponents being Friedrich Hayek and Milton Friedman) and rational choice theory came to frame much public debate (Fine, 2001). This resulted in the individualization, not only of social problems, but also of our proposed solutions to them. Discerning this trend very early, and analysing its impact on our understanding of social inequality, Ulrich Beck, in his highly influential work, *Risk Society*, wrote:

> Intensification *and* individualization of social inequalities interlock. As a consequence, problems of the system are lessened politically and transformed into personal failure. In the detraditionalized modes of living, a *new immediacy for individual and society* arises, the immediacy of *crises and sickness*, in the sense that social crises appear to be of individual origin, and are perceived as social only indirectly and to a very limited extent.
>
> (Beck, 1992: 89)

In terms of Beck's analysis of life in a modern risk society, the commonly cited causes of youth homelessness – mental health, drug and alcohol abuse, family conflict/violence, unemployment, etc. – are all predominantly conceived of as individual problems. As such, the exponential rise in the numbers of people suffering from a mental illness is not primarily considered a social issue, but rather as an individual problem in each individual case. The fact that many people who suffer such illnesses successfully 'manage' them and are able to meet their obligations within the social contract (e.g. hold down a job, find and maintain secure accommodation, etc.) lessens the explanatory impact of mental illness as a social cause of homelessness for someone who has 'failed' to manage their illness. All citizens in a risk society are expected to become their own reflexive project, to manage every aspect of their lives, maximizing strengths and improving upon their weaknesses. The fact that some people are, through education and/or ability, able to do this more successfully than others is not a concern – in a risk society, inequality is a social fact, not a social problem. Homeless people, then, are merely failed self-managers and the solutions to their problems always lie in self-improvement, in their accumulation of more human capital.

It is in the area of youth homelessness that issues of individual and societal factors, agency and constraint become most acute. For in neoliberal terms, at what point does an individual become responsible for the fact that her parents are drug addicts, that her uncle sexually abused her at 13 and that the public schools she attended were drastically underresourced and largely dysfunctional? How, and at what age, does a child victim become a failed self-manager?

Despite the trend towards neoliberalism within public policy debate, there is widespread agreement among homelessness researchers and policymakers that homelessness is a consequence of the interaction between individual and structural factors (Fitzpatrick *et al.*, 2000; McNaughton, 2005; Neale, 1997). However, in practice, many researchers continue to privilege either structural or individual causal models when discussing the antecedents of homelessness among young people (Clapham, 2003).

Structural causes

In their review of British research on single homelessness, Fitzpatrick *et al.* (2000) claim that most researchers favour structural accounts of homelessness. As Neale (1997) suggests, such analyses are founded on the view that macro social and economic factors cause homelessness. Proponents of this view argue that political responses to the problem of homelessness should be directed at the social rather than the individual level. In terms of single adult homelessness (though not specifically youth) Fitzpatrick *et al.* (2000) identify housing demand, management of public housing, poverty, unemployment and social security, and changes to family formation as the key structural causes. More generally, research indicates that homelessness is typically associated with unemployment or underemployment, low or inadequate incomes, poverty, and diminished access to and availability of affordable housing (Anderson, 2003).

Structural accounts of the specific causes of youth homelessness emphasize the role of social, policy, institutional and economic factors and contexts, the changing nature of the family and familial relations, contemporary understandings of adolescence as a life stage, education, health, child protection and juvenile justice policies, legislation and service provision (Kemp *et al.*, 2001; Symons and Smith, 1995). For example, Flatau *et al.* (2007) find that young people are more likely to leave home if their parents are unemployed and that such young people are also less likely to return home or receive financial support once they have left. They also note that children from stepfamilies are more likely to leave home earlier than those from other family types due to high levels of family conflict.

Critics of structural models of youth homelessness note the failure of researchers and policymakers to articulate exactly how individual and structural factors intersect and interact (Beer *et al.*, 2003; Clapham, 2003; Hill and Bessant, 1999). In particular they note that this way of understanding the causes of homelessness for young people is socially deterministic and fails to take account of young people's power and agency. In other words, they claim that the structural models of youth homelessness imply that there are over-arching structural factors that determine people's behaviour, preventing them from acting independently on their own or on behalf of others. Other criticisms of structuralist accounts relate to the limitations of existing homelessness research methods, in which there are no adequate measures of the impact of social structural context on this phenomenon.

Situational/individual causes

Individual level accounts of the antecedents of homelessness focus on personal or familial characteristics – what some have termed situational factors (Beer *et al.*, 2003; Crane and Brannock, 1996; Fopp, 1993; Morgan and Vincent, 1987). Research on the individual causes of homelessness typically focuses on homeless young people's subjectivity, identity, agency, personal characteristics, temperament, or engagement in particular practices. These studies often examine the causal role of so-called personal characteristics such as mental illness, alcohol and drug abuse, school learning difficulties, etc., in the genesis of youth homelessness. They also investigate the interaction between young people's personal characteristics and family level factors such as family violence, abuse and neglect, family structure, and financial hardship.

Structural and individual

In an effort to theorize the complex, intertwined relationship between structural and individual level factors in the genesis, experience and maintenance of homelessness among young people, Beer *et al.* (2003) draw on a conceptual framework for understanding social disadvantage articulated by Williams and Poppay (1999). The latter outline four overlapping conceptual domains that are critical to our understanding of social disadvantage, including homelessness.

The first domain, the *welfare subject*, encompasses young people's identity, agency or capacity to act, their social position and sense of self. Beer *et al.* (2003) point to the need to examine the social, spatial, cultural, political and economic structures that influence young people's sense of self and identity. Our understanding of young people and the ways they conceive of themselves, including their experience of homelessness, must recognize how they shape and are shaped by contemporary gender relations, ethnicity, sex, sexuality and socioeconomic position as well as how they intersect with, relate to, and are influenced by a range of structural forces such as globalization, welfare reform, labour market restructuring and transformation of education sectors. This view of young people acknowledges and foregrounds their capacity to act, to feel, to resist and to transform their lives while also taking due account of complex interpersonal and structural relational context for their actions.

The second domain, *social topography of enablement and constraint*, refers to the social/spatial distribution of resources, risks and opportunities for young people. Williams and Poppay (1999) understand risk as socially, economically and politically mediated and geographically distributed and understood in differing ways across societies and communities. This framework allows for an understanding of and response to risk of homelessness that is both structurally and interpersonally constituted. For example, some young people in particular communities are more exposed to abuse, conflict and family breakdown. Their responses to these life circumstances vary according to their age, their social networks and the available forms of social, economic and institutional support.

The third domain is the *institutional and discursive context of policy formulation*. This comprises the key organizing concepts (e.g. risk, community, etc.) that inform social science research, welfare professional, political and policy discourses, as well as institutional structures. Following other structural analyses, Williams and Poppay note the direct and indirect effect of social, economic and political factors on a phenomenon such as homelessness. Their framework calls for an analysis of the role of these factors in creating, maintaining or arresting social disadvantage, including homelessness among young people. Accordingly, homelessness among young people must be understood as influenced by welfare reform policies, education policies, particularly those directed at marginalized young people, as well as specific policy frameworks driving the direction, distribution and priorities for homelessness service delivery.

As well as a focus on specific homelessness related policy, Williams and Poppay argue for the need to examine the effect of broader *social and economic changes and policies* on the distribution and experience of social disadvantage. In the context of youth homelessness, this approach calls for an examination of the impact of economic policies such as labour market reform, and social phenomena such as changing nature of the family and household formation.

Self-reported reasons

To propel the analysis of youth homelessness beyond the social/individual, agency/constraint dichotomies and to move it away from the causes of homelessness, homelessness research has often turned to a subjective or situational understanding of 'reasons for leaving home'.[1] By asking young people to reflect on the reasons they left home, we can gain insight into the working of the social context to which they are responding and within which their choices and actions are constrained and/or enabled.

The subjectivity of these insights is both a strength and a weakness. People's interpretations and analyses of their circumstances can be, in objective terms, misleading. At the very least, they represent only one side of a multisided story. For example, a young person might cite their stepfather's violence as the reason they left home, but neglect to mention their own drug use as a factor in their family's conflict, let alone the context of intergenerational disadvantage within which all these factors occurred. (It was for this reason that our interviews with young people were lightly directed rather than entirely open-ended.) However, once the subjective nature of this information is recognized, its omissions and emphases can also be read as reflective of the social discourses that influence the way young people perceive themselves and their interactions with others. The fact that young people cite typical 'at risk' behaviours – family conflict, sexual and physical violence, substance use and trauma – as reasons for them leaving home both reinforces the validity of 'at risk' analysis, but also questions the framing effect this discourse has on the way young people interpret their experiences.

The research literature on young people's self-reported reasons for leaving home generally presents quantitative data on individual, familial or situational factors leading to homelessness. When findings about young people's stated reasons for leaving home are collated into population level statistics they reveal the relative importance of particular individual level reasons for homelessness nominated by research participants in a given study. This information can be useful, as it can give service providers, educators and policymakers an indication of individual level issues for the population of young people who are likely to access homelessness services. As such it can assist in identifying some of the support services that may be required by these diverse populations of homeless young people.

Although useful, quantitative 'reasons for leaving home' data are limited. Such studies typically report the relative percentage of young people who identify a single reason as important for leaving home, presenting the findings as if they always nominate only a single reason (e.g. 50 per cent nominate violence and only 10 per cent nominate substance abuse). The percentage of young people who identify particular constellations or clusters of reasons for leaving home is rarely, if ever, reported. Thus we fail to learn the percentage of young people who nominate learning difficulties and personal substance abuse, or any other combination, as their reasons for leaving home. Moreover, we remain ignorant of how these reasons for leaving home cluster according to gender, sexuality, ethnicity or place.

Qualitative research, like that component of our own, provides a more detailed picture of how young people experience and explain their reasons for leaving home. By allowing young people to create autobiographical narratives that have the potential to accommodate family and broader social factors, such research reveals not only the clusters of various reasons for them leaving home, but also the interconnections between these reasons (Hyde, 2005). In this way, what in an exclusively quantitative study may be cited as a single reason for leaving home, say, drug use, in a qualitative study might be contextualized by a biographical story that touches on a single mother's schizophrenia, periods in foster care, and learning difficulties.

This form of research, too, has its limitations. Apart from the obvious one applicable to all qualitative research of not knowing the degree to which one should extrapolate from individual experience in an attempt to understand social phenomena, studies that ask young people their reasons for leaving home or for becoming homeless sometimes find that the participants are confused about or find it difficult to articulate how this event transpired.[2] Many young people also report that their understanding of why they became homeless has changed over time, as a consequence of the critical distance accorded by time itself, space from the other people involved, and a more mature perspective gained through greater experience (Mallett *et al.*, 2003). Such data also sometimes fail to link young people's nominated reasons for leaving home to single or multiple events that have occurred in their recent or distant pasts (e.g. a death in the family). Nor does it always reflect the longstanding processes (e.g. family violence or poverty) that can culminate in a young person's early home leaving (Crane and Brannock, 1996), and as such typically downplays structural factors (McNaughton, 2005).

These criticisms exist within the more general critique of reasons for leaving home data that it reinforces, often unintentionally, unidimensional, individualistic understandings of the causes of homelessness.

Young people's nominated reasons for leaving home are interpreted as personal characteristics of the young people themselves and are 'confused with and become causes or explanations for [their] homelessness' (Fopp, 1993: 12). As a result, young people can be held primarily responsible, or what Fitzpatrick *et al.* (2000) term 'personally culpable', for their homelessness due to their engagement in certain socially transgressive practices such as drug abuse, crime, or school refusal. Others are held indirectly responsible for their homelessness because of their self-identified behavioural difficulties, for example, mental illness or learning difficulties. The latter group are effectively pathologized and/or thought of as individually deficient and this deficiency is then thought to be the cause of their homelessness. Similarly, individual family characteristics can be confused with causal explanations for homelessness. Families that engage in particular practices (e.g. violence, alcohol and drug abuse, etc.) are considered dysfunctional and thereby held responsible for homelessness among young people.

Once these significant limitations are acknowledged and accounted for, research (particularly combined qualitative and quantitative longitudinal research like our own) into young people's stated reasons for leaving home or for becoming homeless can continue to provide important insights into how young people subjectively experience and explain their homelessness. The power of these insights is greatly enhanced if, as is the case with this study, the stories of the young people's experiences are, wherever possible, told in their own words. This then gives the subjectivity of these accounts a context, a texture and a fuller meaning, so that the reader gains not only information but also a sense of the young people themselves: their hardships, humour, confusion, vulnerability, perceptiveness and resilience.

Analytical metaphors

Another way that youth homelessness researchers have attempted better to understand and explain young people's complex reasons for and experiences of homelessness is through the development of analytical models, or metaphors. Over the past decade there has been an increasing recognition, particularly in Australia and the UK, of the need to understand homelessness as a process rather than a situation or event with discrete individual level causes (Anderson and Tulloch, 2000; Fitzpatrick, 1999; Fitzpatrick *et al.*, 2000; Hutson and Liddiard,

1994; MacKenzie and Chamberlain, 2003). It is through the use of three metaphors – *homeless trajectories, homeless/housing careers* and *homelessness pathways* – that such researchers have attempted to incorporate a sense of process in their accounts and analyses of young people's experiences of becoming and being homeless.

Trajectories

The idea that youths have or are on trajectories was borrowed from youth employment research, wherein it was argued that a young person's socio-economic background more or less determined the nature and status of their future employment (Roberts, 1995). Gender, ethnicity and place/locality were later added to this research mix. Like the arc of an arrow, the notion of people having trajectories contains a predictive element, so that knowledge of a young person's current circumstances is thought to be a reasonable guide to the future direction of their life course (Martijn and Sharpe, 2006). In this way, while the trajectories of a young person suffering a mental illness and of another who is a heavy drug user might initially lead to both becoming homeless, it might be predicted that their experiences of homelessness and their trajectories beyond it would diverge.

This approach shares many of the shortcomings and advantages of the rhetoric of 'at risk' (to which it is sometimes attached, as in 'at risk trajectories'). Where 'at risk' presupposes a normality that is under threat, the notion that people's lives follow predictable trajectories attributes a fixity to life that, beyond traditional cultures, seems misplaced. While on the one hand the trajectory metaphor implicitly acknowledges the contingency of life – that one thing leads to another, that one choice or action triggers a series of consequences – on the other, it fails to account for the full extent of life's contingencies – that within those series of consequences there is a series of other choices and possible actions that could redirect the course of a life in ways not predictable from the outset. Hence, as an analytical metaphor, 'homelessness trajectories' offers only a broad brushstroke picture. If applied too literally, it risks underemphasizing, or even eliding, the important roles played by choice, chance and contingency as causes of homelessness and in the ways people both experience and exit homelessness. Again, though, as with the predictive concept of 'at risk', this must be balanced against the fact that the use of trajectories in a policy context can result in the implementation of successful preventative programmes.

Careers

If the metaphor of 'homelessness trajectories' downplays the importance of agency and choice, that of 'homeless careers' gives the
superficial impression that becoming homeless is a desired lifestyle
choice, a goal to be set and reached. On this level at least, it fails to
'convey the loss and trauma of homelessness' (Fopp, 2003: 14). As
with trajectories, the concept of careers was imported into youth
homelessness studies from research into youth transitions. In that
context, the term 'career' denotes 'the sequence of statuses through
which young people pass as they move from childhood dependency to
adulthood' (Coles, 1995: 9). Contrary to the superficial sense that the
concept of careers privileges agency, in fact it risks doing the opposite,
referring not so much to the element of initial choice implicit in that
word, but more to the sense that a career has set stages to it – that
once you embark on one it will take you on a more or less set course;
'that each step in the sequence can be shown to determine future
steps' (Coles, 1995: 9).

Within youth studies, young people are referred to as having, for
example, 'employment careers', 'family careers', 'drug using careers'
and 'criminal careers' (MacDonald *et al.*, 2005). A young person's
'homeless career', then, is only one aspect of their overall trajectory.
As with the terms of 'at risk' and 'trajectories', the notion of a
'homeless career' is employed primarily as a predictive mapping tool,
aimed at increasing the effectiveness of service interventions. Based on
quantitative data, a homeless career provides a generalized description
of the process by which young people typically become homeless.

Chamberlain and MacKenzie's (1998, 2006) model of the youth
homelessness career is a prominent Australian example of this type of
approach (for a similar approach in other contexts see Hutson and
Liddiard, 1994; Jones, 1993, 1995; May, 2000). They describe a four-
stage process whereby young people move from being at risk of
homelessness to a situation where homelessness becomes their way of
life. In moving through these stages (at risk, in and out of home,
involvement in the homeless subculture, homelessness as a way of
life), young people go from short-term to long-term to chronic homelessness. Chamberlain and MacKenzie emphasize that their model of
the youth homelessness career is an ideal type; a heuristic device
aimed at delineating the fundamental characteristics or elements of
the process that leads to homelessness and chronic homelessness in
particular. In a later work dealing with general homelessness, they
explain the nature and function of an ideal type:

An ideal type is an analytical construct that abstracts certain key features of a phenomenon from the myriad of individual circumstances and contingencies. This concept can then be used to compare similarities and differences between cases. Thus, ideal types are analytical models that are constructed by researchers for the purposes of understanding the world.

(Chamberlain and MacKenzie, 2006: 199)

They do not claim that their model of youth homelessness careers encompasses or represents everyone's route into homelessness and beyond. Rather, by nominating stages of homelessness, the model attempts to identify points in the process where the implementation of various service interventions might prevent young people from transitioning into chronic homelessness.

While similar to homeless careers, housing careers are not concerned with people's shifting identities or their interpersonal relationships, but rather simply chart people's housing histories (Meert and Bourgeois, 2005). This materialist approach to understanding homelessness attempts to provide objective descriptions of housing standards, incorporating factors such as price, physical space and location (Clark *et al.*, 2003). In this way, a young person's housing career might begin in the family home and range across temporary stays in friends' parents' houses, a refuge, supported medium-term accommodation, friends' shared rental houses and sleeping rough.

Pathways

As with homeless trajectories and careers, the analytical metaphor of homelessness pathways can be employed as an aggregate of the experiences of a number of people which are then abstracted into an ideal type. In addition to this, though, a homelessness pathway can also operate as the trace of an individual's unique biographical journey into and through homelessness, making it more applicable to qualitative research. As Clapham argues:

The concept of a housing pathway has been developed as a framework of analysis. It is essentially the application of a metaphor rather than being a theory (although theories may be developed from it). In the same way it is not a research method, although it may sit well with some particular research methods.

(Clapham, 2003: 122)

In contrast to the trajectory and career models, pathways approaches to homelessness are, or at least have the potential to be, broad in focus (Meert and Bourgeois, 2005). While it is acknowledged that social structural factors impact on pathways, these are not the focus of this form of analysis. Rather they are understood as a backdrop to individual or household pathways. Founded on the understanding that people's housing or homelessness status may fluctuate over their life course, pathways approaches often include, but are not confined to, analyses of people's housing and homelessness careers. Anderson notes that at its most basic, a pathways approach traces an individual or household's journey into homelessness, their experience of homelessness and their exit from homelessness into stable accommodation' (Anderson and Tulloch, 2000).

The greatest advantage of the pathways 'framework of analysis' over that of the trajectory or career metaphors resides in its relationship to the issues of agency and social constraint. Where the notion of homeless trajectories seems too overdetermined, the starting point too predictive of the direction taken, and while the points in the process identified by homeless careers might enable intervention, the pathways metaphor both suggests structure (a well-trodden track), and also implies choice (a negotiated journey). Homelessness pathways denote that young people take common routes into, through and out of homelessness (Anderson and Tulloch, 2000), while also allowing for divergence and convergence, forks in the track, made sometimes by external interventions, at others by choice or chance. The structure of a pathway (as opposed to that of a road) is made by those who walk it, directing the behaviour and actions of those who in turn create it. This then is an apt metaphor for the symbiotic relationship between the individual and society, the way that through our collective, repeated actions we create and re-create the social structures that constrain us as individuals. Clapham makes a similar point with reference to Anthony Giddens's account of social constructionism:

He [Giddens] argues that social structures do not have an independent existence, but are produced and reproduced by human agency at both the individual and institutional levels where they serve both to constrain and enable action (Giddens, 1984). Action is consciously intentional but has the unintended effect of reproducing structure. Social practices thus have both an agency and a structural dimension.

(Clapham, 2003: 122)

Pathways are also suggestive of our constant movement through time, from place to place, reminding us that people's experiences of home and homelessness are often transitory and always changing (Anderson and Tulloch, 2000). This contrasts with the trajectory metaphor, which conjures images of people being catapulted through or across time, and the career metaphor which breaks people's movement through time and space into discrete phases.

By capturing something of the dynamism in the relationship between individual choice and action and social circumstance and constraint, as well as of the ever-changing way that homelessness is experienced, the pathways metaphor provides a powerful analytical frame through which to view and understand both young people's reasons for and experiences of homelessness (Anderson and Christian, 2003). This approach more closely reflects the lived reality of these processes than do the more static notions of homeless trajectories and careers.

The way forward

It is due to its dynamism, its capacity to switch between individual experience, choice, psychology and pathology and the social factors that delimit, shape and give meaning to these, that *Project i* adopted a pathways approach to analysing the data and stories we collected of the experiences of homeless young people in Melbourne. In doing so we became part of a growing trend within homelessness research (Anderson, 2003), wherein the pathways metaphor has been employed in studies from a range of academic disciplines (Anderson and Tulloch, 2000; Fitzpatrick, 1999; Horrocks, 2002; Johnson, 2006; Martijn and Sharpe, 2006; Maycock *et al.*, 2008). Being a longitudinal study, *Project i* also benefited from the time dimension implicit to the pathways metaphor; the sense that the young people involved were on a journey, a small section of which we attempted to chart. Our application of the pathways metaphor takes the form of creating loosely structured homelessness pathways that group together the stories these young people told about their experiences of becoming and being homeless, and, where applicable, their return to home. These pathways are based on the young people's movements in and out of accommodation over and through time and the housing situation they were in at the time of their interview, 18 months after their recruitment into the study. In these interviews the young people were encouraged to speak in an open-ended way about their understandings of how they became homeless, their experiences of homelessness, their education and/or employment situations, their familial and other relationships, their contact with social services – particularly homelessness ones – how, where applicable, they ceased to be homeless and how they envisage their future. This broadly biographical approach implicitly acknowledges that the relationship between individual and social factors in youth homelessness (as with all other social phenomena) cannot be usefully abstracted into neatly unravelled analytical strands, but must be understood in the context of individual lives. In this way, our research privileges the young people's perceptions of their own experiences in the belief that the stories we tell of our lives provide the most nuanced means for us to apprehend the way that our choices, actions and behaviours interact with the social context in which they occur.

The Australian social context

From young person to adult

As we noted earlier, during the latter half of the twentieth century the transition to adulthood in Australia was typically marked by key life events, including achieving legal adult status, completion of education, securing a full-time job, leaving home, marriage and having children (Coles, 1995; de Vaus, 2004; MacDonald *et al.*, 2001). There is now considerable evidence to suggest that contemporary young people do not routinely take these well-worn pathways into adulthood (Wyn and Dwyer, 2000; Wyn and Woodman, 2006). As White notes, 'childhood and adulthood are no longer so readily differentiated by financial independence, employment and student status nor by events such as getting a job' (White, 2002: 216). This is reflected in young people's perceptions of adulthood. While traditional signifiers of adult status are still relevant, emotional control in relationships with parents, personal responsibility for oneself and others and the capacity to make independent decisions are now considered crucial markers (Arnett, 1997; White, 2002).

These changes have accompanied significant social and economic changes. The decline of the welfare state, reduced full-time youth employment, altered employment opportunities, changes to family constellations and housing affordability have all affected the timing and routes taken by young people in their journeys into adulthood (Bessant, 1999; Ellis, 1996; White, 2002). One indication of this is reflected in their patterns of home leaving.[3]

When are young people leaving home? Where are they living?

Australian young people are now remaining in the family home longer than those of the preceding two generations. Once they have left they are also more likely to return, especially during times of crisis such as relationship breakdown, unemployment and accommodation problems (de Vaus, 2004; Kilmartin, 2000). While census figures indicate that young women make the transition out of the family home earlier than young men, they leave at a diverse range of ages and for quite different reasons. One reason cited is that they are subject to closer parental supervision and behavioural restrictions (Buck and Scott, 1993).

In Australia, young people typically leave home in their early twenties. The 2001 Australian Bureau of Statistics Census (de Vaus, 2004) revealed that just over half of 20 to 22 year olds (57.2 per cent) and just over one-third (37 per cent) of those aged 23 to 24 live with their parents. Of the 20 per cent of young people aged 18 to 19 who lived away from the familial home, only one-quarter were living alone. Half lived in group households and one-quarter were living with a partner and/or children. Although young people aged 20 to 24 are the most likely of any age group to leave the parental home, half of these return at least once – findings consistent with those of Kilmartin (2000). Kilmartin found that two-thirds of young people in their early twenties were living at home, and that just under 40 per cent had never left home.

Why do contemporary young people remain at home longer than those in previous generations?

Hartley (1990) notes that the main reasons young people remain at home longer are personal, emotional and financial support and the sense of security it gives them. A number of structural reasons have also been proposed. Wyn and White (1997) argue that apart from the structural issues such as employment and housing affordability, the shift to remain at home longer has been directly influenced by government policies. These policies are aimed at retaining young people in education and at home so that they are equipped to participate in the contemporary labour market. Policies of retention are also founded on the assumption that parents are primarily responsible for providing financial support to their young people, including those in their early to mid-twenties (Bessant, 1999; Ellis, 1996).

Education and employment

Over the past decade there have been sharp increases in the number of young people engaged in secondary and tertiary education. De Vaus (2004) reports that by 2001 over half of young people aged 15 to 19 years were in school and tertiary participation rates among this age group had increased to over one-quarter. Tertiary participation rates for 20 to 24 year olds almost doubled over the 14 years from 1987 to 2001. By 2001 only 22 per cent of 15 to 19 year olds and 63 per cent of 20 to 24 year olds were not involved in some form of secondary or tertiary education.

Young people's involvement in education can impact on their capacity to leave home as it may prevent them from becoming financially independent. Although many young people combine work with study, most engage in part-time rather than full-time work. Of those 20 to 24 year olds engaged in tertiary study, more than half (53 per cent) were working part time and only 4 per cent were engaged in full-time work.

Young people gradually move into the labour force between the ages of 15 and 24 years and their engagement in full-time work increases over time. Participation in the labour force changes dramatically with age. A labour force survey in 2002 revealed that almost half of 15 to 17 year olds were not in the labour force, compared to 20 per cent of those aged 18 to 19 years and 16 per cent of 22 to 24 year olds. Unsurprisingly, participation in full-time work also increases with age.

Financial dependence

During their transition into full-time work young people may receive income and/or financial and material support from a number of sources including parents, the government, personal income and partners' income, often from multiple sources at the one time. Regular income support from parents declines over time. Young people's reliance on government income support also declines over time. However, those aged 18 and above rely more on government than parental income support. Over one-quarter of those aged 18 to 19 and one-third of 20 to 21 year olds receive income support from government benefits (de Vaus, 2004). Young people, as they grow older, are increasingly likely to generate their own income. However, in making this transition they typically go from parental financial support to government support to self-support. This process may be protracted for some, particularly for those engaged in full-time education or from socially disadvantaged or marginalized backgrounds.

Schneider (1999) notes that in Australia in the period between 1992 and 1996 the percentage of young people aged 15 to 24 who were financially dependent – defined as those living below the poverty line – rose by 12 per cent with increases most marked for 15 to 20 year olds. From 1982 to 1996, financial dependence among 15 to 24 year olds increased from 37 per cent to 61 per cent among young men and 40 per cent to 62 per cent among young women. Almost all of those aged 15 to 17 years (96 per cent) were financially dependent.

Rates of income poverty (less than half the average income) are higher for young people aged 15 to 24 than for any other age group with over one-quarter (27.1 per cent) of single, non-dependent young people aged 15 to 24 experiencing income poverty. Low youth wages, the collapse of the full-time youth labour market, continuing participation in education and high rents contribute to this income inequality.

The family

Many sociologists have noted that radical changes are occurring in the traditional notion of the nuclear family, particularly over the past decade. Most researchers link these changes in family types, as well as rules, forms and ideals of family life, to the increased individualization which came to characterize the second half of the twentieth century (Beck, 1992; Beck and Beck-Gernsheim, 1995, 2002; Giddens, 1990, 1992; Stacey, 1990, 1996; Weeks *et al.*, 2001). Like other domains of our lives (such as school and work), the family has increasingly become an arena of choice and individual decision-making. Within the family, prescribed roles, responsibilities, obligations and commitments are increasingly negotiated. Where role expectations of fathers, mothers and children were once largely assumed, now family members increasingly reflect on what they will and will not do or accept. People increasingly question who they love or do not love, how they demonstrate care for one another and themselves, and how, where and with whom they want to live (Giddens, 1992). The changing nature of the family is reflected in shifting patterns of family and household types in Australia.

While there is increasing diversity of family and household types, couple families remain the most common form. Census data from 2001 indicate 52 per cent of children aged 15 to 24 live with two parents (not necessarily both biological parents) and 14 per cent live with a lone parent. Brandon (2004) estimates that one-quarter (26 per cent) of children in Australia under 15 years old do not live with both biological parents. De Vaus reports that at the time of the 2001 census 21.8 per cent of families with dependent children were lone-parent families; of these, most live with their mothers. Nearly 27 per cent of children spend some time up to the age of 18 living in a lone-parent family.

In 2001 stepfamilies and blended families accounted for approximately 9 per cent of families in Australia with children under 18 years. Again, the majority of these children live with their mother (de Vaus, 2004). There is very little information on the financial position of stepfamilies or blended families but these data indicated that parents with children in these families, particularly mothers, are less likely to receive financial support from the non-resident parent than those living with lone parents. This difference was even more pronounced in regard to other types of financial support, such as payment of school fees (de Vaus, 2004). However, the percentage of stepfamillies or blended families living below the poverty line is considerably lower than that of lone parents (de Vaus, 2004).

Conclusion

These social trends form the backdrop to the experiences of homelessness had by the young people in our study. The fact that early exiting of the family home is statistically becoming increasingly rare only renders those who do so under sufferance or in difficult circumstances all the more vulnerable. As youth policies, services and discourses adjust and respond to this new, more complex mode of transitioning from adolescence to adulthood, young people who experience homelessness are at risk of becoming more marginalized than ever.

3 Participation and pathways

The hardest thing about leaving home was not seeing my mother every night. That killed me. . . . Just not seeing her and being able to talk to her if I needed it, like even though I didn't talk to her much, I knew that even if I needed to, I couldn't. Not seeing my little sister. I wasn't even allowed around at their house for a while and that hurt.

(Barry)

In this chapter we briefly describe our broader longitudinal study of young people experiencing homelessness, *Project i*. We then focus on the smaller cohort of young people in this study whose diverse pathways into and through homelessness form the basis of the material in this book.

Recruiting participants

Young people aged between 12 and 20 years who had spent the last two consecutive nights away from home (either without a parent's or guardian's permission if under 17 or had been told to leave) were recruited into *Project i* from youth and homeless services in Melbourne, Australia. We initially had two groups of young people: those defined as 'newly' homeless (77 males, 88 females; mean age 17.0 years), who had been living away from a parent or guardian for less than six months although they may have returned home multiple times during this six-month period, and 'experienced' homeless (266 males, 261 females; mean age 17.9 years), who had been living away from a parent or guardian for more than six months. Participants were recruited from 95 youth or homeless services across all regions of metropolitan Melbourne between December 2000 and August 2002.

Following a comprehensive screening procedure, eligible young people were invited to participate in the survey.

What did we do?

Once recruited, all the young people completed a survey which included questions about accommodation history, drug and alcohol use, sexual practices, mental health/illness, HIV/HCV/STI testing and status, family contact, social support, friendships, current and past employment and education, income support, alternative sources of income, survival skills, and service use. Questions regarding drug and alcohol use and sexual practices were administered using an Audio-CASI (computer assisted structured interview).

The newly homeless cohort was surveyed on five further occasions over a two-year period. As a result of intensive tracking strategies, we maintained an 85 per cent follow-up rate at each survey.

In undertaking this longitudinal study of newly homeless young people we were particularly interested in their pathways into and through homelessness. In order to examine these pathways more closely, we selected a subgroup of 40 newly homeless young people who, in addition to completing the surveys, we interviewed 18 months after their recruitment into the larger study. The primary criteria for selecting participants for these interviews were gender, age and level of service use. The sample was selected from the larger cohort of newly homeless young people by generating eight groups from a cross-tabulation of age, gender and service use (high and low). Age was defined by median split (12–16 years and 17–20 years). For each participant, a measure of number of services used was created by summing responses to 18 service use questions on the initial baseline survey. High/low service use was defined by median split (0–2 and 3–9 services used). Five participants from each group were then randomly selected to take part in an interview; these lasted between one and one and a half hours and were undertaken by trained interviewers between November 2002 and August 2003.

The interviews were designed to elicit accounts of the young people's experiences of homelessness and to gain their perspectives on their pathways into and through homelessness. Participants were asked to discuss their reasons for leaving home, their accommodation history, their forms of social support and connection, including their use and satisfaction with services, their engagement in employment and education, and personal practices that affected and/or reflected their health and well-being (e.g. drug and alcohol abuse, self-harm, suicide, sexual practices).

Forty case studies were subsequently developed, based on a combination of these interviews and selected results from the preceding surveys in which these young people participated. By combining the quantitative and qualitative findings, we were able to plot stories about young people's homelessness pathways and examine the associations between personal, familial and institutional practices on their homelessness journeys.

Constructing homelessness pathways

To aid our analysis of these young people's different pathways into and through homelessness we created four categories based on the presence or absence of two interdependent criteria, type of accommodation (whether they were homeless or home) and how long (stability) they had been in this accommodation at the time of the interview. The pathways categories were: street-based homelessness ('on the streets'); service-based homelessness ('using the system'); unstably housed ('the ins and outs of home'); and stably housed ('going home').

Stability was defined as living in the same place for six months or longer prior to the interview. We used two broad accommodation types: home and homeless. 'Home' refers to accommodation in either private rental, family home or partner's family home. We defined these accommodation types as 'home' because all the young people living in these places for a stable period identified themselves as having a home. Homeless accommodation included street-based and service-based living. The assumption that young people are homeless when living in services is based on our finding that 80 per cent of young people identify as homeless when in this situation.

While we could have chosen other criteria by which to categorize young people's pathways into and through homelessness (e.g. age, mental health status, drug and alcohol use), we chose accommodation type and stability of accommodation for several reasons. First, policymakers and service providers have expressed concerns about how best to provide optimal accommodation outcomes for this diverse group of young people. Second, by avoiding the use of 'problem' categories such as mental illness we make no assumptions about the significance of these factors in young people's homelessness pathways. In this way, we also shift the focus away from pathologizing these young people as individuals with 'problems'. In this chapter we describe and discuss each of these four pathways and the young people classified within each pathway.

The 'on the streets' pathway

Contrary to media stereotypes and public perceptions regarding the prevalence of 'street kids', only five of the 40 homeless young people interviewed were actually street based. Sleeping rough in squats or in other forms of transitory accommodation, young people experiencing this most unstable form of homelessness are highly vulnerable. Often they have violent and chaotic family backgrounds and a long and unhappy association with government social services. Typically, the precariousness of their physical situations is paralleled by the instability of their mental states. Ongoing mental health issues, self-harm and suicide attempts are common among these young people. So, too, is frequent polydrug use. Their lack of a semi-permanent physical base makes it almost impossible for them to accumulate material possessions and to maintain a reasonable level of personal hygiene and presentability. This then becomes a significant barrier to them finding and/or maintaining employment. Unable to work, yet needing to buy food and to support drug habits, many young people living on the streets turn to drug dealing, shoplifting and other forms of crime in order to survive.

Of the five young people living on the streets, two were female, the other three male. One, Kimberley, was an Aborigine, while the other four had Anglo-Celtic backgrounds. All five self-identified as heterosexual. When compared with the other 35 people in the study, on average, these five became homeless at a younger age. Jamie and Craig were both 12 when they first became homeless, while Ben, who was the oldest when this occurred, was only 17.

The families from which these young people came varied from single mothers (Kimberley and Jamie), nuclear (Craig), extended (Kayla) and blended (Ben). Kayla, Craig and Jamie shared family backgrounds typified by poverty, violence and neglect. As such, they were forced from their family homes by intolerable circumstances, under the guidance of the Victorian Department of Human Services (DHS). Ben and Kimberley came from financially stable families and their exiting of the family home was more, though not entirely, a matter of their choosing.

At the time of the final interview Kayla, 16, was separated from her baby daughter and living in a secure welfare unit: Craig, 18, was unemployed and temporarily living in a caravan. Jamie, 17, had recently attempted suicide and was camping in a bush squat. Kimberley, also 17, had returned to Melbourne with her boyfriend and was sleeping in her car: Ben, 19, had been sacked from his part-time job and was 'couch surfing' at friends' places.

The 'using the system' pathway

Seven of the 40 young people that we interviewed had been living in medium-term accommodation for at least six months. Accommodated in transitional or lead tenant, supervised housing, their living circumstances were more secure than those of the street-based homeless young people. Even so, all of the young people in this using the system pathway considered themselves to be homeless.

Whereas three of the five street-based homeless young people came from materially impoverished and emotionally and physically abusive family settings, this was true for only two of the seven young people in the using the system pathway. The remaining five had a history of disconnection from and displacement within their families but had not been subjected to sustained abuse, trauma or neglect.

Another possible factor in the comparatively better accommodation outcomes for these young people was that, on average, they were slightly older when they first became homeless than their street-based counterparts; three had left home when they were 15 or younger, three were 16 and one was 17.

However, the single most notable characteristic of these young people was that more than half were born overseas and either immigrated with their parents to Australia or later joined them there after being raised overseas by grandparents. Of the four who were from culturally and linguistically diverse (CALD) family backgrounds, two were from Asia, one was from Africa and one from the Middle East. Only one other young person among the 40 interviewed came from a CALD family background. Why this overrepresentation? We can conjecture that in cases where young people leave home in part because of issues concerning cross-cultural conflict, the disagreement between parent and child is typically deep-seated enough to preclude the young person from returning home, yet not so damaging that she or he is, through drug abuse and/or mental illness, unable to secure reasonably stable, service-based accommodation for themselves. Another factor is that, despite these young people being in conflict with parents' cultural expectations, they have in fact taken on the common migrant emphasis on the importance of education and hard work. Thus, they accessed services that enabled them to continue their studies, maintain part-time employment and thereby achieve their generally ambitious career goals.

As with the on the streets pathway, family configurations within this group were varied. Prior to leaving home Adam was living with both biological parents, Toby and Brittany were living with their single-parent mothers, Maree, Fahra and José were living with a parent and a step-parent and Victor was living with his aunt and grandmother. As with the on the streets young people, all seven in this group self-identified as heterosexual.

At the time of the interview: Brittany (18) was living in medium-term accommodation and was enrolled but not attending school; Fahra (17) was in transitional housing and was doing an Arts degree at La Trobe University; Victor (17) had just moved back into a shared house with his brother and was doing a technical and further education (TAFE) course in digital design; Maree (18) was living in transitional accommodation for young students, working part-time and doing full-time tertiary study; José (17) was living in supervised student accommodation and was studying business and working part-time; Adam (17) was living in supervised medium-term accommodation and studying hard in Year 12; Toby (19) was also in his last year at school and living in a supervised shared house.

The 'in and out of home' pathway

In the time that elapsed between the initial survey and the interview, six of the 40 young people interviewed went from staying in refuges or couch surfing at friends' houses to either living back in the family home or in privately rented shared accommodation. Three of the six returned home in that time, while the other three entered shared households. We have categorized these six as the in and out of home pathway. Their routes into and through homelessness are typified by a comparatively fluid movement between the family home and alternative forms of accommodation. Their journeys, the beginnings and ends of which were arbitrarily defined by the timeframe of our study, 'ended' with them being accommodated in more secure, privately funded housing. Perhaps even more importantly – especially in terms of contrasting them with the young people in both the on the streets and using the system pathways – at the time of their interviews the young people in the in and out of home pathway no longer identified themselves as being homeless.

According to a measure of homelessness defined by accommodation type, their trajectories were extremely positive, tracing a path from homelessness to a renewed sense of home; from insecure, often publicly funded accommodation to more secure, privately funded housing. It is, however, the very fluidity of the accommodation outcomes of the young people in this pathway which suggests that by another measure, one governed by stability, they were in fact less secure, more vulnerable and in that sense 'more' homeless than their serviced-based peers. As we discussed in Chapter 2, for most people the notion of 'home' denotes something more than mere shelter, than simply being housed. In general use, 'home' suggests a stable base, a place from which one can venture forth into the world secure in the knowledge that one has somewhere safe to return. Despite being housed either in shared accommodation or back in their family home, nearly all of the six young people in the in and out of home pathway had serious unresolved mental health and/or drug and alcohol issues that rendered their current accommodation arrangements highly provisional. In fact, compared with those in the using the system pathway, the lives of these young people seem in greater flux, to be more unsettled and unstable.

In contrast to the majority of those in the using the system pathway, five of the six young people in this pathway had Anglo-Celtic family backgrounds, with the other one (Christie) having an Italian heritage. Four of the six were female, two were male, and all self-identified as heterosexual. In terms of family composition, none of these young people came from a blended family. Three (Kate, Lauren and Christie) had both parents at home, and the other three (Tim, Lucy and Damon) came from single parent (female) families. Tim and Lucy had both been placed in foster care early on in their teenage years, but with disappointing results. It is interesting to conjecture whether or not the absence of step-parents played a positive role in the general willingness of these parents to accept their children back into the family home after they had fled from or been forced to leave it. While our research sheds no direct light on this matter, the generally negative impact of step-parent relations evident across the 40 interviews suggests that the absence of this added dynamic might assist in family reconciliation more often than not.

The financial status of the families from which these young people came varied from solidly middle class (Kate) to impoverished (Lucy). Only Lucy, Christie and Tim could be said to have come from neglectful or chaotic families, though nearly everyone in this pathway described their family as troubled and their family life as typified by conflict. In contrast to the parents of those in the using the system pathway, half of the young people in this pathway reported that one or both of their parents suffered from a mental illness, and at least one parent of two of the six was drug or alcohol dependent.

When interviewed; Kate (16) was attending school and living with her boyfriend; Lauren (18) was living back in the family home and was working full-time; Tim (16) was enrolled in a vocational training course and living in a shared house with friends; Lucy (17) was living with her mother and her mother's new fiancé and enrolled in the final year of secondary school; Christie (18) was working part-time and living in a shared house; Damon (19) was back living with his mother and working as an apprentice in a furniture factory.

The 'going home' pathway

The last homelessness pathway identified is characterized by young people experiencing a relatively brief period of homelessness, followed by either a return to the family home or entry into another form of stable private or public housing. Of the 40 young people interviewed, over half (22) followed this pathway, making it by far the largest of the four. By the time of the interview, 12 were back living in their family home, with members of their extended family or with their partner's family. Another eight were in private rental accommodation and two were living in public housing. Eight of the 13 young women in this pathway were living with boyfriends, five in private rental accommodation and three at their partners' parents' house.

The one element that clearly distinguishes this pathway from the others is time. That is, the young people in this pathway were homeless for shorter periods of time than those in the other three pathways. Seven of the young people were homeless for less than three months, another seven for less than six months, six for less than a year, and the remaining two for less than 14 months. At the time of their interviews, they had all been securely housed in private or public accommodation for longer periods (i.e. for at least six months) than their in and out of home counterparts. In our analysis of young people's homelessness and their vulnerability to homelessness, the length of time that someone is securely housed is a key indicator of stability. This then suggests that the young people in the going home pathway were less likely than those in the in and out of home pathway to become homeless again in the near future. Like their in and out of home peers, some in this pathway had unresolved mental health and drug issues, but the very fact that they had resided in one place for six months meant that, whatever their other issues, they were not compounded by accommodation insecurity.

Similar to those in the on the streets and using the system pathways, the family configurations within the going home pathway were widely varied, with 13 of the young people coming from single-parent families (ten mothers, three fathers), four from nuclear families, three from blended families (though one of these was a broken blended family in which the stepfather had reared the child), with the remaining two young people having been raised by their grandparents. Only two people in this pathway described their families as being highly chaotic. In both these cases, the young person had been placed in DHS care as a child. Of the 22, only two came from materially deprived backgrounds, significantly less than the three of five with similar backgrounds in the on the streets pathway.

Another distinctive feature is that very few of the young people experiencing this pathway reported that their parents had mental health or drug and alcohol issues. For example, only three indicated that their mothers had a clinical mental illness (i.e. schizophrenia or depression). This contrasts starkly with the parents of those in the in and out of home pathway, 50 per cent of whom suffered from a mental illness. There were similarly low rates of reported alcohol and substance abuse among the parents of the young people in the going home pathway. As has been observed, these parental factors are often crucial in both the family conflict that leads to a young person becoming homeless, as well the ability of their parents to respond to that event in a way that encourages ongoing family contact and the possibility of future reconciliation.

Beyond, but also including these ongoing family connections, relationships in general were crucial to the journeys through homelessness taken by these young people. In every case in this pathway, the young person's journey out of homelessness was aided by their relationship with a family member (often one of the extended family), a service worker or a boyfriend or girlfriend. (This will be discussed in greater detail later.)

The large number of young people experiencing this pathway precludes us from telling the stories of all of its constituents, as has been done for those in the other pathways. Instead, we have selected five young people who followed this pathway to stand for all those in the going home pathway. While these five have, to some extent, been chosen because their stories illustrate experiences common to those in this pathway, they are not in any strict, quantifiable sense representative of the whole. In fact, their selection was based on the power and poignancy of their stories as much as any notion of representativeness.

Compared with the other three pathways, the young people in the going home pathway left home at an older average age, that being 17. This was the average age of the five young people whose experiences of homelessness are discussed below, with three of them having left home at 17, one at 16 and the other at 18. Three of the five were female, the other two male, which again roughly mirrored the 13 female, nine male composition of the wider group. The Anglo-Celtic ethnic origins of these five also reflect those of the others in the pathway, who uniformly shared this heritage. As with all of the 40 young people interviewed, these five young people self-identified as heterosexual. Their family configurations before becoming homeless all but cover the full range of options present in the wider group, with only the nuclear family being unrepresented. Tom and Suzie were raised by male single parents (with Tom's being his stepfather); Emma and Phoebe were brought up by a combination of female single parents and grandparents and Nick came from a blended family.

At the time of their interviews: Tom (19) was doing an apprenticeship and living with members of his extended family; Phoebe (19) was working in a supermarket and living with her boyfriend in a private rental property, Suzie (19) was trying to finish secondary school and was living in a shared house with her boyfriend; Emma (20) was living with her boyfriend in a private rental property and was working part-time as a waitress; Nick (18) had recently begun a traineeship and was living in the family home.

In the next chapter, we describe the pathways into homelessness experienced by these 40 young people and examine the similarities and differences between members of the four pathways in an attempt to discover if the reasons for leaving home provide us with insights into their pathways over the next 18 to 20 months.

4   Becoming homeless

> When my mum kicked me out the last time I thought, that's it, that's enough, I've copped enough beatings, I've copped enough 'you're wrong'. I have copped enough 'You're the reason my family broke up. You're the reason why I'm not happy; you're the reason why my grandma's sick. You're the reason why this, you're the reason that. It's your fault, everything's your fault.' I'd had enough of it. I'd had enough. I couldn't take it any more. Like I was really – I was angry. And I still am. But I don't wanna have that anger. Because it's not healthy.
>
> (Joanne)

Under what circumstances did young people in this study become homeless? The answers to this question enable us to shed light on two issues. First, the stories they told about leaving home allow us to understand in a unified way the multiple circumstances surrounding this event and their interrelationships. Second, our four pathways were not developed on the basis of young people's entry into homelessness. Hence, the stories we report here enable us to determine the impact, if any, of the young people's reasons for leaving home on their subsequent journeys through homelessness. We take each pathway in turn.

'On the streets' pathway

Of the five young people in this pathway, two (Kimberley and Ben) chose to leave, the other three were told to go. This choice, or lack of it, represents a significant dividing line within this pathway and our account and analysis reflects this distinction.

Dropped out – seeking independence

Of the five families, Kimberley's single mother and Ben's parents and step-parents offered the most stability and support. Kimberley and Ben had boundaries imposed on them reflecting parental expectations regarding their children's current behaviour and future orientations. Kimberley's response to her mother's midnight curfew was to disregard it. 'If I was grounded . . . I usually tried jumping the back fence at about five in the morning, climb through my window.' Under the influence of her boyfriend, Kimberley thought she would rather live 'under my own rules'. Telling her mum that she wanted to travel, Kimberley left home. Reflecting on this time, laughing about it, she said:

> I thought it would be easy before I left but it was so much harder than I thought . . . It was so much easier living at home, and I was thinking it was hard living at home. I felt lost. I felt so alone and I felt really upset when I didn't know if I was going to find where I was going. I didn't know what was going to happen to me.
>
> (Kimberley)

In a sense, Ben left two homes, first his mother's and then his father's. After his parents' divorce, he lived with his mother, who later remarried. Ben continued to have a good relationship with his mother until he finished school and dedicated himself to partying. After a working holiday in the USA, he moved in with his father, his step-mother and his newborn half-sister. Ben was disappointed to discover his father was no more relaxed about his partying lifestyle than his mother and stepfather had been:

> It kind of all came to a head when they said, 'Look, you're gonna have to get a job and, you know, start doing something with your life. You're not just gonna sit up at Jeremy's place smoking pot all day.' And I'm like, 'Yes I am!' So, yeah, I kind of had enough warnings and then one day they just said, 'Oh, look, we've had enough; you've got to leave.' So I went . . .
>
> (Ben)

While, strictly speaking, Ben was asked to leave his father and stepmother's house, his repeated refusal to alter his behaviour in accord with their expectations represented a chain of choices that made his leaving home almost inevitable. Hence, unlike Kimberley who made a positive choice to leave, Ben made a passive choice to do so. Knowing what was at stake, he chose not to change and thereby gave his father and stepmother the power to choose the timing of his leaving.

Influenced by problematic friends and living lifestyles centred on the acquisition and taking of drugs, both Kimberley and Ben rebelled against their parents' attempts to provide boundaries for their behaviour. In both cases this resulted in a pattern of conflict that culminated in the young people rejecting the kinds of support their parents offered and ultimately in them choosing to leave home in search of greater freedom and adventure. Kimberley declared, 'I don't like being told what to do anymore. My rule is that I can do anything. The rules are there are no rules.'

In their own terms, Kimberley and Ben did not leave home in flight of hardship or maltreatment, but rather to pursue their independence. Speaking of his new circle of friends, Ben drew a clear distinction between people like him who had left home from choice and those who had been forced from home by poverty or abuse:

> Most of my mates have kind of basically dropped out . . . they've been out of home for a few years – not because they're kinda from, you know, poor families or they have broken homes or anything, it's just that they're independent people, I guess.
>
> (Ben)

Kicked out – fleeing abuse

Kayla, Craig and Jamie came from exactly the types of families Ben had in mind when distinguishing those of his friends and, by implication, his own. All came from stressful, volatile families, in which poverty, parental drug or alcohol abuse and trauma contributed to their leaving home. As children they experienced extreme violence and neglect from parents who, for a variety of reasons, were unable to provide them with stable home environments. All three had been the focus of interventions by the Department of Human Services (DHS), with Craig and Jamie having been placed in foster homes.

Ironically, in trying to stop Kayla from leaving home, her father reinforced one of her primary reasons for going – to escape family violence:

> And he goes, 'You're not leaving, I want you to stay home. Please stay home, you're hurting your mother – you're hurting me and her.' And I didn't want to go, but he pushed me against the wall . . . and I pushed him back and he pushed me back even harder and fucking elbowed me in the

face. The bad thing was my older sister actually smacked my head into the gutter on the side of the road, and she full-on pounded into me in front of my parents and they sat there and watched for ten minutes before they took her off me, and I thought, 'Mum, why didn't you do something?'

(Kayla)

The trigger for Craig leaving home was the repetition of a well-established pattern of family conflict and arbitrary violence meted out by his mother. Squabbling with his older brother over control of a Nintendo, Craig found himself the focus of his mother's fury as she burst into the room and 'started hitting me with a rubber hose'. Craig retaliated, pushing his mother to the floor, threatening to stab her in the throat:

I wanted to. I don't know why I didn't though. I was only twelve, they wouldn't've been able to put me in gaol. I would've gotten away with it. I wish I did. Oh, I do. Like, she's been an absolute mole to me my whole life. . . . She's not a good mother . . . Her approach with me is 'Out of sight, out of mind.'

(Craig)

Jamie's history of family abuse started very early, with his mother accused of poisoning him when he was only five months old. 'That's when Human Services first got onto us. . . . Human Services wanted to take me and my sister off Mum and Dad, and that's when all the abuse in our family started.' Both of Jamie's parents were addicted to heroin. When Jamie was eventually removed from his parents and placed in a foster home, the cycle of violence and abuse that had encircled his life to that point was continued rather than broken. With remarkable generosity, he recalled:

I like my foster care father, he did his best for us. But at that time, when we first got into foster care . . . he wasn't used to people like us, you know, little shits. We weren't that violent until we actually got there, but we copped everything from the metal end of straps across the forehead to pieces of wood with nails in 'em. . . . it was just shock horror.

(Jamie)

The most stable period in Jamie's life was the six years between the ages of five and 11, when he and his sister lived with their Nan. 'For the first time in our lives we got a proper parent who cared about us, looked out for us.' Unfortunately, though, the trauma of his early years had filled Jamie with an anger that produced its own violence.

Aged 12, he rebelled against his Nan's strictness and, disobeying a court order, moved back with his mother. Predictably, this arrangement did not last long. 'Things got very abusive after I moved back to my mum's. . . . My mum got pissed one night, threw a bottle at my head and that's when I thought, "Nuh, it's time to get out of here." I went on the street.'

Where a key factor to Kimberley's and Ben's decisions to leave home was their resistance to the limits their parents placed on their behaviour, for Kayla, Craig and Jamie the reasons they left home were rooted in their parents' inabilities to regulate their own behaviours around drugs, alcohol and violence. Ironically, a perceived excess of stability (experienced as rigidity) and a total lack of it produced similarly tragic results: people as young as 12 living on the streets.

Ownership of negative behaviour

A striking characteristic that these five young people shared was a willingness to take responsibility for their part in the events that led to them becoming homeless. None of them thought of himself or herself simply as a victim. Kimberley and Ben fully acknowledged their roles in the family conflicts that led to them leaving home. Kimberley explained:

> Me and Mum were just fighting every day. I was being a little shit. I know how hard it was for Mum and that, to raise three kids on her own. I know I put her through a lot of shit and I've told her how sorry I am and stuff, but you don't realize it until you're out and see what everybody else goes through and find out how hard life really is on your own.
>
> (Kimberley)

Ben was similarly honest about his negative attitudes towards his parents prior to him becoming homeless:

> When I was living with my mum I used to run away all the time, 'cause I didn't get along with my stepdad. But I don't think they would've kicked me out if I'd stayed there. But instead I moved [to my dad's]. Like, I got along great with Mum for years, but things started to fall apart when I finished school. I was just partying a lot and just pretty much being a stubborn little turd.
>
> (Ben)

Despite the violence and deprivation they endured as children, wrongly or rightly, Craig, Kayla and Jamie still accepted some responsibility for the conflict in their families. When asked what led to him leaving home, Craig replied, 'Years and years of torment on my mother by me. But it was a two-way street, she'd give and she took and I gave and she took.' For Kayla the main source of the conflict was her drug use:

> I used to have a really good relationship with my mum and dad and then when I hit 13 I got into the wrong crowd and I started sniffing paint, and I started chroming. And my mum was so hurt over it. It kept going for two years, until I was about 15. . . . It just hurt my mum so much, and she just had to call the Department and say, 'Look, take her, we can't have her any more.'
>
> (Kayla)

Even Jamie, who was the most violently abused of the five, reflected on his Nan's harshness and realized that 'she was just doing whatever she could to keep us off the streets'. He acknowledged that when he was 11 and 'everything started going down the creek' it was because he had 'turned very violent', but that his violence and anger stemmed from memories of 'what my foster parents had been like . . . the little details of the violence'.

Drugs and alcohol

All five of these most vulnerable homeless young people spoke of drug use as a factor in their leaving home. For Kimberley and Ben the drug use was all their own, for Kayla it was a combination of her drug use and her father's drinking, while for Craig, and particularly Jamie, it was their parents' addictions that were crucial.

Whether as a symptom or a cause, drugs were central to Ben's conflict with his parents and step-parents. When confronted with the choice of restricting his drug use and remaining at his father's home or leaving and being free to 'party', Ben chose the latter. Describing his new lifestyle, Ben said:

> Most of my time now I probably spend at the beach, or at my friend's house near the beach. . . . Usually we just sink piss down at the beach. Yeah, I don't know, occasionally we get together and play music, do something constructive. But usually we just hang out and catch up with each other and try and see if we can do some more dope, get off our faces.
>
> (Ben)

While much of the violence in Kayla's family was fuelled by her father's alcoholism, Kayla's use of drugs caused conflict with her mother. 'It was like all my friends and all my family and my mother started disappearing because, you know, my whole attitude changed and I was only after one thing: drugs, drugs, drugs.'

While Craig's father's alcoholism contributed to the chaos of his family life, for Jamie, his parents' addictions were pivotal to his childhood deprivation and were therefore significant causes of his homelessness. Unlike Kimberley, Ben and Kayla, Craig's and Jamie's own drug use was not a key factor in them leaving home. Given that they did so at age 12, it is perhaps not surprising that most of their experimentation with drugs occurred after they became homeless. Even so, both had started smoking marijuana before they left home.

Summary

As we have seen, the routes into homelessness for the young people in this pathway were characterized either by a desire for greater independence, associated with the pursuit of drug-centred lifestyles, and/or the need to flee violent and chaotic family lives. It is noteworthy that neither parental nor personal mental illnesses were cited as reasons for leaving home, though all five in this pathway suffered from reactive depression after they became homeless.

'Using the system' pathway

Where the routes into homelessness for the young people in the on the streets pathway could be analysed in terms of seeking independence or fleeing abuse, these categories are less relevant to the seven young people experiencing this second pathway. With the exception of Brittany, these young people were not attempting to escape impoverishment and material neglect or leaving the restrictions of a caring home. For most, their route into homelessness began with a sense of being displaced within their families and ended with them leaving home in order to pursue conventional education and employment goals. The dislocation of the four young people from culturally and linguistically diverse (CALD) backgrounds involved physical separation from one or both parents during or after the immigration process. Brittany's displacement was also physical, as she was placed in foster care at the age of 18 months. In the cases of Toby and Adam, the displacement was more psychological; a sense that they did not belong in the families into which they were born.

Displacement and disconnection

Until the age of five, José was raised by his maternal grandmother in the Philippines. 'I never called my mum my mum until maybe – I don't know, 13, 12 . . . It was only a couple of years ago.' As an adolescent living with his sister and mother and his mother's boy-friend, José found his mum to be 'very strict' and often extremely angry. In her rages she sometimes threatened to kick him out of home. After one such outburst, José called her bluff, packed a bag and stayed at his friend's house for a week:

> That pretty much scared her because she didn't – she thought I was gone. Because, like, I've never said 'No' to my mum in my life. Like, I've always respected her 'cause she was the only person there.
>
> (José)

After successfully pleading with her son to return home, it wasn't long before José's mum once again ordered him to leave. 'So I did, the next day, and I took everything. And I don't think my mum really meant it, I think she just said it.'

Maree's mother left her two daughters in Malaysia when she came to Australia, the older child with her mother (the child's maternal grandmother) and the younger, Maree, with her ex-boyfriend's mother (Maree's paternal grandmother). When Maree was seven, her mother began a relationship with a man that Maree has never liked. When the couple had a new baby, the family was effectively split in two. Maree felt that her mother no longer treated her and her older sister like daughters, but 'more like slaves. . . . We have to make sure that, you know, this is done and that is done. Like, it's just so much stress that you can't even concentrate on your homework.' Part of the conflict between the mother and her two older daughters was cross-cultural. What Maree experienced as intolerable restrictions on her freedom, her mother – comparing her daughters' lifestyles with her own growing up in Malaysia – perceived as being liberal and indulgent. 'She said she's really modern . . . that she gives us a lot of freedom. . . . She thinks she's not being restrictive at all. She just thinks she's educating us the right way.' After enduring yet another fight with her stepfather, Maree felt that she 'just couldn't stand the pressure anymore' and enacted her longstanding plan with her sister to leave home together.

As with Maree, physical dislocation and cross-cultural conflict were key elements in Fahra's route into homelessness. Born in Iran, Fahra's parents divorced when she was three:

> I lived with my mum until I was seven years old. The law in Iran is for the kids to be given back to their father as soon as they turn seven. So, I just had to go back and live with my dad. They lived in different cities. My dad and my mum, they had this thing, you know, like a revenge sort of thing. So my dad's revenge was for her not to see me and my older brother.
>
> (Fahra)

As a child, Fahra loved her mother deeply, and having that bond broken at the age of seven made her distrustful of others – particularly her father's second wife – and fiercely self-reliant:

> I've always been, like, independent. I make up my own decisions. I never let anyone – 'cause, just like, back then, when I separated from my mum, when I was seven years old, I knew I was on my own. I was a very mature kid. I was the kid who never played, you know, like. I learnt how to cook and clean and wash dishes.
>
> (Fahra)

Once living in Australia, Fahra's independent streak was encouraged by her friends and the broader culture but strongly discouraged by the patriarchal elements of her culture of origin. Interestingly, though, it was not her father but her older brother who actively played the role of patriarch, setting himself up as the enforcer of Iranian custom, the protector of his sister's virtue:

> And because of, like, our culture and everything, like, my brother, he's very strict. He's very proud. . . . And my brother was very strict with me. I wasn't allowed on the phone. He had to come and check whether I was talking to a girl or a guy. And for me that was, like, embarrassing. I was talking to my friend on the phone and he would just grab the phone and see if it was a girl or a guy.
>
> (Fahra)

Her brother's obsessive over-protectiveness provoked ongoing conflict regarding Fahra's behaviour and his desire to monitor and control it. 'My brother thinks he owns me. Like, he might call me ten times a day, "Where are you? What are you doing? Who are you with?"' When she announced that she had found a boyfriend on the internet and was going to visit him in Adelaide, both her brother and father were outraged. Much like Maree's departure from home, Fahra's leaving was premeditated, so that once she turned 16 she made good on her oft-repeated threat to leave her father and brother if they did not treat her with greater respect.

Victor's family dislocation was extreme and was experienced by him as abandonment. Born in Tanzania, he migrated to Australia with the rest of his family when he was seven. The family lived together in Melbourne for one year, then, suddenly, unexpectedly, his parents returned to Tanzania with his two younger brothers, leaving Victor and his older brother behind. Years later, Victor still had no idea what motivated his parents' sudden departure, or why they left without him. 'They went back to their business, I think. I don't know. It's something I am trying to forget about. . . . I haven't seen my mum and dad for a long time; a big gap. I don't know who they are.'

Initially, Victor and his brother were placed in foster care, but before long they were taken to live with their aunt and grandmother. This, though, was not a happy arrangement, partly for reasons of cross-cultural conflict similar to those experienced by Maree and Fahra, but predominantly because the aunt seemed to dislike her nephews. Most of her anger was directed towards Victor's older brother, the constant conflict leading him to flee her home. With the older boy gone, Victor then became the focus of her discontent:

> When [my brother] left she didn't have anyone to pick on, so, yeah, she started to pick on me. I was sick of it and I isolated myself from her. You know, didn't come out of my room. I got in trouble for going to a festival and coming home in the middle of the night. She didn't want me to go first of all, but then when I came home late at night, she cracked it, and a few days later she asked me to leave.
>
> (Victor)

In effect, when his brother left their aunt's house, Victor's sense of dislocation and abandonment was complete. In most ways that matter, Victor had become homeless when he was eight years old, when his parents abandoned him.

In different ways, the routes into homelessness of the three young people with Anglo-Celtic backgrounds – Brittany, Adam and Toby – covered some of the same terrain traversed by the young people with CALD family backgrounds. Brittany shared the experience of being physically separated from her parents. It could be argued that in fact her route into homelessness began when she was a baby, with the absence of her father and with her mother's schizophrenia. When Brittany was 18 months old the DHS placed Brittany in foster care, where she remained until she was 14 years old. Recalling her time in foster care, Brittany said, 'It was okay until I was 12. And then I had to leave . . . 'cause I was sexually abused in foster care. And all they

[DHS] cared about was covering their arse.' Disillusioned with social services and the people who work in them ('I just started to realize that they don't really care about you; they're just doing their job'), Brittany returned to live with her mother for the first time in 12 years. From the outset, the move 'home' was a disaster. 'My mum's just a bitch. Every day she bashed my brother. I'd defend my brother, and then she'd bash me.' After three years of constant conflict, Brittany's mother 'kicked her out' permanently. 'I was used to it because she used to kick me out all the time.'

In contrast, Adam came from a strong nuclear family, but he shared a form of cross-cultural conflict with the young people from CALD backgrounds. In his case, the conflict derived from his parent's commitment to fundamentalist Christianity. As a young teenager, Adam repudiated his family's belief system and its attendant, all-encompassing lifestyle. His sense of dislocation was psychological and emotional rather than physical. He felt he did not belong in that subculture and that no one in it was willing to listen to him:

> I was going to the school, the Christian school which my mum taught at, and my dad worked at the church, which is part of the school . . . I really hated it and it just didn't agree with me and when my parents couldn't understand anything that I was going through and no one at church would either, and I just couldn't find anyone to talk to, I just thought, 'I hate this; I hate living with my parents.'
>
> (Adam)

Similar to Maree and Fahra, Adam's and his parents' expectations regarding freedom diverged:

> My parents were really, really restricted with me . . . a lot of the time they were treating me like I was eight, ten years old. Like, I'd ask, 'Can I not go to church this weekend 'cause I don't feel like going to church any more, I don't think it's for me?' But I wouldn't say that 'cause I was really scared to say that, but I didn't wanna go to church. 'No, you're going to church, you have to go church. If you live under this roof, you're going to church!' And it was the same situation with every little thing, every little thing that could possibly happen. 'No, we're the parents, we decide what's going on here.'
>
> (Adam)

The conflict escalated over time and, after one particularly brutal argument with his father, Adam 'ran away' from home. Unlike Maree and Fahra, this was an unpremeditated act, one that resulted in him catching a train to Sydney, where he quickly ran out of money and sought assistance from the police.

In many ways Adam's route into homelessness fits neatly into the 'seeking independence' category. In the face of his parents' rigidity and lack of understanding, he decided he did not 'want to live with my family anymore. I want to be able to make my own decisions and I want to make my own mistakes.' In one sense, though, his experience runs counter to the stereotype of a young person rebelling against parents. Like José, Maree and Fahra, Adam was not rebelling against 'mainstream' parental expectations but rather the reverse. He was seeking freedom from his family's involvement in a fundamentalist Christian culture in order to participate more fully in the 'mainstream', to focus on things like study.

Like Adam, Toby's sense of dislocation and disconnection from his family was psychological and emotional. He too sought greater independence. However, his route lacked the element of (sub)cultural conflict that characterized Adam's experience. Toby's mother provided him with a reasonably stable home life; it just wasn't the life he wanted to live. Reflecting on that period, he took full responsibility for the circumstances of his leaving home. Whereas Adam felt his parents were not willing to listen to him, Toby rebuffed his mother's repeated invitations for him to talk to her about his life:

> Yeah, like I never – I didn't really speak with my mum, like she'd try and speak to me, but like I'd just ignore her and like do my own thing, like. I felt a bit uncomfortable.
>
> (Toby)

Toby's mother's desire for emotional connection with him, for his approval, left him wanting more space:

> I wanted my own space and she was sort of like in my space, even though it was her place and like, more than anything, she should've felt that I was in her space, 'cause she couldn't really do very much 'cause I didn't approve of what she wanted to do, like go out or whatever.
>
> (Toby)

Where many adolescents feel powerless in the face of their parents' unrealistic expectations, seemingly unable to gain their approval, for Toby the power balance was inverted. In leaving home he was not fleeing his mother's disapproval of his behaviour but rather her need for his approval of her behaviour. His desire for independence stemmed from a need to break his mother's dependence on him, to renounce power as much as to assert it. In one sense, his motivation for leaving home was similar to that of Adam and their CALD counterparts; he left home not to rebel but to become more conventional, to escape familial relationships that set him apart from other teenagers.

Violence

When compared to the families from which the majority of young people in the on the streets grouping came, those in the using the system pathway were generally more financially stable and far less chaotic. Despite this, familial violence was a contributing factor in five of the seven in this grouping becoming homeless. In Adam's case, the parental violence was reactive, a physical expression of broader, ongoing family conflict. For Brittany, José, Maree and Fahra, the violence was systemic, a regularly recurring element in their families' lives.

Maternal violence was common in this grouping. In three of these five instances of familial violence it was the mother who was the perpetrator. Brittany's mother regularly 'bashed' her brother and beat Brittany if she attempted to intervene. For Maree and her older sister, violence was the means by which their mother enforced her strict regime of domestic labour:

> We're basically adults and she's like, you know, physically trying to hurt us if she's not happy about a certain thing. I suppose it's because of power; she just feels that because we're growing up she's losing power.
>
> (Maree)

While it was Maree's mother who regularly meted out the violence, she and her stepfather also regularly fought. These arguments only became physically violent on one occasion. 'He only hit me once, like slapped me around the face until I bled.' Fahra's experience of male violence was more regular and, in keeping with his adoption of the role of patriarch, was administered by her brother, not her father:

> My brother pushed me, and I fell onto the ground and I injured my nose really bad. . . . It was swollen and I had, like, basically my whole face was black. And, I mean, before that, he had hurt me, and my teachers realized, so they called child protection services, because I was under 16 at that time. . . . And, he had an intervention order, like, on me, so he couldn't come anywhere near me for a year. So they made him move out, but he still came back all the time. He just moved back in.
>
> (Fahra)

Flaunting the intervention order, Fahra's brother continued to physically intimidate her. In the end, his violence was central to Fahra's decision to leave home.

In Adam's case, his father's violence was reactive, an escalation of their heated arguments about religious belief and church attendance. As with Fahra, for Adam the violence represented a tipping point in the family conflict, an indication that things had gone too far, that he needed to leave the family home. 'I guess when my dad started getting violent with me, that was really just the icing on the cake. I knew then that this isn't fun, this isn't what family is meant to be. I wanted out.'

Step-parents

Blended families and step-parents were an essential element in the family conflicts experienced by four of these seven young people. In the cases of Maree and Fahra, their parents' new partners played stereotypically negative roles. Maree often fought with her stepfather, who treated her with disdain. Illustrating his inappropriate behaviour, Maree spoke of how, when she was younger, her stepfather would watch porno videos in front of her. Despite having been present in her life for most of her childhood, Maree had no respect or affection for her stepfather and refused to acknowledge that he had any authority over her. 'I don't care who he is, how long he's been there, he's not my father and he doesn't have a right to tell us what to do. . . . I don't like him. I don't care about him. I don't want to know about him.'

Fahra spoke of her lack of trust in her stepmother based on Fahra's belief that her stepmother was jealous of her maturity and of her relationship with her father. One incident in particular stood out in Fahra's memory as testament to her stepmother's deep dislike of her:

> I knew my stepmother didn't like me, so I was never happy with, like, letting her do things for me. So I thought I'll just do them myself because maybe she's going to break this or maybe she's going to – and one day she did, you know. She put acid in my shampoo. And like, thank God my dad came home early that day. . . . as soon as I put it on my – like on my head, I just started screaming and my dad came in and he realized what was happening. He took me to the hospital.
>
> (Fahra)

While Maree's and Fahra's relationships with their step-parents were fairly typical, the effects of Toby's and José's parents' new relationships were far less conventional. Both their mothers had boyfriends but, in Toby's case, it was not the presence of any one of his mother's boyfriends that became a factor in his route into homelessness. Rather her need for him to approve of her having boyfriends in general, and specific men in particular, became a source of conflict. Interestingly though, by the time of our interview (18 months or more after leaving home), Toby had more sympathy for his mother's situation and regretted his rejection of her. 'I probably shouldn't've done half of the stuff that I did. . . . Looking back, like, you think about these things and – 'cause then to, like, grow more you tend – I'm more aware of it now. I'd like to be more aware of people's feelings.'

In stark contrast to the stereotype, for José, his mother's long-term boyfriend was a source of conciliation, not conflict. As the communications between José and his mother worsened, the boyfriend tried to console each party and be the mediator:

> And like, one time when I left home, I went to Jerry, my mum's boyfriend – I go to talk, I told him that, you know, I can't handle it. And he just goes, you know, just try to be good, and he's like – I don't know, like he was sticking up for both sides: me and my mum.
>
> (José)

Drugs and alcohol

In spite of drugs and alcohol being a common ingredient in family conflict leading to homelessness, it is striking that none of these seven young people cited either their own or their parents' drug or alcohol use as a factor in their route into homelessness. Only Fahra spoke of the use of drugs and alcohol prior to becoming homeless and did not link it to family conflict:

> My brother uses drugs, and my dad drinks. I can't really tell you if he's an alcoholic or not, but he's harmless when he drinks. But for me, I don't like to see that. I don't like alcohol . . . I hate the smell of it; I hate the taste of it. And for me, that's like insecurity, you know, when you're with someone who's drinking or using drugs. My brother, he's, on marijuana and he smokes marijuana everyday.
>
> (Fahra)

Summary

The routes into homelessness of the young people in the using the system pathway were typified by their sense of dislocation from and disconnection with their families. For over half of them, their sense of not belonging contained an element of cross-cultural conflict regarding expectations. Other common factors included systematic parental violence and conflict borne of blended families and step-parents. The almost total absence of drugs and alcohol as elements in their routes into homelessness is noteworthy and raises the question as to whether or not, and to what degree, this influenced their accommodation outcomes once they became homeless and framed their experiences of homelessness.

'In and out of home' pathway

Mental illness was commonly cited as a cause of homelessness by young people in the in and out of home pathway, as was drug and alcohol abuse. None of these six young people left home to seek greater independence, nor were any of them fleeing extremely abusive homes. Instead, four exited home amidst personal and/or family crises, while the other two were forced to leave as a consequence of their own difficult behaviour. These two categories frame the following analysis of these young people's routes into homelessness.

Crisis

All four females had serious and ongoing mental health issues. In addition to their own mental illnesses, Lucy, Lauren and Kate also spoke of their parents' mental health problems. Unlike many other young people for whom depression or other mental illnesses comprised one part of a complex backdrop to them becoming homeless or was a reaction to this event or state of being, for these four young women mental health issues were central to them leaving home.

In Lauren's, Kate's and Christie's cases, these issues were exacerbated by a specific crisis within their wider families. The underlying tensions in Lauren's family were heightened by her mother's involvement in a serious car accident:

> I was at home and I'd just had another major argument with my parents. There was tension in the house and no one wanted to be there. My brother was hardly ever there . . . Mum – I think Mum was probably suffering from depression as well, 'cause she'd had a car accident not long before. And Dad didn't care about anything at the time; just didn't want to know about it. I just don't think he could deal with Mum's accident, and I

> think my brother was doing Year 12 at the time, I was suffering from
> depression and it was just . . . I think it just got to him and he knew he
> couldn't do anything.
>
> (Lauren)

The mother's accident was a tipping point for a family struggling to cope, triggering depression in Lauren's mother and father and resulting in family dysfunction. Ultimately, in the heat of an argument, her mother asked her to leave the family home.

Kate's family, too, had endured a traumatic time prior to her leaving home.

> Before I left home it was quite a disaster . . . All of a sudden I had about
> two deaths in the family – Mum's mum and Dad's dad – in the space of
> about three months and my mum was full-on depressed and my parents
> had a falling out with their closest friends. . . . It was just full on . . . I just
> thought everything was falling apart.
>
> (Kate)

This sequence of distressing events left Kate's parents 'stressed out' and undermined tolerance within the family. Things which ordinarily would not have been an issue suddenly became the source of serious conflict. Also Kate's clinical depression and her heavy marijuana use were heightened at this time:

> When they told me to leave it was out of anger. It was completely like,
> 'Fine, get out.' And I'm like, 'Fine, I will.' And I walked out and they were
> just like, 'She'll be back.' . . . I stormed out crying in a tantrum, and my
> parents didn't believe I would actually go; they kind of didn't care 'cause
> they thought I'd be back in the morning. . . . The next day they called me
> and wanted me to come back home and said that I was always welcome
> to come home. But I refused to, because I was just so angry that they'd
> kicked me out in the first place.
>
> (Kate)

Christie's conflict with her mother echoed another rift in her wider, extended family. As with Kate and Lauren, the trauma of this external issue magnified the pre-existing tensions in the parent/child relationship:

> A big family feud started . . . My gran's health is deteriorating and, you
> know, my mum and my aunts were fighting about, um, how to look after

her. . . . I think it was very stressful on my mum, you know, she'd be crying a lot.

(Christie)

Christie and her mum had never really got along and in Christie's mind at least 'my mother hates me'. Throughout Christie's teenage years their relationship became a series of rolling disagreements and disputes that periodically snowballed into a major argument. Christie acknowledged her role in the conflict and the negative impact her mental illness had on the situation:

> I was very depressed at the time. The tiredness kind of became depression and, um – so I was depressed, I was really easily irritable and, yeah, just all the shouting and fighting and I was missing a lot of school at the time because I wasn't feeling well and I – I'd still be going out at night time at that stage and my mother didn't like it. She didn't like who I was hanging around with, thought they were a bad influence.
>
> (Christie)

Although Christie's mother had threatened to evict her many times before, ironically no such threat was made during the fight that finally resulted in her leaving. In fact, after this fight it was Christie's mother who first left home, momentarily casting Christie as the fretful one left to imagine the worst:

> My mum and I had had a really, really big fight and um I just went into my room and I suppose I started packing just in garbage bags. And um, when I got out, mum had gone. I think she had gone for a drive and I remember sitting and thinking to myself, 'You know, if she doesn't come back, or anything happens to her, you know, this is going to be my fault, 'cause we'd had an argument. Um, you know, if she doesn't come back alive, it's gonna be my fault.' But anyway, I just went to a friend's house and slept on the couch there for a while.
>
> (Christie)

In Lucy's case, her father was absent ('he just sort of made his own life') and had a history of schizophrenia. Her mother suffered from depression and panic attacks and was an alcoholic. Two years before Lucy left home, an anonymous caller notified the DHS about her mother's erratic behaviour. Lucy, at that stage, was suffering her own prolonged bout of depression. If anything, over the next couple of years, Lucy's home life worsened:

> And my mum, like she was getting drunk, and when she was seeing her
> ex-boyfriend, he was like an alcoholic too, they'd get drunk together.
> Basically, it was having an impact on me, I suppose. I was just scared. At
> the time I was just really depressed and I just didn't want to live with her
> because I was sick of coming home and seeing her drunk, and I was sick
> of fighting with her about everything. I couldn't get along with her at all,
> and we would have basically probably ended up killing each other or
> something.
>
> (Lucy)

When Lucy told her mother that she was thinking of accepting a
placement in foster care her mother accused her of wanting to leave in
order to receive the government youth allowance. Feeling guilty,
manipulated, but also genuinely concerned, Lucy deferred leaving.
'But then, you know, I got so sick of it. We just started fighting again
and then I'm like, "Okay, I want to do this," so this lady organized it
and I went into foster care.'

Problematic behaviour

Unlike the routes into homelessness of the four young women that
were dominated by mental illnesses exacerbated by external crises,
those of Tim and Damon were characterized by their own problematic, sometimes criminal, behaviour. Both Tim and Damon had
absent fathers and, in Tim's case, a mother who often drank to excess.
It seems likely that the rejection felt by Tim and Damon contributed
to their general rage and their disregard for their mothers' attempts to
place limits on their behaviour.

Tim's parents separated when he was five years old. Initially his
mother attempted to raise him and his two siblings on her own, but
after a while she moved the family into her mother's house. According
to Tim, his grandmother didn't like him because he was 'very
disobedient'. Tim's home life was typified by conflict and his life at
school was no better:

> I wagged school . . . I was always, always having problems. . . . School
> sucked. I've hated school ever since I can remember. That's always been a
> problem. . . . Me and my brother always fought. We'd always just have
> arguments. We were little shits, basically. . . . I just didn't get along with
> my mum. When I did start to go out myself – like when I was 11, 12 –
> everywhere I'd go she'd ask me, 'Where've you been? What've you been
> doing? Who are you going with? What time are you going to be home?
> What exactly are you doing?' Maybe she was trying to be protective, but

it was probing into my life too much, I felt. I got sick of it; we'd always have arguments. We'd have arguments about school, have arguments about cleaning my room. We'd just have arguments about anything and everything and finally it got to the stage where every time we saw each other we were arguing.

(Tim)

Tim's use of drugs was a constant source of tension, until one day his mother ordered him to leave the house, threatening that if he returned she would call the police. In truth, she had made arrangements for him to live with his father. The first couple of months of him living with his dad went well, but then when the new school year began 'things turned bad'.

He was doing the same things as my mum was, except if I didn't answer he'd whack me one. . . . He was just a normal person, nice guy, you know, but everything we did together – fireworks. Big drama! I stayed there for another six months and then I ran away from there.

(Tim)

Reflecting on his past behaviour, Tim gave a brutally honest, unflinching self-assessment:

When you're young you don't take responsibility for things, but I think I was a little shit and it was half my fault too. I can understand that I was a little shit. I didn't do anything I was told to do, like young kids are meant to . . . listen to their parents, go to school, be a good person, not get into trouble. At the time I didn't think it was my fault at all. I thought I was being completely reasonable about it all. At the time I thought my mum was just a drunk ball-breaker when I first got kicked out, but I was a little shit too.

(Tim)

Damon's parents separated when he was four and his father has been living interstate and so totally absent from Damon and his siblings' everyday lives. Damon was bullied by his older brother who Damon believed was favoured by his parents. Damon's childhood resentments reached a crescendo six months prior to him leaving home. Whereas in the past he had shared a bedroom on his brother's terms, smoking his joints outside, suddenly he decided, 'Nah, I'm taking over the room. If you wanna come in, you have to put up with the smell, otherwise, don't come in here.'

In the end though it was not this fraternal tension that triggered Damon's departure from home, but rather a conflict he was having with one of his neighbours. Like Tim, in his teenage years Damon had developed a serious drug habit and became involved in various criminal activities (mainly dealing) in order to support it. When a neighbour accused Damon of stealing a bass guitar that Damon claimed was in fact his, the underlying tensions between them erupted into raw aggression. Fortunately Damon's mother arrived home before the men came to blows. Somehow she defused the situation and managed to get her son inside their house. In an uncontrollable rage, he proceeded to destroy most of his belongings, hurling them around his room. Like Tim, in hindsight Damon viewed what happened next sympathetically from his mother's perspective:

> She just couldn't control it, couldn't control it any more with the extent of the aggression between me and the neighbours. She couldn't go on every day with it, so she pretty much – I left that night, I just went, 'Yeah, I'm going to a friend's place where I can cool down,' and then when I came home the next day I wasn't allowed in the house. She was home, and she normally isn't, and she just said, 'Stay outside, you're not allowed in the house, you've just gotta wait.' So I just waited and the police came and handed me an intervention order.
>
> (Damon)

Violence

Compared to those in the two earlier pathways, these young people were rarely victims of domestic physical violence. Only Tim and Christie spoke of being hit by their parents and both represented their parent's violence as reactive and contextual rather than systematic and/or malicious, thereby, in their minds, normalizing if not excusing it. Christie expressed a generous interpretation of her mother's punishment, placing it in historical context as a practice passed on down the generations. 'Her childhood was very bad, like her mum just ignored them. It was back in the old days where you'd hit your kids or smack, I suppose. And that's kind of the way she treated me. I think that's because of her mum.'

The only other mention of physical violence prior to becoming homeless was Damon's aggression towards his neighbour. By his own account, while this anger was not directed towards his mother it created an intolerably violent atmosphere in the family home.

As we have seen, heated arguments and verbal violence played a role in each of these young people becoming homeless. Of the four evicted from the family home, all were told to leave in the midst of a verbal brawl, in the heat of the moment. While it is not hard to imagine a distressed parent later wishing he or she could retract such a directive, it is also reasonable to conjecture that the lack of parental physical violence enabled this directive to be overturned in time. This would suggest that physical violence is a threshold issue; that when sustained physical abuse results in a young person becoming homeless, the threat of such violence recurring operates as a strong and reasonable deterrent to them ever returning home.

Mental illness

While all of the young people in the using the system pathway suffered from reactive depression after they became homeless, only one, Victor, had a severe, pre-existing mental illness. This contrasts with young people in the present pathway in which parental and/or adolescent mental illness was a key factor in four of these young people, all female, becoming homeless. While all four had mental health problems themselves, two, Lucy and Kate, said that mental illness 'runs in the family'. Lauren too said that her parents suffered from reactive depression after her mother's car accident. These three cases all suggest that the fragility of the parents' mental health made it impossible for them to cope with their daughters' mental illness. In this way, and given their conciliatory gestures later on, it is possible to interpret Lauren's and Lucy's parents' responses to the young women's suicide attempts as an inability to care rather than lack of care.

Drugs and alcohol

An even stronger point of contrast between the young people in this pathway and their counterparts in the previous pathway is their use of drugs and alcohol. While their own or their parents' use or abuse of drugs and alcohol was not a reason for leaving home among the young people in the using the system pathway, this was far from the case for those in the in and out of home pathway. Combined with and compounded by mental illness, the use and abuse of drugs and alcohol was a major contributing factor in five of these six young people becoming homeless.

Prior to being forced from their homes, the lives of Kate, Lauren and Damon had all become primarily focused on the acquisition and consumption of drugs. Their use of drugs and involvement in the cultures and lifestyles that attend to them became a constant source of concern for and conflict with their parents. All three spoke of how the need to feed their habit became their daily priority:

> My main priorities would be, when I was living at home, get ten dollars for my marijuana and another two dollars or something for food, for the munchies afterwards. That's what I used to do every day. I used to wander around Knox City with my friend and scab in the shopping centre.
>
> (Kate)

The cost of Damon's habit quickly accounted for all his available income and savings and ultimately led to him becoming a dealer. Distressed by these developments, Damon's mother encouraged him to undergo a detoxification programme, which he eventually agreed to do:

> I went to detox before leaving home. The only reason I went in there – I had no intention of getting off it – I only went in there to shut my mum up. Just so I could say, 'All right, yep, I've done detox. Right, leave me alone.' But, um, I always knew that no matter how many times people tell me to get off it, I'm just gonna do it to spite them. I mean, I'll go out there specifically just to spite them and do it.
>
> (Damon)

Summary

The dominant shared elements in these young people's routes into homelessness were severe parental and personal mental illness, external family crises, personal drug use and, in two cases, family conflict caused in large part by the young people's self-assessed problematic behaviour. It is noteworthy that there was an absence of systematic parental violence in this pathway, which may have been a factor in enabling these young people to later reconcile with their parents and, in some cases, to return home.

'Going home' pathway

As with the other three pathways, family conflict was the main trigger for young people in this pathway becoming homeless. These conflicts were often around issues concerning the young person's desire for greater independence, their attempts to push their parents' boundaries. For young women in this pathway, parental disapproval of boyfriends was the most common trigger for the fight that led to them becoming homeless. By choosing to date a boy that their parents considered unsuitable, these young women were exercising their agency and asserting their independence. Their boyfriends represented their power to make choices beyond parental control and thereby became the focus of the conflict between them.

In contrast to the in and out of home pathway, whole family crises (in which external events disrupted normal family life) did not feature as reasons for becoming homeless. Interestingly, the reasons these young people left home can be evenly divided between those forced to leave and those seeking greater independence, much as they could be for those in the most vulnerable on the streets pathway. Of the five examples that we consider in the going home pathway, three were seeking independence and the other two were made to leave by their parents. The congruence of reasons cited by those with the best and the worst accommodation outcomes demands further consideration. In particular, it raises the question: What factors led to the independence-seeking young people in the going home pathway achieving much better accommodation outcomes than their independence-seeking equivalents in the on the streets pathway? How did similar motivations result in such starkly contrasting housing outcomes (albeit, provisional ones)? It is, then, this trope of agency and constraint, choice and necessity that frames our discussion of the routes into homelessness taken by these five young people from the going home pathway.

Seeking independence

Phoebe, Tom and Suzie all had complicated family backgrounds, though none of them could be described as abusive. Rather than fleeing abuse or neglect, in leaving home they were escaping the conditions and limitations placed on them by people who had cared for them and continued to care about them.

Phoebe's mother suffered from severe schizophrenia and was unable to look after her daughter. Hence Phoebe was raised by her grandmother until she was 15, at which time her grandmother died. 'I still feel very close to her and I still think about her more than anyone. So, every day I'll think about her.' For the next two years Phoebe lived with her uncle and aunt and their three much younger children where she was treated well. Despite her drug habit, her relatives continued to support her, and it was Phoebe who decided to end this comfortable living arrangement. Ironically, she did so because it was too good, because the contrast between 'this perfect family life' and her own traumatic past was too great for her to reconcile:

> I just felt wrong where I was, even though it was the best for me, I felt it was best for them to just let them have their own little family because I just felt – I don't know, I just felt like – um, I felt guilty for being there. . . . [But] I was like, 'I'm really lucky.' So I felt I just had to be happy, I couldn't feel bad.
>
> (Phoebe)

But Phoebe did in fact 'feel bad'. She also felt compelled to confront those feelings and to resolve the dissonance between her external and internal realities:

> I moved out 'cause I just felt I needed to understand myself more and I realized then that I'd just sort of blocked it out. Because I had this happy atmosphere, I didn't need to think about it and then I was like thinking about it again, so . . . I wanted independence. . . . I felt that I had so many things that were important in my mind, like so many things that I wasn't being exposed to in that house. It was all sort of normal.
>
> (Phoebe)

Phoebe's departure from the material comfort and emotional stability of her uncle and aunt's home was not a rebellious assertion of independence, but rather a quieter recognition of her need to find her own way forward, a way that took account of her past. While she recognized the virtues of her relatives' lifestyle and remained grateful to them for sharing these with her, Phoebe chose independence over comfort and convenience in the hope of healing past hurts and of forging a more sustainable, reconciled happiness into the future.

As with Phoebe, Tom's family life was complicated and characterized by pain, but also by care, albeit from unconventional quarters. Tom's father was an alcoholic who 'used to get very violent towards Mama'. He left Tom's mother when Tom was three months old and Tom had only seen him once since then, when he was seven. His mother's new partner was also an alcoholic, but a reformed one:

> Jim was never violent with us when he drank; he was always sober with us. . . . He's going to AA meetings and trying to stop, trying to keep from drinking. . . . My relationship with him was like a father–son relationship, you know. And he trusted me and he let me do things.
>
> (Tom)

When Tom was 14, his mother walked out on Jim and the children. The new arrangement was unconventional, with the mother moving two blocks away, coming daily to help look after the children. Despite her assistance, Tom said, 'She wasn't there all the time like a mother should be, so I took on the mother's job.' While Tom resented being forced to carry such a heavy burden of responsibility, he was also accepting of it and was committed to the welfare of his siblings. Negotiating a new type of relationship with his mother, while working closely with his stepfather, Tom was vital to the smooth functioning of this reconstitution of the family:

> I took on the full responsibility for looking after the kids. Jim was working all the time, so I was there for them. . . . I was going to school at the time; I wasn't working. . . . I mean, all my life I've been looking after the little kids. . . . Going to school and looking after the kids, so there really wasn't anything else in my life apart from looking after the damn kids.
>
> (Tom)

Unorthodox as it was, this complex family configuration seemed to work until Jim and the children moved to another suburb. Tom described their new address as 'that sort of crappy area where not everyone was able to be trusted'. Somehow that sense of suspicion and mistrust infiltrated the family unit and undermined Tom's good relationship with his stepfather. Tom did not explain, or did not know, what caused him to lose Jim's trust (something he had greatly valued), but now whenever a misdeed was committed, Jim no longer turned to Tom as an ally, but rather as the prime suspect. Worst of all, Jim no longer trusted his stepson to care for the other children. 'He was sort of making me feel unwanted around him and he didn't really trust me with the kids anymore. So, really, what was the point of me being there?' Having invested so much of himself in the task of looking after his younger siblings, once he was given the message that his services in this area were no longer appreciated, Tom at first felt bereft and abandoned, 'like a black sheep', but then he felt the exhilaration of his freedom. With his reason for staying at home taken from him, he chose to leave, to focus on himself. Ironically, Tom's independence-seeking route into homelessness inverted the usual pattern of the adolescent chaffing against his or her dependence upon parents, and instead arose after he was relieved of the burden of having others dependent upon him:

> I felt free then. You know, I left home and I didn't have any responsibilities anymore, so I felt free. I just wanted to start up my life again, so I did that. I took on new responsibilities, for example, work and living arrangements.

> . . . Just stuff I couldn't do for the past 18 years by myself, so I've had to go
> out and find out how to do that.
>
> (Tom)

Of the three, Suzie's case more closely fits the stereotype. Her desire
for greater independence grew from her sense of being oppressed by
her father's attempts to place limits on her behaviour and movements.
Suzie's mother had died when Suzie was nine, leaving her father to
raise the children. He was strict and critical of Suzie's behaviour and
in her words 'never really got used to having a girl in the house'. They
fought 'non-stop', mainly over issues related to Suzie's growing
independence. This underlying tension was given a new, more intense
focus when Suzie entered into a relationship. 'I got a boyfriend that
he really hated, which drove him even more insane and he just went
pretty nutty.' Not only did this relationship come to symbolize her
father's fear about her growing up, away from his own sphere of
influence, but it played on his prejudice:

> My dad wasn't too comfortable about the cultural differences, that my
> boyfriend was Pakistani and . . . Muslim and stuff. He wasn't very com-
> fortable with that. . . . I've wanted him to learn that I'm going to choose
> who I'm with, not him.
>
> (Suzie)

With neither able to compromise, it seemed it was only a matter of
time before Suzie would depart the family home. Whether she was
forced to do this or chose to is something of a moot point. In the end,
she was ordered from it by her father. 'The final straw was like my
dad told me I had to get out within two weeks. And I went, "Yeah,
good, I'll be away from you."' While she is right to say that 'he told
me to leave; he gave me no choice', on one level Suzie chose to allow
her father to decide the timing of what had come to seem an inevitable
event. 'I'd been wanting to move out. Like, I wanted to get away from
it.' So, although Suzie did not choose the timing of her departure,
much like Ben in the on the streets pathway, the choices she had made
prior to this in exerting her independence in the face of her father's
intransigence set up a dynamic that turned choice into necessity.

This points to the limitations of agency as a way of interpreting
such relationships. For how meaningful is it to suggest that by
asserting her independence Suzie was ultimately 'choosing' her
departure from the family home? Perhaps if through some external
intervention (e.g. family counselling) she had been made conscious of

the longer term consequences of her rebellious behaviour, we might then be able to think of her route into homeless as directed by a series of conscious choices. The story of Suzie and her father cautions us against applying the notion of choice and constraint too reductively to the lives of all the young people in this study.

Forced to leave

If Suzie's case is positioned close to the classificatory border between young people choosing to leave home and those forced to do so, Nick's story occupies a similar position on the other side of that same fine line. As with Suzie, Nick's home life was dominated by ongoing and recurring conflict with his father. 'Me and my old man weren't getting along, and like jumping down each other's throat. Like, always yelling at each other and like just general verbal abuse.' The pair argued about everything, but particular triggers included 'the way I dressed, the people I hang around with . . . why I'm not working and why I'm not doing this and that'. The point of contrast with Suzie's case is that, unlike her, Nick had not reached the point of wanting to leave home of his own accord. Therefore, when his father told him to leave the family home he was not giving voice to a position that both parties mutually, if tacitly, acceded to. Nick's eviction came as a shock and an affront to him, as though he had had no idea that his behaviour and the dynamic between his father and himself might have produced this outcome:

> I was absolutely distraught, you know. I was so upset, you know. Like I got kicked out of home, you know. I was – I didn't care for nothing in the world. . . . You know, I done criminal activity and I just couldn't care, you know.

> (Nick)

Of the 22 young people in the going home pathway, Emma was one of only two who came from an abusive, chaotic family background. Emma's mother was addicted to heroin and when, as a teenager, she gave birth to her daughter, she was incapable of caring for her. As a result, Emma's maternal grandparents adopted her and masqueraded as her parents (pretending that her birth mother was her older sister) for much of her childhood. Trying to compensate for her mother's neglect, Emma's grandparents resisted Emma's push for greater independence as they attempted to protect her from her mother's self-destructive lifestyle. Predictably this only resulted in Emma rebelling.

'I'm 18 years old, like at the time I was, and I should be out, going out alone, by myself in the world. And, you know . . . they wrapped me in this big cocoon or some shit.' Once Emma developed her own drug habit, her grandparents 'tried to help me heaps and, ah, it didn't work'. In exasperation, they finally asked her to leave. Against her grandparents' advice, Emma moved in with her mother. Within a few weeks, though, the mother and daughter were fighting constantly. Then one day all the minor arguments culminated in a 'big blue. She's like really, really selfish and I told her that one day, so she kicked me out.'

Emma's family background and her route into homelessness share some similarities with those of Kayla and Jamie in the on the streets pathway, which were characterized by heavy personal drug use in the first instance, and neglect borne of parental drug abuse in the second. These similarities make Emma's contrasting experiences through homelessness all the more noteworthy, if not instructive. How did someone with a similarly chaotic family background and her own serious drug habit manage to resolve her homelessness so much quicker than the likes of Kayla and Jamie? To what degree is Emma's more direct journey through homelessness attributable to the foundation of care and ongoing support provided to her by her grandparents?

Drugs and alcohol

Of the four pathways, the young people in the using the system pathway were the least affected by drug and alcohol abuse. Those in the going home pathway were the next least affected; 50 per cent stated that they had never had a problem with drugs. While regular recreational use of alcohol and marijuana was common, and party drugs (e.g. ecstasy) were occasionally used, most in this pathway did not cite their drug use as a factor in their route into homelessness. Hence, the fact that Phoebe and Emma said that their drug use did contribute to their leaving home is misleading in terms of the overall population in this pathway.

Phoebe's marijuana habit was one of the things that made her feel uneasy about living with her uncle and aunt and her young cousins. She began smoking at 16, around the time of her grandmother's death, and soon her marijuana use became central to her sense of self. 'When you smoke marijuana it becomes part of you and like, really a part of you. Like that's who you are; you're a marijuana smoker.' Phoebe's quest for independence was entwined with her desire to reconcile her view of herself as a renegade marijuana smoker with the conformist, 'normal' home life she was leading at her uncle and aunt's house:

> My illusion was that if I was out, you know living by myself, I'd get to know people I wouldn't usually get to know. I don't know, just – 'Cause I just I felt like I was a strange person so I should be living a strange life, not just a normal life. It just felt wrong. I just felt really – I don't know, I was just – I was always stoned as well.
>
> (Phoebe)

It was 'mainly because of my drug use' that Emma was asked to leave the home of her grandparents. Then, when living with her mother, who was herself a heroin user, it was her mother's own prioritizing of drugs above all else that caused the conflict that led to Emma being 'kicked out'. In this way, personal and parental drug use were key factors in Emma becoming homeless.

Suzie's and Tom's attitudes to and experiences of drugs were more typical of the majority of the young people in the going home pathway. Suzie had never been a regular smoker of marijuana. 'I've only ever been one of those people who smoke it about once every six months and then regret it, because everything spins' and Tom told us, 'I haven't had any drug use in the past.' This attitude to drugs was common among the young people in the going home pathway, reflecting the lack of influence of drug use on their routes into homelessness.

Mental illness

Unlike those in the in and out of home pathway, mental illness among both the young people and their parents was not a major factor in the routes into homelessness for those in the going home pathway. Of the 22 young people, most reported that they experienced no mental illness prior to becoming homeless. Of the five cases under discussion, only Suzie cited mental illness as contributing to the conflict that led to her becoming homeless. In listing some of the things she and her father fought over, she said, 'Like school for example, because I had just – like I suffered from anxiety, which I still do, and at that time I wasn't leaving the house much, I wasn't going to school, I wasn't going to my exams.' Nick also said he suffered from depression, though he did not link this to his route into homelessness. 'I just deal with it by myself. I just swallow it down in my gut.'

These young people's generally better mental health was reflected in lower rates of suicide attempts and episodes of self-harm. Whereas roughly 50 per cent of the young people in the other three pathways had attempted suicide and/or had repeatedly self-harmed, only two of the 22 in the going home pathway had attempted suicide, and while seven had self-harmed, only three of these had done so repeatedly.

Violence

While domestic violence featured as a reason for leaving home in the on the streets and using the system pathways, this was not so among those in the going home pathway, most of whom had no experience of domestic violence. All six of the 22 in this pathway who had experienced violence at the hands of their (step-)parents said that these episodes were the result of violent outbursts that occurred at points of crisis and high stress, rather than them being premeditated and/or malicious. Of our five featured cases, only Emma mentioned violence as being an aspect of her life prior to leaving home. Talking of the fights she had with her mother she said, 'We're very much similar, and she'd tell me what she thought of me and I'd say what I thought of her, and it was on, you know, we'd have punch-ons and things like that.' As with the in and out of home pathway, the lack of arbitrary domestic violence in the lives of the young people in this pathway seems to have increased the possibility of them forging positive relationships with their parents into the future, with many of them eventually being able to return to the family home.

Summary

The routes into homelessness of the young people in the going home pathway were characterized by family conflict arising from young people either actively seeking independence or behaving in ways unacceptable to their guardians or parents, who felt compelled to ask them to leave. Generally, drug and alcohol use, mental illness and violence were not key factors in these young people leaving home, which, we assume, helped them to quickly resolve their homelessness.

Conclusion

Although our four pathways were defined in terms of young people's accommodation outcomes 18 months after the study began, and up to two years after they became homeless, it is clear that our pathway classification revealed significant differences in young people's routes into homelessness. While family conflict emerged, as it usually does, as the key factor, there were subtle (and not so subtle) differences in how this conflict was enacted for each of the pathways. The most commonly cited triggers for leaving home, as well as family conflict (violence, mental illness, drug use), were nominated to a greater or lesser extent by young people in each of the four pathways. In spite of some variability among young people in each pathway, the overwhelming impression from their stories is how these common causes for leaving home intersected in distinctive ways in each pathway and were given particular weight. For example, drug and alcohol abuse of young people and, often, family members, figured in both the on the streets and in and out of home pathways. However, in the former this was often associated with sustained violence and neglect, whereas in the latter violence and neglect did not feature. It is these nuanced constellations of reasons that potentially allow us to anticipate young people's pathways through homelessness.

In the following four chapters we describe young people's journeys through, and in many cases out of homelessness, highlighting, as in this chapter, the similarities and differences between young people within and between the pathways.

5 On the streets

> We're on your doorstep and you see straight past us. It's like you've purposely turned a blind eye; it's hard. . . . I'd like to see an organization that would give homeless people work, even if it's only the cheapest you can possibly pay. Youse might not believe this, but we find it hardest to find jobs. We haven't got somewhere to go at night where we can wake up in the morning and go, 'All right, time for work.' We've not got money for transport. We've got no money for food. We have to do everything from scabbing up money for food, to scabbing up money even for a drink, like we haven't got house taps 'cause we're on the streets, mate. Ain't no house tap, so it's very, very hard.
>
> (Jamie)

Whether homeless from necessity or by choice, life on the streets entailed similar experiences for the five young people in this pathway. Even so, the differences between Kimberley's and Ben's reasons for becoming homeless, their seeking of independence, and Kayla's, Craig's and Jamie's flight from abuse influenced the way they interpreted their experiences of homelessness. What follows is a discussion of those experiences, the common elements as well as the different attitudes the young people brought to them, and the understandings they took away.

Accommodation

With the exception of Ben, everyone in this pathway had been living on the streets or in highly unstable accommodation for an extended period of time (longer than 18 months). All five spoke of having made multiple moves since leaving home, with Ben having moved the least, about 12 times, and Kimberley the most, approximately 100 times.

Kimberley's extraordinary mobility is in part explained by her desire to travel and by the need for her boyfriend to avoid the law, as warrants for his arrest had been issued in every state except Victoria. While Kimberley and Archie had rented 'scummy flats' for brief periods and at one time had lived in a old bungalow with an outdoor shower, they more typically slept in a tent or in their car. 'Since we've been in Melbourne we've just been sleeping at truck stops and rest areas and stuff. . . . About every hour or two you have this huge truck pull up. I prefer to sleep at the rest stops.'

Ben continued to draw a distinction between him and his 'dropped out' friends and other homeless young people whom he termed 'morons' and 'useless people'. Despite this, Ben's accommodation history since leaving home was very similar to those of the people from whom he sought to distance himself.

> I was in the supervised house for three months, then I moved in with my girlfriend at the time. I was there for three or four months and then we got a unit together. We lived there for six months and then we both moved out of the unit and went our separate ways. Then I moved into a share house – the bachelor pad. . . . I started kind of not getting along with people that were there so I moved out a couple of days ago. Since I've moved out I've just been staying at friends' houses. I slept in my car last night.
>
> (Ben)

Ben despised living in supervised accommodation. Given that his primary motive for leaving home was to seek greater freedom, it is not surprising that he was disappointed to find himself living in another house where his behaviour was supervised and subject to strict rules:

> I moved into a shelter for homeless people, then into a supervised shared house. There were three others in the house, including the supervisor. . . . I really, really didn't like the supervisor guy. . . . I would've been happy about being out of home if I'd just moved in with a mate or kind of got a place with a mate; got a room on my own. But because it was in this supervised place, it just made me feel like a dirty little homeless bum. You know, because you have to check in with your worker and you can't have anyone in your room, and you can't have your bedroom door shut if there's someone over and no one can stay the night. And, you know, it just makes you think you're a bloody prisoner or something, like you're under house arrest.
>
> (Ben)

After her mother told her to leave the family home, Kayla stayed in a series of refuges and hostels. During this period she became pregnant and after the baby was born she and her daughter moved back home. Everything went well for six weeks, until her father discovered she was using heroin again.

> Then my dad found needles and he kicked me out after Christmas, with the baby and all. I moved to my sister's, then I moved to my daughter's other grandparents, back to my sister's, back to the grandparents, to my own unit, into a caravan park, then to a refuge and then on the streets. . . . I remember sleeping in a park a few times. . . . No, it wasn't really good at all. And it was around the corner from my mum's and she'd see me in the street and she'd walk straight past, like I wasn't her daughter. I used to break down crying all the time.
>
> (Kayla)

Craig too spent considerable time in refuges and medium-term supervised accommodation. At the time of the final interview, Craig was living alone in a caravan. He had been sharing it with someone he met at a refuge, but his co-tenant stole Craig's food and failed to pay his share of the rent. Having gone their separate ways, Craig was revelling in his newfound freedom. 'I love being by myself. No one has to tell me what to do, when to turn the lights off 'cause they wanna go to sleep . . . Food's always in the cupboard when I go back to it.'

More than any of the others, Jamie had avoided refuges and assisted accommodation programmes.

> I've been on and off the streets for the last five, six years without accommodation, without people backing you up all the time, like your parents being there for you. It is, it's very hard. . . . From 12 until I was 16 I was on the streets with my mate. I hit 13, went back home to see how my mum was doing. First thing I got shoved in my face was a big hash cake. As soon as I was smashed I went out and burged cars – got done, got locked up. Never went back to see Mum again until I was about sixteen.
>
> (Jamie)

At the time of the final interview Jamie was exploring a new way of meeting his accommodation needs, one that underlined his determined self-reliance:

> I'm still on the streets, but I've put myself into a different category. I'm in between, I'm not exactly on the streets, I'm sort of making my own squat

up at the moment. Definitely homeless, but not roofless. There's a heap of bush and it's owned by the government and, yeah, I plan on doing something with it. Put up a few poles, a tarp.

(Jamie)

Violence

For Kayla, Craig and Jamie, the violence that had shaped their childhoods and had helped propel them from their family homes continued to stalk them in their lives on the streets. External threats aside, in Craig's and Jamie's cases the violence was from within. Jamie articulated both his ownership and the lineage of his violence when he said, 'You know, everyone does their own thing and makes themselves what they are, but it's a lot to do with what's around you. Like, I believe I picked up my violence from my family, and also my foster care homes.'

Living on the streets, there was no shortage of potential outlets for Jamie's violent urges. Tutored by a mate in 'how to be violent streetwise', Jamie mixed property crimes with assaults and armed robberies. 'What I did was roll as many people as possible, which means holding people up with knives and telling 'em you'll either get their money or take their life. When you're in that state there's not much other things you can do.' At times he was frightened by his own fury:

I've gotta admit, from my past if you annoy me or you get me agitated, I won't stop until the damage is done. Straight away I'll just snap. It's not a good thing. It actually scared me for quite a while. I'm aware that when I get angry, I have to get the hell out of the area or it's my life or someone else's.

(Jamie)

Craig's anger towards his mother was undiminished, but by the final interview there had been a more general shift in his disposition. Comparing himself with the person he had been when he first left home, he said, 'I am less angry and violent now. I don't even really remember when it happened; it just happened that I lost all my anger. I still get angry, but I just don't express it anymore.' Perhaps more consciously, Jamie too had become less violent over time. 'Luckily I woke up. I realized, "Nah, it's not the way." Two years ago, I decided I wasn't going to do it anymore. I was sick of rolling people. It wasn't a good thing to do.'

In Kayla's case the violence of her family relations was repeated in the dynamics of her relationship with her older boyfriend, the father of her daughter, who like her own father was physically violent towards her. 'He had a strong hold over me and I couldn't say no. His attitude was like, "You go out, you go get the money, you do this, you do that." We used to fight over five lines of gear . . . it was a pretty full on violent relationship.' Like Jamie, though, Kayla took positive steps to alter her situation, to remove this source of violence from her life:

> We were actually living in a caravan park and we were getting evicted and I thought, 'Here's my chance to leave him,' because I was getting so hurt and my daughter was in the middle of everything. I actually moved into a youth refuge, and he couldn't be there. I had our daughter and he was coming round every day and all of a sudden I just said, 'Look, it's over. Go away, I don't want you anymore.' He hounded me for quite a few months until he got locked up.
>
> (Kayla)

While Kimberley did not discuss how violence impacted on her life on the streets, Ben spoke of it as an ever-present threat, as something he needed to negotiate and avoid on a daily basis:

> I'd just like to be able to walk down the street and not have to worry about, you know, walking past someone and accidentally catching their eye, 'What are you fuckin' lookin' at?' You know, I just get sick of having to face the same crowd every day. . . . The drug dealers think you want to buy their drugs and, you know, if not, they think they can roll you for your money. And you just think, 'Man, all you fucking filthy scums, just leave me alone. Just let me walk to the shops and back, you know.'
>
> (Ben)

These accounts suggest that the distinction between young people who left home in search of greater freedom and those who were forced from home through parental neglect and abuse is reflected in their experience of violence on the streets. Ben, who had not suffered from parental violence, became prey to street violence, while Jamie, who had been a victim of violence throughout his childhood, once on the street became its perpetrator.

Mental illness

All five of these young people living on the streets experienced significant mental health problems, particularly depression. As Jamie succinctly put it, 'It's very easy to get depressed on the streets.' In the course of the study, Kimberley, Ben, Craig and Jamie all self-harmed and Kayla suffered from an eating disorder. 'I stopped eating for a couple of months, off and on. And speed really made my weight go down a lot, and when I stepped on the scales I couldn't believe I was 42 kilos. I was so sick I could hardly move.'

Ben, who on the surface seemed the most confident and mentally robust, in fact suffered from clinical depression and anxiety and regularly self-harmed. Kimberley too had a history of depression. 'I did have anti-depressants when I was living at Mum's, but I didn't really want to be on them anymore. I feel a bit better when I'm not on them.' Jamie's struggle with depression led to him attempting suicide. 'I hung myself a couple of months ago and one of my mates come through with a knife and he had to cut me down and take me to hospital.'

Despite the severity of the mental health problems experienced by these young people, the treatment of them was at best sporadic and at worst non-existent. Over the course of the study, only Kayla and Ben sought and received medical attention for their mental illnesses. None of these young people had experienced time in psychiatric hospitals.

Drugs

Drugs were a constant presence in the lives of young people in this pathway, both before they became homeless and even more so afterwards. However, at the time of the interview, with the exception of Ben, all were trying to limit their drug intake. At that time Kimberley was smoking marijuana 'about twice a week, 'cause, like, if you're smoking everyday you just don't get the effect anymore and then you get this feeling of moving on to higher drugs'. Although her friends all expected her to 'progress' to speed and heroin, Kimberley was certain she would not, in part because she hated needles, but also because of her struggle to break her boyfriend's heroin addiction. 'I just told him, "If you love me, you'd choose me over that shit." So he stopped, 'cause I told him I was gonna leave him if he didn't; 'cause I don't do that shit. And so he stopped it and he hasn't done it since. I'm really proud of him.'

Unlike Kimberley, Kayla had a near fatal attraction to needles. Describing the course of her addiction, she said:

> I thought, 'Oh yeah, I'll try heroin, it won't hurt.' But then you slowly get addicted to it and your body gets really dependent on it. And it's really

hard to say no. And when you don't have any you get hot and cold spells, you're not able to get out of bed; aching joints. And, you know, just looking at the track mark on my arm . . . I still look at it today and get that little temptation. . . . I think my brain's just got a thing for steel, maybe. I think it's just . . . it's the whole needle thing. You know, that's what gives me the whole adrenalin rush. But I know it's really dangerous. . . . It used to make me feel like I could do anything. It used to put a lot of confidence in me. And now it just makes me feel like shit, and I hate it when people who love me see me like that.

(Kayla)

In the four months prior to the final interview Kayla had 'dropped' six times and the last overdose very nearly killed her:

I was sitting on the toilet and I'd smacked my head against the floor. When my friend came in I was all blue and there was no pulse and he started yelling and they had to give me CPR [cardiopulmonary resuscitation] . . . I wouldn't come to and they had to give me two doses of Narcaine. I still didn't come to and the heavy duty squad team had to come in and give me another two heavy doses of it. It was pretty full on. I ended up in the hospital that last time and that's when they put me in secure welfare. That's when I thought, 'Nuh, I'm going, I really need to clean up.'

(Kayla)

At the time of the final interview Kayla had recently completed a detoxification programme and was hoping 'to keep straight'.

Craig's drug taking greatly increased once he became homeless and moved into supervised accommodation. 'My whole DHS [Department of Human Services] period was pretty much spent using drugs.' His drug of choice was marijuana, though for a year and half he used speed, which turned him into a 'clean freak', obsessively polishing a single spot for hours on end. He also experimented with magic mushrooms. For Craig the attraction of drugs was that 'people seemed nicer when I was stoned . . . the bullshit didn't seem to be there. People just seemed real genuine, they didn't seem like they were lying to me face, or just saying shit just to get out of some shit. I don't like seeing the crap.' Even so, by the time of the final interview Craig had ceased using speed. 'I don't even know that I've really stopped. Like, I just haven't felt like doing it again. I got bored with it.' As with his improved anger management, Craig's decreased drug use seems to have happened by chance, without any act of choice or dedicated effort on his part.

Jamie's parents' drug addictions were central to the chaos and abuse of his childhood, and after leaving home his own drug use continued this destructive pattern in his life.

> I'd got myself into trouble without realizing, mostly drug abuse trouble. Got myself into the wrong group. . . . I didn't realize what I was playing with. I was only 12 at the time. By the time I knew about it, it was too deep. I'm still going through it at the moment and there's nothing much I can do. Everyone on the streets is in danger.
>
> (Jamie)

Jamie experimented with every drug he came across – coke, ecstasy, marijuana, acid, heroin and speed. He used heroin twice because 'I believed I had to try it before I judged my parents'. It was to speed though that he became addicted:

> As soon as I experimented with it, I loved it. I wanted more and more, couldn't give it up, just wanted it. It's like you're in heaven, mate. You don't have to think about stuff. Comedowns would stuff me up; you just get agitated and pissed off and if someone says something you don't like you snap. And like, ever since we were young I've been a violent person and I snap quite easily, so it wasn't good stuff for me.
>
> (Jamie)

At that stage in his life, Jamie didn't care about the risks of drug taking, the side effects. He didn't feel he had anything to live for. 'It was either do it or I kill myself.' In more recent times, Jamie came to the conclusion that 'if I like a drug, I shouldn't touch it again because I will not stop'. With the benefit of this insight, by the time of the interview he had dramatically reduced his drug intake. 'I still smoke to keep my anger down, but I don't take speed anymore. I don't take coke, I don't take heroin, acid, anything – maybe once a month for a good time, but other than that, nuh.'

Superficially, it seems ironic that of these five most vulnerable homeless young people it was only Ben, the one who came from the most stable, middle-class family, who at the time of the final interview had not moderated his drug use. In fact, though, this is consistent with the differences in these young people's reasons for leaving home. Unlike Kayla, Craig and Jamie, whose chaotic family backgrounds were in part the results of parental substance abuse, Ben wanted, even more so than Kimberley, to leave home to pursue his partying lifestyle. For him, taking drugs was emblematic of his freedom from parental constraints, of his independence. Where for Jamie a reduction in his drug use might be seen as a positive development in his flight from the abuse that marked his childhood, for Ben it would indicate a redefining of his conception of freedom, one no longer necessarily oppositional to the limits his parents and step-parents had attempted to place on his behaviour. To put it another way, if Jamie were to stop using drugs it would be a break from his destructive past, while if Ben were to do so it would be a return, and would entail tacit acknowledgement that his drug taking had negative effects, from which his parents had been trying to protect him.

Education and employment

In terms of education and employment, Ben was again the odd one out in this pathway. Having left home later than the other four, he had by then completed Year 12 (final year of secondary school), something none of the others had achieved. Until immediately prior to the interview, he had held down a part-time job throughout the 18 months of the study. He was also enrolled in a professional writing course at a technical and further education (TAFE) college. Looking back, Ben acknowledged that the loss of his job marked the beginning of a downward spiral in his life:

> A few months ago I got fired and I kind of went down hill from there. . . .
> When I was living in the unit . . . going to school and working as well and,
> you know, doing everything right, I felt in control. It's just that kind of, you
> know, comfort of having a unit, a base to go back home to.
>
> (Ben)

Kimberley's itinerant, hand-to-mouth lifestyle did not allow time for considerations of education and employment. Her concerns were too immediate, focused as they were on securing another food voucher, stealing a tank of petrol from a service station or finding a quiet rest stop to park in for the night. Kayla was similarly too preoccupied with a daily struggle for survival to act on her dreams about future work and education. In her mind, she had to beat her heroin addiction before she could embark on such endeavours.

For Craig and Jamie, employment or their inability to secure it was a defining aspect of their identities as homeless young people. When asked to give an example of something that made him feel better about himself, Craig answered, 'Oh, when I apply for a job and actually get a call back; even if it's to say you haven't got it.' The desire to be treated decently implicit in this response is made explicit in Jamie's account of his attempts to find work:

> I've handed out more than three hundred resumés just in central Melbourne, and so far I've got three calls back. Because of the way we look, we get judged, we won't get jobs that easy. You know, the same day we get employment is the same day we don't have time to cause mischief; we get our lives together.
>
> (Jamie)

Engagement with services

As we have seen, Kayla, Craig and Jamie had contact with DHS from very young ages. Once living away from home, however, only Kayla had an ongoing engagement with government and non-government services and workers. The other four accessed services strategically for practical support (such as employment, income, legal aid) when they were desperate. Otherwise they preferred to maintain their independence, valuing that more highly than the support and security that welfare organizations might offer them.

Kayla's long-standing engagement with DHS worked in her favour when she initially became homeless and later when her heroin habit made it impossible for her to look after her baby. At both these critical junctures she was admitted to a secure welfare unit where her most immediate physical and medical needs were met, something for which she was extremely grateful:

> I was lucky enough to be involved with the Department for them to put me at my resi unit. . . . I was there when I was 13, up until I had my daughter and I'm very lucky that I'm down there. But it's a really high risk unit and there's only 18 people in the region that they put there and they actually picked me as one of them.
>
> (Kayla)

Craig's and Jamie's experiences of DHS were far less positive. Jamie had little time for DHS but praised the work of the Citizen's Advice Bureau:

> The old ladies have been the nicest. These old blokes, they're sort of like, 'Right, you're on the streets, it's your fault. Go do something about it.' Mostly it is very nice and very respectful; it actually made me feel that not all rich people aren't worth it. But these days they only help you four times a year. I'm not sure if they realize, but 20 bucks don't go three days,

especially when you're on the streets, 'cause if you don't take drugs, your
friends do, and if they get you by with food, you've gotta get them by, so
– it's very backwards and forwards on the street. If not, you're dead. I
guarantee ya.

(Jamie)

Ben was affronted by his experience of living in supervised
accommodation because it grouped him with the very people from
whom he wished to distinguish himself. From then on, he only
accessed services when circumstance demanded it. When asked which
services he used, he replied, 'Centrelink give me money occasionally.
And if I need a food voucher – if I've got no milk or bread or
anything – I'll go and see a welfare agency and get it, a food parcel
or a food voucher. But apart from that, I don't.'

For Kimberley and her boyfriend, accessing services from a welfare
agency was like stealing petrol – something you had to do sometimes
to survive. Before they became itinerant, they devised a way of
obtaining food vouchers from the same welfare agency in the town in
which they lived. 'You're not allowed to get one every second week,
you're only meant to get one every six months . . . we'd just take it
in turns in going in there and just make up bullshit stories and why
we needed it and they'd give us 30 dollars, one each, each time.'
By positioning themselves in opposition to such welfare agencies,
Kimberley and Ben were able to occasionally access services without
feeling they were compromising their hard-fought independence. In
fact, Kimberley saw her knowledge of the available services, of how to
work them, as underlining rather than undermining her independence.
'I feel a bit more independent than I did when we first left 'cause I've
been here, I've done it before and now I know what to do, know
where to go, know where to get help from.'

Despite their overall negative experiences and assessments of
welfare services, both Craig and Jamie spoke of the positive influence
on their lives of individual welfare workers. Craig remembered two
workers with whom he had had good relationships. 'There was one
particular worker that I liked, Ross, and he was one of the residential
workers, but then there's case management workers that work in the
actual office and one of them again stood out, and I actually keep in
contact with him.' For someone as isolated as Craig, the affirming
effects of these relationships with workers might be crucial to his
ability to forge a positive future for himself. Certainly in his mind they
represented some form of compensation for his general sense of
disappointment regarding DHS and its dealings with him.

Jamie's example of the positive influence of a worker on his life points to the possibility that these relationships, sometimes merely one-off conversations, can act as turning points in the lives of such highly vulnerable young people. Reflecting on the time immediately after his suicide attempt, Jamie said:

> There was actually a worker who came down and sat down on the steps with me, turns around and tells me about how I have got a future. And ever since then I've been trying to do what I can to help people in my same position. It's just amazing how that felt. . . . I didn't believe in myself, but stuff like that makes me sit back and go 'Whoa,' you know, people do care.
>
> (Jamie)

Relationships

With the exception of Jamie, who had no ongoing relationship with his parents, the other four all had some sort of continuing relationship with one or both of their parents. In Kimberley's case the move from home greatly improved her relationship with her mother. No longer forced to live by her mother's rules, she stopped fighting with her. 'As soon as I moved out we just got along so much better, we're actually friends instead of enemies. . . . We love each other. I ring her up all the time, different state or wherever. I ring her every day. I've got a homelink [reverse charges] number.'

The fact that Kimberley's mother had enabled and encouraged her daughter to ring home free of charge suggests that she had reluctantly accepted Kimberley's choices and was doing what she could to support her in them. The knowledge that her mother still cared about her provided Kimberley with an emotional security that the other four young people lacked. Then again, Kimberley may need this more than the others, given that her other key relationship was with Archie, the older boyfriend with a long history of drug addiction and crime. At least by keeping the lines of communication open, her mother had provided Kimberley with another source of support should she ever decide to leave Archie or if, as seemed likely, he was returned to gaol.

Beneath his bravado, Ben was hurt by the ultimatum his father delivered which resulted in him leaving home. Then when his father, stepmother and half-sister moved interstate, he felt abandoned. 'I felt very angry. I was pretty shocked for a while . . . I was like, "Hmmm, that's a bit of a severe dent in the father–son relationship." I was told not to come back. That was a finality thing.' Although he said it was 'nice to go up and spend a week with them' occasionally, he also said that 'it's almost like my friends have become my family'. The friends he referred to were a group of mates that, like him, had chosen to 'drop out' and party rather than to 'use their brains'.

> Basically we support each other and sort of – Most of us are in the same financial predicament or, you know, got similar kind of life struggles. So we just support each other, 'cause there's no one else. . . . Yeah, and we support each other just with relationships and things like that, sorting out family problems that we're having and stuff.
>
> (Ben)

Having been forced to choose between his partying lifestyle and the support of his family, and having chosen the former, Ben now looked to his friends for emotional and material support.

More than the others, Craig was emotionally isolated. He had little contact with his family and lacked either a circle of friends or a girlfriend. His relationship with his mother remained volatile, and although he got on reasonably well with his father their times together were often thwarted by the presence of his mother. 'You know, he's a good bloke my dad. We can – I can go over there with a slab of beer and we can have a drink together. [Then] my mum walks in the door, "What are you doing with beer, Reg?"' When interviewed, Craig was relieved to be living by himself, his days defined by a trip to the shop and his obligations to work for the dole and to complete a community service order working, ironically, as a kitchen hand in a shelter for homeless men, a place in which he used to stay.

At the end of the study, Kayla's family relations remained fraught. In the aftermath of her near fatal overdose, her father responded appropriately while her mother failed even to visit her:

> When I was in detox my dad hadn't heard from for me for nearly a year. . . . He was crying . . . and he came running down to where I was with this big Pooh Bear, this big teddy bear. I seen him coming through the door, but I didn't see my mum, and that's what really hurt.
>
> (Kayla)

Given that it was Kayla's father who had the history of being violent towards her, it is ironic that it was now her mother who had become the focus of her disappointment:

> Knowing my parents – I mean my dad's a really good help, but knowing my mum's not there which – and she never used to talk to me when I was

younger and she hasn't supported me and she – you know, she knows I've got a baby and she doesn't support me whatsoever. Nobody does. I feel pretty alone at the moment.

(Kayla)

Contradicting this sentiment, in the same interview Kayla spoke of the sense of security she derived from being in the company of her new boyfriend, Patrick:

Being around him is the only place I feel safe. . . . He's caring, he's really supportive and he doesn't say the wrong things. He doesn't hurt me at all. . . . He's there all the time and he's at me, making sure I go to my appointments, picks me up. . . . Patrick's been a really good help, he's been the only one there to pull me out of it.

(Kayla)

Jamie too had entered into a new positive relationship by the end of the study. With typical insight, he articulated the importance of being loved to one's sense of self-worth – the transformative power of care:

The last two years I've been waking up quite a bit. I realized that it wasn't just us street kids who care about ourselves and it was other people as well. We always used to think, you know, no one's on our side. Now I've got a girlfriend; she's what's made me think of myself. By thinking of her, I'm thinking of myself. I didn't look after myself, I went through drugs after drugs after drugs, tried to get out of reality 24/7. She's the one who woke me up to it. If I keep going that way, I won't be here. . . . My girlfriend keeps me healthy. She wants me to look after myself. Looking after her makes me look after myself. By caring about her, I care about the things she cares about.

(Jamie)

Abused as a child by all those he should have been able to trust, as a young person Jamie faced the world with fear and suspicion, negotiating his way in it with the anger and violence they had instilled in him. However, once his girlfriend demonstrated true concern and affection for him, once she showed herself to be both trustworthy and trusting, Jamie responded in kind and, out of concern for her, discovered a previously unknown capacity to care about himself. 'Looking after her makes me look after myself.'

For Kayla and Jamie the development of relationships with new, caring partners had acted as turning points in their lives, enabling them to contemplate not only their survival but futures that would take them beyond their experiences of being young and homeless.

Positive futures

Surprisingly, perhaps, a key characteristic that these five young people shared was a positive attitude towards the future. As indicated by their shifting behaviours regarding drug use, they saw their lives as changing, as in transition, and could all envisage better futures for themselves. Apart from Ben, whose plans were characteristically somewhat grander, their hopes and aspirations were conventional and typically involved stable employment, long-term relationships, children and secure accommodation.

Kimberley simply hoped to 'get a house, settle down and don't move anymore'. She wanted to live in 'a peaceful area . . . keep her boyfriend out of trouble and just try to make a go of it and not stuff up'. Craig's future hopes were similarly modest. He wanted to get a job, move out of the caravan and 'find meself a chick, have kids'. Encouraged to contemplate the sort of work he might do, he half jokingly suggested he wanted to be a glazier because 'I wanna make my own fish tank'. Then, less whimsically, he suggested, 'Probably just factory work or something. Forklift driver, maybe.'

Kayla's aspirations were more specific. 'I want to go to school or TAFE or something, or get a job or do some kind of traineeship, something to keep me occupied.' She saw her experiences as a young homeless person as both a potential asset to her hoped for career as a youth or childcare worker but also as an impediment, something that qualified her as it disqualified her for such work:

> My worker wants me to give a talk to 13 and 14 year olds about chroming and that. . . . I eventually want to work towards being a childcare worker . . . my worker's actually trying to get me into that kind of stuff. I think about it and I think, 'Oh, that sounds really, really good,' and then I think, 'No, I can't do it,' because of the situation with my own daughter. . . . I really love kids, you know, I think I can relate to them. It's either that or being a youth worker or something.
>
> (Kayla)

Despite persistent doubts that she will 'always end up falling back' into her addiction, Kayla hoped for an ordinary life, one she could share with her daughter:

I would like to be able to keep straight and have my own unit. I need a minimum of two bedrooms, because my ultimate goal is to get my daughter back. . . . I'd just like to see myself living, living a normal life like every other girl I see out there walking on the street.

(Kayla)

Having been told by his favourite TAFE lecturer that to become a good writer he needed to 'go out and go to lots of good parties and collect your material and go overseas', Ben's hopes were more dreamlike than those of the others tinged, as they were, by the ghosts of Hemingway and Fitzgerald:

I thought, 'Well, yeah, okay.' I want to go travelling. . . . Travelling and being paid to do it; being a foreign correspondent or something. I'm just gonna have to write and send it to publishers and gradually – I'll just have as much difficulty as any other writer, I guess.

(Ben)

Superficially, Ben presented as someone with an excess of self-belief. His drug use was merely 'partying', something he could control. He was no 'moron' and had chosen to 'drop out' and therefore, within his own logic, he could choose to 'use his brains' any time he liked and drop back in to middle-class life. He didn't doubt that he could become a foreign correspondent; it was merely a matter of his choosing. The fact that, despite being enrolled in the writing course, he hadn't 'written in a while' was of no consequence – all he needed was 'to be focused'. Ben's bravado was a failed attempt to mask his severe depression, his propensity for self-harm. As we have seen, there were moments in the final interview when his delusion fell away, when he acknowledged the true precariousness of his situation. For example, he admitted that he was 'enslaved to the evil herb' or that the loss of his job had propelled him on a 'downhill' trajectory. Having made one crucial choice, to leave home to pursue his partying lifestyle, Ben wanted very much to believe that he was still exercising his agency, that his past decisions had only fleeting consequences and his future would forever yield to his will.

Of the five, Jamie's hope for the future was the most modest. Having failed in his attempt to kill himself and having now found someone who cared about him, Jamie merely hoped to retain his newfound desire for life. 'As long as you've the will to keep surviving, you can get there. With all the stuff I've done in the past, I'd like to believe I have that will.' Beyond this most basic aspiration, Jamie refused to speculate.

Conclusion

The routes these five young people took into homelessness were guided by issues of choice and constraint, victimhood and agency. Kimberley's and Ben's routes were defined by their choices to rebel against the various constraints their parents attempted to impose on their behaviour. They both actively chose to leave home to obtain greater freedoms, to live by their own rules. In contrast, Kayla, Craig and Jamie were forced from their homes by their parents' violence and neglect. For them, leaving home was not an assertion of independence but an act of survival; not a flight to freedom but a flight from abuse. When Kimberley and Ben took drugs it was an act of rebellion; when Jamie took drugs it was an act of conformity, a continuation of a family tradition.

These differences in family background and reasons for leaving home framed the ways these young people interpreted their experiences of life on the streets. Despite the chaos of their daily lives, Kimberley and Ben maintained a belief that they were in control: Kimberley that sleeping in truck stops was part of a travel adventure; Ben that his constant partying constituted research for future writings.

While not viewing themselves as victims, Kayla, Craig and Jamie, having been forced to live on the streets, saw their lives as, in Jamie's words, 'very, very hard'. For them, life to this point had largely been a negative experience, a force that seemed set against them, one they could only react to and never act upon. Kayla, in particular, acknowledged the dire nature of her circumstances and sought assistance from government and non-government welfare services to change them. Jamie wanted to improve his situation but was more independent in his efforts to do so. However, he experienced his attempts to assert his will, to find work or accommodation, as thwarted by a recurrent pattern of prejudice and disregard. 'You can't get yourself on top if everyone's putting you down.'

By the conclusion of the study, both Kayla and Jamie had survived near-death experiences (Kayla her dramatic overdose and Jamie his suicide attempt) and had subsequently entered into new, loving relationships. In both cases, the conjunction of this lowest point in their lives with the development of the most affirming relationship they had yet experienced acted as a turning point. Jamie's attempted suicide and Kayla's heroin addiction can both be seen as ultimate expressions of their flights from abuse. But having survived their attempts to kill themselves and having discovered partners who cared for them, there was a suggestion in their final interviews that they might now be able to make positive choices about their futures. Unlike Kimberley and Ben, for whom freedom was defined by the ability to take drugs, in some ways to choose homelessness, for Kayla, Craig and Jamie, to assert their independence over their pasts would be to impose positive patterns of behaviour on the chaos and neglect that had been their inheritance.

6   Using the system

I'm more independent. I know I can take care of myself better. I've learnt different responsibilities that come by when you live by yourself. . . . I know where to shop, how to budget. You know, how to talk to people . . . you have to be nice to people these days to get somewhere. You can't be selfish or disrespecting. And I try and like live my life the way that my parents were supposed to live. You know, I try not to make the same mistakes.

(Fahra)

The sense of dislocation that resulted in these seven young people leaving their family homes also prevented them from returning to them. Feeling forced to be independent, they used the services available to them to access transitional or medium-term accommodation. While slightly less vulnerable than those in the on the streets pathway discussed in Chapter 5, the young people in this pathway continued to self-identify as homeless.

Despite their lack of a 'home' and their tenuous sense of security, most of these service-based homeless young people achieved a level of day-to-day stability in their lives that enabled them to focus on their schooling and to maintain part-time employment. Knowing of the shortage of services for young people in their circumstances, many experiencing this pathway counted themselves lucky to be housed in medium-term accommodation. Luck, though, was probably only a minor factor in their accommodation outcomes. Whereas three of the five street-based young people came from materially impoverished and emotionally and physically abusive family settings, this was true for only two of the seven young people in this pathway. As we saw in Chapter 4, the remaining five had a history of disconnection from and displacement within their families but had not been subjected to sustained abuse, trauma or neglect. This, it seems, accorded them greater psychological stability and personal resourcefulness when confronted with the challenges of homelessness, which in turn resulted in them being more successful than their more traumatized peers in accessing available services.

This greater stability was also reflected in the comparatively controlled ways that these young people used drugs and alcohol, with none of them self-identifying as having an ongoing drug or alcohol 'problem' or as users of injected drugs. While all these young people had experienced mental health issues, for five of the seven these were isolated episodes triggered by specific life crises rather than chronic afflictions, as was the case for four of the five in the on the streets pathway.

Whereas for the young people in the on the streets pathway homelessness generally came prior to their accessing of services, for those in the using the system pathway it was often the other way round. By accessing services before leaving home or while staying with friends, they improved their longer term accommodation outcomes. It was this ability to successfully engage with services that largely framed their experiences of homelessness and set them apart from their street-based peers. The following discussion traces the pattern of that pathway, focusing on the young people's engagement with services, before turning to the issue of accommodation and other shared elements in their experiences of homelessness.

Engagement with services

Importantly and critically, everyone in this pathway was effective in accessing the services they required to meet their immediate needs, particularly regarding accommodation. In fact, by the time of their interviews five of the seven young people classified in this pathway claimed that all their service needs were being met. Together with Brittany, who had had a long engagement with the Department of Human Services (DHS), Adam and Victor were high users of services beyond those dedicated to accommodation. While these two young men engaged with a similar range of services (including health, housing, income support, employment and education), they did so in quite different ways and for very different reasons. Adam sought out services to pursue his well-defined educational goals. Victor, given his severe depression, depended on services for his very survival. Four others in this pathway had also received help from dedicated mental health services.

All the young people in this pathway sought assistance in finding accommodation either prior to or soon after becoming homeless. This, it seems, was instrumental in them achieving better accommodation outcomes than those in the on the streets pathway. For everyone apart from Adam, the event of becoming homeless had been prepared for in some way, either planned for or rehearsed. The young people who had planned for this event were those who had left home of their own accord, while those who had rehearsed for it were the ones who had been repeatedly threatened with homelessness, only on this occasion the threat was enacted.

For Maree and Fahra, leaving home, while triggered by specific events, was a premeditated and planned for act. Both realized their situations at home were unacceptable and, while hoping these would improve, they prepared for the likelihood that they would not. In both instances, school welfare teachers played crucial roles in providing a sympathetic ear as well as practical advice regarding available housing services. Maree explains:

> Before me and my sister moved out we got it all planned out. We weren't just going to move out and just live on the streets or whatever. We actually talked to our student welfare teacher about our situation. . . . We told him that because of all the stress that our mum was giving us, we just, like, we just want to move out. And he said he'd assess our situation and if it's unreasonable, he'd find us a new home. . . . And, yeah, he just basically made some contacts and we had a look at a medium-term accommodation place. And on the day after we moved out we decided to move into it.
>
> (Maree)

Acting on the advice of her school welfare coordinator, Fahra contacted a youth accommodation service and explained her situation. There was a waiting list for places in medium-term supervised houses and Fahra was told she would have to wait for a vacancy. In the meantime, the violent episode with her brother that compelled her to leave home occurred (see pp. 58–59). Fahra moved out and couch surfed at friends' houses until she was offered a place in a supervised house. It seems reasonable to suggest that had she not had the foresight to enquire into and register with this service her accommodation outcome and general experience of homelessness would have been far worse.

In a sense, Toby both rehearsed and planned for his final departure from home. Although he left home voluntarily, he soon returned, though only in order to wait for a position in a supervised house to become vacant. As with Maree and Fahra, it was Toby's school counsellor who directed him towards a youth housing service. Despite the heavy demand on such services, Toby was able to leave home and move into a refuge almost immediately. Acknowledging his good fortune he said, 'Yeah, there was only like four residents there at the time. So, like, it was pretty lucky. I was lucky to get in, 'cause like there's a long waiting list, apparently.' To his surprise, however, Toby found living in the refuge as difficult as living with his mother. He had a personality clash with one of the female residents and after only two weeks of staying there he was asked to leave. Before travelling for a week or two, he visited another non-government agency which encouraged him to put his name down on a waiting list for accommodation in a lead tenant house:

> The counsellor there suggested that it was best that like I go home until I got a spot, 'cause like it's better than staying in refuges. So um, I went up to the country for a little bit and then – I had to go home eventually, so I went home. That was only for like, um, oh, I think, like a month or so, and then I was told there was a spot for me.
>
> (Toby)

In José's and Brittany's cases, the preparation for homelessness took the form of rehearsal. José's mother had often threatened him with eviction and had 'kicked him out' once before. These threats had become part of the cycle of conflict between them. As such, the idea of being homeless had been normalized for José, so that when it finally occurred he was not altogether intimidated by the reality of his circumstances. As with the earlier time that he was told to leave, he initially stayed at a friend's house. Maintaining his studies, he sought assistance regarding accommodation from his social worker at the government welfare network, Centrelink. She referred him to a youth accommodation service that, in time, offered him a room in a supervised house for secondary school students.

Brittany was 'practised' at being homeless. 'I was used to it because she [her mother] used to kick me out all the time.' When it became obvious that this latest eviction was to be the last, Brittany contacted her support worker from DHS and through her found accommodation in a refuge.

For Victor, the rehearsal for becoming homeless was performed by his older brother. Having witnessed his brother go through the same process, when his aunt evicted him too, Victor turned to his brother first for support and then as a role model, copying some of his successful strategies for survival:

> Well, the first night I went to my brother's house, but he was going away somewhere. Then I stayed another night with my brother's housemate. This is like Christmas Day. So I rang the Salvation Army and all that to get a few numbers for places to stay. And after that my brother came home, so I went back to his house and stayed there for about a week. When the council opened up, they put me up in a refuge.
>
> (Victor)

Victor then accessed medium-term accommodation services through the Centrelink office that his brother had gone to when he was looking for housing.

Of the seven young people in this pathway, only Adam's departure from home was unprepared for, an impulsive response to what became the last of a series of verbal and physical fights with his father. Despite the suddenness of his leaving and the fact that he fled inter-state, when he found himself without money Adam sought assistance from the police. His rebellion, then, was against his family's funda-mentalist Christian subculture, not the wider society. Hence he was willing to cooperate with authorities in every regard except when they suggested that he return home. This combination of compliance and resolve (together with obvious intelligence) enabled him to navigate his way through the system towards an accommodation outcome that best suited his needs – a room in a well-run supervised house that allowed him to enjoy some freedom and to concentrate on his studies. Attached to a regional family services non-government organization (NGO), Adam had a case worker and occasionally had family counselling. As with most of the young people in this pathway, he was aware of his good fortune:

> Almost two years ago I made a decision that I wasn't going to move back home, 'cause it's like, I didn't care about where I might end up, but I wasn't going to move back home. But if I hadn't got connected with a place like this I would've – I don't know where I would've ended up.
>
> (Adam)

Criticism of services

Apart from Fahra's and Maree's comments regarding the degraded physical state of their supervised housing (see below), the only other recurring criticism was that the services, particularly DHS, pressured the young people to return home. Having endured highly stressful, often violent and abusive home lives, many homeless young people experience a service's exploration of the possibility that they might return home as offensive, a form of betrayal. For them, the mere suggestion of this possibility indicates that the service in question has not listened to their side of the story and is in fact an advocate for their parent(s)' position. Brittany said, 'Human Services was on my mum's side. Like, they were supporting everything she said against me.' Adam was similarly unhappy with the department, believing the worker assigned to his case was biased towards his parents' perception of the situation, was trying to 'close it down'.

> I guess it was because he talked to my parents first and he got my parents' side of the story straight away, and they pretty much told him, 'There's nothing wrong with our family. He should be able to come back home, there's no reason why he shouldn't.' But that wasn't true. There was a lot of things going wrong with our family . . . But, um, yeah, like straight away they just took the point of view that 'Oh, you're gonna move back home.'
>
> (Adam)

In Maree's case it was her youth worker who, having contacted Maree's mother and discovered she wanted her daughter home, then encouraged her client to return there. The ensuing dispute caused a permanent rift in Maree's relationship with that worker and only served to reopen old wounds between mother and daughter:

> Annie [the youth worker] kept convincing me to go back to my mum. And I said, 'Yeah,' but when I saw my mum I just changed my mind. Because I refused – I said, 'No,' to Annie, 'I don't want to go home' – she got really angry with me. . . . When she got angry with me I just didn't have much confidence in her anymore. I just didn't want to tell her anything. . . . I just felt like I couldn't trust her. . . . I just decided, 'Right, fine, I'll go to another service.'
>
> (Maree)

This is a delicate area for homelessness services to negotiate. Whereas in these instances exploring the possibility of a return home was interpreted as betrayal, in other cases (like some in the two pathways to follow) it produced positive outcomes. Beyond the question or suggestion of them returning home, what seems most important is that such young people are listened to, that their side of the story of their leaving home is heard and taken seriously.

Accommodation

Of the seven young people in the safely serviced grouping, only Adam had experienced street-based homelessness, and only for a matter of days. Four others had couch surfed, but infrequently and only for short periods. Although at the time of the interview each of these young people had been homeless for at least two years, they had experienced relatively few moves since leaving home. As we have seen, all seven successfully accessed emergency accommodation immediately prior to or soon after they became homeless. In most instances, they went first to a refuge and from there moved to a form of medium-term supervised accommodation. Whether they elected to leave or were forced from the family home, they all actively sought help and advice in securing alternative accommodation. In general terms, it was their exercising of agency and their determination to create a better future for themselves (and, as most of them acknowledged, a degree of good fortune) that ensured they had better accommodation outcomes than their street-based peers. What follows is a more detailed account of their experiences of living in supervised accommodation.

In keeping with their surprising lack of rebelliousness, the young people in this grouping typically judged their new accommodation as much for its stability as for its freedoms and its ability to facilitate their studies. José remarked:

> I live at a student housing place. It's, like, seven people, and, um, yeah, it's more a student place, for like schooling and study. I feel good because there's like people there to, you know, guide me through to VCE [vocational certificate of education], finish off school. So, yeah, I've got people there that support me, which is good. Mainly it's adults, and supervisors, and students there as well. . . . I'm comfortable with the place. . . . I just feel welcome in the place. . . . like I'm not scared to go to my own home.
>
> (José)

Adam made similar comments about his accommodation:

> It's pretty good, pretty structured. You know what's expected of you and it works pretty well. Ninety-eight per cent of the time it's really good. So yeah – and I'm going to school every day still. . . . I get along well with the lead tenants and the tenants. It's a pretty stable place, like I've been there 18 months and the girl that I live with has been there since last October.

. . . It's just they provide us with really stable accommodation and it's, yeah, really good for learning life skills. It's been really helpful.

(Adam)

Even when some of the young people were critical of their accommodation, their criticisms were based on a desire for more homely, stable places in which to live. Fahra spoke of her own attempts to improve the house she was living in, of how she had painted her own room. She criticized the service provider for not maintaining the house properly, for not making it more liveable and more conducive to people studying:

They should come and check out the place. Does it need painting? How do these kids feel when they're sitting in this house? Make it a place that we would want to spend time in. Make it a place that, you know, we would want to study in, sit down in – 'cause everything's so dirty, the walls are dirty, the carpet is dirty. You feel like you're just in this, like, house where no one lives.

(Fahra)

For others the main difficulties in adjusting to living in shared accommodation were social rather than physical. While Maree shared Fahra's disgust for the uncleanliness of her accommodation, she found living with a group of strangers a far greater challenge. Self-described as shy, she said it took her a few weeks to get used to living with 'really loud and friendly' people. After a while though she 'fully adapted' and felt more relaxed than she had at home and began to enjoy her greater freedom. Even so, she often retreated to her own room, her 'comfort zone', where she was surrounded with her familiar belongings. She also regularly escaped to the State Library, so as to better concentrate on her studies. Discussing why she enjoyed working there, she said, 'Because other people are studying and, you know, they're producing things and I just feel like people are there to work, and looking at everyone working, it just sort of comes naturally for me to work as well.'

As Toby's brief and unsuccessful time in the refuge suggests, he too struggled to adjust to living in shared accommodation. He felt that such a house could never be a home because 'there's no love there' and felt embarrassed by his fellow tenants, seeing himself as the 'only normal one'. The whole experience was isolating for him. 'There isn't anyone that I can rely on. Like, you have to look after yourself more.' He also found it stressful having 'to meet new people again' and to

abide by the house rules. This lack of love and the unexpected constraints on his freedom seem to have engendered Toby's earlier
reflections on and reassessment of the home life his mother had
provided for him before he chose to leave it.

Victor too became increasingly isolated after becoming homeless,
though in his case this was a continuation of a trend that had
developed while he was living with his aunt and grandmother. As with
Maree, though more extremely, Victor retreated to his room, a private
space over which he felt he had some control. 'I spend a lot of time in
my room. . . . In my spare time I just go to my room and sleep. I don't
want to do anything else. I just can't be bothered. . . . So even though
I can't sleep, I just lie there, do nothing.' A textbook description of
symptoms of depression, Victor's account of his inertia and
withdrawal gave voice to the depth of his psychological distress.
While he was the most severely affected, all the young people experiencing this service-based pathway were, to varying degrees, afflicted
by mental illnesses once they became homeless. It is to this common
element in their experiences of homelessness that we now turn.

Mental illness

Despite the relative stability of their accommodation, the psychological stability of these young people was challenged by their experiences of becoming homeless and mental illness (mainly depression)
became a prominent feature of their experiences of homelessness.
Feelings of rejection and abandonment triggered reactive depression
in all seven young people and resulted in five of them self-harming
and/or attempting suicide. As we have seen, only Victor had a strong
history of mental illness prior to leaving home, though part of
Brittany's struggle with her own mental illness after becoming homeless was separating it out from the legacy of her mother's schizophrenia. 'I didn't trust anyone. And I was pretty suicidal back then
'cause I couldn't understand what was going on, 'cause my mum's
schizophrenic.' Fortunately, Brittany's case worker reassured her that
most of the issues surrounding her family conflict rightfully belonged
to her mother and made an appointment for her to see a psychiatrist.
Brittany was greatly relieved when the psychiatrist declared that 'I
wasn't mad'.

At the time of his interview, Victor had recently been discharged
from a specialist adolescent psychiatric unit where he had spent time
prior to leaving his aunt's house. He was admitted there on this
occasion because he had attempted suicide. Although, when asked

directly, his only stated reasons for this suicide attempt were 'ongoing', in telling of his desire to spend all his spare time alone in his room he revealed the direct connection between his childhood abandonment and his current struggle with clinical depression:

> I don't like to get too close to people, so I just keep my distance a bit. I just keep my distance in case anything ever happens, in case people go away, you know, like what my parents done. Each time they kept going away I drifted further away . . . So I isolate myself from it. Yeah, you get hurt in a way.
>
> (Victor)

Although Victor had ongoing contact with an outreach adolescent mental health service, he preferred the less intrusive youth service offered by his local council.

> When I come here I have a much better time. I have like a good time and I enjoy myself. Like at the other services I don't, because I don't really like to deal with psychiatrists at all – doctors like that. That's why I decided to come here, 'cause I like being here. I like to interact with the workers here more than with any other workers. . . . I like services that are friendly to be at and where they're not pushing me all the time.
>
> (Victor)

Like Victor, Fahra and José both suffered from depression and had self-harmed and tried to commit suicide. Farah explained the circumstances surrounding her suicide attempt:

> Usually if my friends are around, you know, we talk and stuff like that, but if they're – there's been a couple of times when my friends weren't around, or I was just – I just went, like, I just hit the bottom, you know, and I cut my wrists. But, not deep enough.
>
> (Fahra)

Both Fahra and José sought professional help and were prescribed antidepressants. Interestingly though, neither of them continued to take their medication. Fahra said that the drug made her 'drowsy, blank and stupid – I couldn't think', and José claimed to have never liked swallowing tablets or 'taking drugs to make myself feel better'. José was trying to combat his depression by 'keeping control' – going to school, not doing drugs, and making his life as stable as possible.

Both Maree and Adam also experienced reactive depression soon after they became homeless. By the time of their interviews, however, they had both recovered their psychological equilibrium. For Adam the turning point came when a counsellor reassured him that his conflict with and negative feelings towards his family were understandable, that he was not alone in feeling the need to leave home and that, in the circumstances, his response was 'normal'. Since then he had tried to maintain a positive outlook and to nurture his self-esteem by doing what he termed his 'hobbies' – playing his violin, going to the gym, riding his bike and going out with friends. Maree too seemed to have emerged from her depression now that the new life she had created for herself – full of study, work and time spent with her boyfriend – had caused her conflict with her mother and stepfather to recede.

Health

The fact that two of the young people in this grouping most severely afflicted by mental illness also had the worst general health outcomes underlines the interconnection between psychological and physical well-being and the ways both are affected by homelessness. At the time of his interview Victor had been ill for an extended period. He often suffered from stomach cramps and headaches, the former caused, he thought, by a lack of food. He believed though that 'too much thinking' was the primary cause of his ailments. According to his self-diagnosis, excessive thinking caused his insomnia and the lack of sleep made him susceptible to illness.

Fahra also complained of suffering from an excess of contemplation. 'So for me life is hard – I think too much.' In her case the interconnection between her mental and general health issues was even more explicit and consciously understood. In the first month after leaving home she lost 12 kilos. Rendered extremely weak and regularly fainting, she underwent tests for a range of ailments, including leukaemia and heart disease. The results of all the tests were negative, yet at the time of the interview she was still struggling to gain weight:

> No matter what I eat I don't put on weight. And when I'm stressed I – like it's weird, I can like lose two, three kilos in one or two days. I just like melt into depression. And I get headaches. I've got problems with my eyes . . . I'm telling my psychologist about this, because I think I know that it's all coming from stress. And the stress is about school. Where am I going to be living next? What am I going to do for money next week? Food? Rent?
>
> (Fahra)

Throughout her final year of secondary school, Maree, like Victor, was plagued by general ill health. She ascribed this decline in her health to her diet, which was framed by an underlying desire to not eat at all for fear of becoming fat, yet in reality consisted of junk food. Maree knew the dangers of this practice and by the time of her interview had 'decided to, you know, eat more healthy now. . . . I'll just eat whenever I'm hungry, and, you know, the stuff that I'm eating isn't that much junk'.

Drugs and alcohol

Consistent with the fact that none of these young people cited drug or alcohol use as a factor in leaving home, substance use or abuse was not a prominent feature in their experiences of homelessness. While the conflict of their family lives and the trauma of becoming homeless affected the mental health of all of them, only José attempted to ameliorate his situation or anaesthetize himself against the pain of it through the use of drugs. José's drug use was a direct response to what he called 'bad' and 'depressing times', which were typified by conflict with his family and relationship problems with 'girls'.

> For six months I had a big drug problem. I was using a lot. Like, maybe, three times a week, or something like that. Like marijuana, ecstasy, um – What else was I taking? Speed. Like other types of street drugs as well, but not heroin. I've never touched heroin.
>
> (José)

José knew he had 'lost the plot' and sought help from a psychiatrist. He was aware that the drugs he was taking were making his depression worse. 'Well, I stopped, fully stopped about three months ago.' In keeping with the general concern for education exhibited by those in this grouping, he explained his motivation for stopping thus: 'I had to change, like I knew drugs would affect my schooling as well.'

Toby occasionally used marijuana and while he did not 'rely' on it he enjoyed the fact that it made him laugh, something he otherwise seldom did. He had experimented with other drugs without really 'going for it full-on' and saw himself as 'pretty strong with it, like I know that I wouldn't be dependent on it'. For the others in this pathway, a commitment to education similar to José's ensured they remained clean. Adam had never used illegal drugs. With an innocence nurtured by his sheltered religious upbringing, he confessed to having tried cigarettes and alcohol. For different reasons, Fahra, having witnessed her father's drinking and her brother's dependence on marijuana, was similarly uninterested in drugs and alcohol. For her, using drugs or alcohol was a sign of weakness, of 'insecurity'. For Maree, the decision to steer clear of drugs and to remain focused on her studies was a conscious one, motivated by her determination to vindicate her flight from home:

> I knew I was not going to be influenced by drug abuse and things like that. I knew that I could do well at school, just to show Mum that she was wrong, that we can survive without her, and we would do well because we're living out of home.
>
> (Maree)

Violence

Unlike drugs and alcohol, violence did play a part in these young people leaving home, often proving to be the tipping point or providing the trigger for their departure. Interestingly, violence did not register in their accounts of their experiences of homelessness. As with the issue of drug and alcohol use, this represents a major point of difference between the experiences of these young people and those of the young people in the on the streets pathway, some of whom were regular perpetrators and/or victims of violence once they became homeless. This suggests that one of the many benefits of being housed in relatively stable accommodation services was that it removed these young people from the constant threat of violence that pervades life on the street.

Education and employment

After accommodation outcomes, the next most common characteristic exhibited by members of this grouping was a commitment to education and work, which again distinguished them from their street-based peers. Along with Adam, all four young people from cultural and linguistically diverse (CALD) backgrounds remained in both education and employment throughout the 18 months of the study. Victor was a partial exception, as he was unemployed during his admission to the adolescent psychiatric unit. Even so, despite his homelessness and severe depression, Victor managed to complete the final year of secondary school (Year 12) while also working 30 hours a week. At the time of his interview he was enrolled in a technical and further education (TAFE) course in digital design, which he found disappointingly boring. 'We draw lines. That's what we do. We're learning how to draw lines!'

When interviewed, Maree, José, Fahra and Toby had all completed Year 12 and were enrolled in various tertiary degree courses. Brittany and Adam were both completing Year 12 at the time of their interviews. While wanting to study ('I can't wait to go to uni'), Brittany was finding it a challenge to attend school each day, the main barrier being 'getting up in the morning'. In contrast, Adam was highly focused on his studies, which were all directed towards his long-standing goal to become a doctor. 'It's a bit hard sometimes . . . but I've just gotta try my hardest and see what happens.'

In terms of paid employment, all but Toby and Brittany were regularly in work. Their jobs were all in the service industries, working in cafés, restaurants, shops and clubs. Fahra spoke of a recent incident with an employer who 'obviously wanted me to do more than just work'. The owner of the café was 'very rude' and exploitative. He paid low wages and 'he just thought that he owns you'. Feeling 'disrespected', Fahra resigned in disgust on her second day.

Relationships

Family

Whereas four out of the five young people in the on the streets pathway had regular contact with their parents, in the using the system pathway this was the case for only three of the seven. Perhaps this occurred because, having secured stable accommodation and accessed other support services, these young people were more able than their street-based peers to remain independent of their troubled family relationships. Only two, José and Adam, said their relationships with their parents had improved since they left home. Describing his current relationship with his mother, José said, 'Now it's really good, because, like, I'm not there as much but I still see her, like. You know, I've come more closer to her than I used to be.' For Adam, it took eight months of separation before he was able to really talk to his father again. It was around that time that his father apologized to him for his part in their conflict and this proved crucial to the improvement of their relationship. Also important were the insights Adam had gained during those eight months from living with strangers in a shared house:

> I've learnt to deal with conflict a bit more, especially with the house and learning to understand that some people do disagree with me. [Laughs] I

> guess . . . like learning to understand other people's points of view. And,
> yeah, learning to get along with my parents again and my brother.
>
> (Adam)

More recently, Adam found that the family counselling he was attending had helped him maintain communication with his parents and to resolve his ongoing conflict with his brother.

Maree too had regular contact with her family, though unlike José and Adam her relationships had been little altered by the move away from home. The fact that Maree visited her mother once a week was testament to her loyalty rather than any improvement in her family relations:

> Once a week I go there. I've got to do that, rinse the clothes out, and do
> that. I've got to sweep the floor, mop the floor and vacuum the floor . . .
> sometimes even her room. And she expects me to vacuum my little
> sister's room as well. . . . And I just don't feel like I'm part of that family.
> And I don't like my stepdad . . . and I just don't think that she treats me
> like a daughter.
>
> (Maree)

Having left home together, Maree and her older sister continued to have a close relationship, though the intensity of their bond had lessened with the appearance of her sister's boyfriend. Of this Maree said, 'I can understand why, like, she values him more than she values me.'

Despite his earlier quoted regrets regarding his past poor behaviour towards his mother, Toby did not speak of his current relationship with her. He did, however, ruefully admit that if given his time over he would probably behave the same way again, be 'still on the same path'. Brittany had no contact with her mother, but saw her grandmother and her uncles once a week. She enjoyed the company of her uncles, who were only ten or so years older than her and she often went out with them. In contrast, Victor avoided any contact with his aunt. At the time of the interview he had moved out of his supervised accommodation and was back staying with his brother; the only person in the world that he felt close to. On each of the few occasions he had returned to his aunt's house to visit his grandmother he had ended up arguing with his aunt. 'I try to stay away from there. . . . I just tend to keep to myself.'

Fahra too avoided her family home. Whenever she did return she discovered nothing had changed, that all the old conflicts quickly reappeared:

I go back and I see exactly the same pictures, exactly. Like everything just comes back to me. I know that I can't even stay there for half an hour, you know. My family, like, we never agree on anything. We're just three different people, my brother, my dad and I. . . . I just think my family are crazy. I would never be able to live with them no matter what. They're different people. It just feels like I was – I'm like the fruit, you know, on the wrong tree.

(Fahra)

Friends

Of the seven, only Fahra, Maree and José spoke of having boyfriends or girlfriends. For José, this was in the past tense. More recently he had become a committed bachelor, preferring to keep his female friendships free of romantic entanglements. Fahra met Bijan, her boyfriend, on the internet. Despite living in different states and enduring long absences (they hadn't seen each other for six months at the time of the interview), the relationship had lasted for over 18 months and seemed to satisfy both parties. Bijan was seven years older than Fahra, 'but for me he's not even mature enough. I like mature guys'. They talked regularly on the phone and visited each other whenever they could afford the bus fare. Regardless of his physical distance, Fahra felt genuinely supported by Bijan:

> For me he was there when I needed somebody to talk to and especially when I was having problems at home. And he's there for me, like, financially if I needed help. He's there for me if I need anything. But it's hard because it's long distance, we don't see each other often. We fight a lot because we don't see each other. You know, like, when are you going to come?

(Fahra)

In contrast, Maree saw her boyfriend every day. She often spent time at his parents' house and on cold nights would sleep over because her house had such inadequate heating. The only tension in their relationship stemmed from the fact that the boyfriend tended to distract Maree from her studies. 'He's annoying. He's really – he does stupid things, just childish. And, like, you know, it annoys me. And him being there, I can't really concentrate; he's so distracting.'

While Adam did not have a girlfriend, his closest friend was a girl, someone he had known all his life and who had always supported him:

I have quite a lot of friends at school who are quite important to me, but in particular I have one friend who was at my old school, the Christian College who was, who's – I've known her since I was five years old and for the entire time she has always been right there with me. She's always, you know – she's just the best. She understood what I was going through and stuff 'cause she was going through similar things with her parents.

(Adam)

Consistent with his desire to be romantically unattached, José had a large circle of friends with whom he 'hangs out'. No one friend seemed more important to him than another and his emphasis was on freedom, flexibility and a lack of social pressure. Describing the ingredients of a good time, he said: 'It's like, have a laugh. Go to places. And yeah, just try to relax and have a good old conversation.'

Victor and Toby were the most isolated among these young people. When asked if he had a girlfriend, Victor said he 'didn't really like relationships'. He did speak of male friends who he sometimes saw, but their social horizons were extremely narrow. 'I enjoy the company, but we don't do stuff. We just sit around and do nothing; play PlayStation. They come to my place, we go to another guy's house, play Gamecube or something.' As we saw earlier, for Toby homelessness was an isolating experience in which he was forced to look out for himself. He seemed to hold no hope that he would make friends with his fellow residents, rather, speaking of his shared accommodation, he declared, 'There's no love there . . . I'm just there for myself and to sort things out.'

Professionals

Four of these seven young people spoke of having good relations with one or more welfare workers or teachers who had helped them in some way. In the cases of Fahra and José, teachers had encouraged them and given them confidence when they were feeling low. Fahra simply said, 'My teachers loved me.' Speaking of a teacher in his tertiary course, José said, 'She, like, really lifts my spirit up, makes me feel good about myself . . . She tells me I'm a bright boy, um, you know, like she just says a lot of good stuff to make me feel good about myself . . . it makes me happy.' When he first became homeless, José also had a good relationship with a social worker at a youth homelessness outreach service. He regularly met with this worker and was able to talk freely to him; it was through this connection that he found his medium-term accommodation. Remembering the ease of their relationship, it was with a tinge of sadness that José admitted, 'And then now I don't see him. I don't see him at all.'

Maree's relationship with her youth worker was more pragmatic, devoid of emotional investment. 'She advises me in what to do and helps me on what I need. . . . I'm pretty satisfied 'cause everything that I asked her – problems that I have – are usually solved.' There was more affection in Adam's admiration for his case worker, the coordinator of his supervised accommodation. 'Whenever there's a problem in the house she'll – she always has a really good way of going about it, talking to all the people . . . she's a really nice person, as well, she treats us all with respect.'

The positive effects that such small acts of kindness and encouragement can have on the life of a vulnerable young person are immeasurable. What we do know though is that they often function as crucial turning points (as was the case for both Adam's and José's relationships with their case workers) and help build vital self-esteem.

Positive futures

As with their street-based counterparts, all but one of the service-based young people viewed their future with optimism. The exception was Victor who, when asked what he thought would be happening for him in the future, revealed the depth of his depression by saying, 'At the moment, nothing.' The long-term goals of the others were even more ambitious than those of the street-based young people. Perhaps, though, given their greater stability and their dedication to education, they were also more realistic.

Fahra could speak four languages and it was this facility and her interest in politics that encouraged her to contemplate working as a diplomat or for an international organization:

> I'd like to work maybe for the UN, or for the government. Maybe a politician, if I'm lucky. Stuff like that. I'm really interested in literature and politics and I'm good with languages, so that's my first interest. And I'd like to still – you know, if things don't work out with my boyfriend, I want to be independent, have my own place, have a nice car. You know, have a good life. I want to be able to afford what I want, you know. So, I want to work hard. I know I will work hard for it if I've been given the opportunity.
>
> (Fahra)

Fahra also spoke of her and Bijan living together, marrying and having 'kids and a happy life'. She wanted to have children almost immediately but had 'put the facts all together' and decided she should wait until she was 24, so that in the meantime she could save her money, 'buy a house and travel'.

Adam too had set his sights high, but in a more targeted and measured way. He had long dreamt of becoming a doctor and was studying hard in Year 12 in the hope of gaining entry into a medical degree. He knew this was an ambitious goal and was doing what he could to maximize his chances, but he also had a contingency plan in case his attempt failed. 'I was thinking of doing a science course if I don't get into medicine, but I'm applying everywhere across the country. . . . Well I hope to get to medical school. I hope to be the best doctor I could be.' In terms of relationships, Adam's aspirations were more modest. Envisaging his studies taking him on a trajectory very different from those of his current friends, he simply hoped that he would be able to maintain contact with his old friends while making new ones. And also, 'I wanna definitely still stay in contact with my family, 'cause they'll always be my family.'

Like Adam, Maree's long-term ambitions were directly connected to her short-term goals. In keeping with her practical approach to confronting the challenges of homelessness, she realized that in order to 'rent a private property with my boyfriend' she would have to defer her university course for a year and work full time in order to save money. 'And so it'll probably take longer. Yeah, so I just want to be, like, a midwife and have a career. Get married and have kids.'

When contemplating his future, José did not mention relationships but was very clear about wanting to build on his current business studies, to develop his communication skills and to enter business. ''Cause I've been doing nightclub work, and like I wouldn't mind to maybe manage one day, or something like that. Like, own one.' Toby's aspirations were more focused on material wealth and social status, but lacked any clear plan as to how these might be attained:

> After uni, I'll hopefully like get a good job and then like make shitloads of money. . . . I wanna live in Toorak [an exclusive suburb]. In the next couple of years, if I have the money to, I'd like to get into Toorak. . . . It'd feel prestigious and, like . . . the rich people just seem to like have fun, like hold house parties and dinner parties.
>
> (Toby)

Unlike the futures envisaged by Adam, Maree, José and even Fahra, Toby's was a fantasy. His thoughts about his possible future career were slightly more realistic in that they acknowledged possible obstacles. 'I'm just like attracted to the areas like the legal area and criminals and all that like. I'd like to do law, but I won't get the marks, so, like – I think there's a course, criminal justice or justice systems, where eventually you can manage like a business kind of thing.'

Brittany was also attracted to the law and acknowledged that 'I've got to get to school' if she wanted to become a lawyer. One can conjecture that young people like Toby and Brittany are attracted to the legal professions because they represent both a continuity with but also a break from their pasts. On the one hand the law is a professional world that they have some knowledge and experience of, yet on the other it promises to impose order on a world that they have experienced as being largely chaotic. Certainly it seems Brittany's attraction to the law and law enforcement was rooted in her childhood experiences. 'I always wanted to be a cop. And when I moved in with my mum, I wanted to be a lawyer.'

Conclusion

Despite the overrepresentation of young people with CALD backgrounds in this pathway, cross-cultural conflict was an overt factor for only three of these seven young people becoming homeless and one was Adam, for whom the conflict was a matter of belief-based affiliation rather than ethnicity. As we have seen in Chapter 4, a more general characteristic of these young people's pathways into homelessness was the shared sense of dislocation and displacement that they felt in relation to their families. All of the young people from CALD backgrounds (as well as Brittany, who was placed in foster care as a baby) were physically separated from their parents for an extended period during their early infant years. This created a lasting legacy of a sense of separateness and, in Victor's most extreme case, of utter abandonment. For Toby and Adam the sense of separateness was not physical but psychological. Simply, they felt that they did not belong in their families. Not merely black sheep, they felt like goats; entirely different species.

When compared with the on the streets pathway, the most striking difference is that none of the young people in the using the system pathway cited drug or alcohol abuse as a factor in their routes into or experiences of homelessness. This lack of dependence on substances seems to have enabled them to more successfully access accommodation and other services and to sustain a more stable lifestyle. Apart from the negative physical effects of drug or alcohol abuse and the impact these may have on a person's ability to study and maintain steady employment, their consumption causes financial stress which, as seen with those in the on the streets pathway, often leads to young people being drawn into criminal activities in order to support their lifestyle. By remaining largely free of drug and alcohol abuse even after becoming homeless, the young people in this pathway were able to focus on other goals, such as acquiring and maintaining stable accommodation, and their eduction and employment.

While the overall stability of these young people distinguishes them from their street-based counterparts, the fundamental sense of dislocation from their families that stopped them even contemplating returning home is what clearly demarcates them from those in the in and out of home pathway. It is to these young people that our attention now turns.

7 In and out of home

> The week before I went back I was writing in my diary stuff like, 'Oh, how could you be so stupid? Like, if you go back home, she's just going to start drinking and then you're gonna like break down.'
>
> (Lucy)

In terms of secure shelter, as well as familial care and affection (two of the more intangible elements contained in a broader notion of 'home'), the young people in this pathway were far 'less' homeless than those in both the on the streets and using the system pathways. At the time of their interviews, all six in this pathway were either living back in their family home or in a privately rented shared house. Yet the unresolved nature of many of the issues that originally led them into homelessness made their current accommodation situations unstable and suggested that future homelessness was a distinct possibility. Despite being privately accommodated, the young people in the in and out of home pathway shared more in common with those in the on the streets pathway than with those in the service-based one. The characteristic that the young people in these pathways shared and which distinguished them from their contemporaries in the using the system pathway was their ongoing dependence on drugs. Whether safely housed or living on the streets, young people who are drug dependent are less stable and more vulnerable than those who are not. This single factor has flow-on effects in other important areas of their lives (education, employment, mental and general health, relationships, involvement in criminal activity, etc.) and renders whatever accommodation arrangements they may have as more provisional.[1]

Apart from their accommodation 'outcomes', the other significant single factor that separated the in and out of home young people from those in the two pathways already discussed was their parents' desire to resolve the conflict that had propelled their child from the family home. The parents of four of the six young people in this pathway sought professional help to address their family conflict. This preparedness to share responsibility for the conflict and/or to assist the young person with his or her own issues (e.g. drug and alcohol dependence) was further reflected in the fact that half of the young people had been able to return home.

Important as drug use, mental illness and ongoing parental concern were for these young people, their experiences of homelessness were also framed by the fact that they maintained their friendship and extended family networks. Couch surfing at friends' or partners' parents' places ensured that they remained in their local communities and enabled three of the six to avoid using crisis or medium-term accommodation services. This contrasts particularly strongly with the journeys into homelessness taken by those in the on the streets pathway, most of whom severed their place-based connections, moving away either to flee parental abuse or to follow their quests for greater independence.

Accommodation

Couch surfing

Of the three young people who did not access crisis accommodation, Kate was the only one who spent time on the streets, and only for one night. When her parents told her to leave, Kate walked to a nearby park and spent the night in an adventure playground, huddled in a large concrete pipe. 'It was freezing up in the hills. I was writing in my diary all night; didn't get any sleep. . . . I had a breakdown that night, or something. I was just totally depressed. It was horrible. I didn't sleep at all. I was just crying the whole night.' Kate's experience of homelessness might have ended there and then, for she knew her parents had not really wanted her to leave, that they would have accepted her back:

> I felt really dirty actually, sleeping out. All I wanted to do was go home and have a shower and have something to eat. But because I was so stubborn, I didn't. I knew I'd be more than welcome to, but I was just so up on my high horse. No, they kicked me out in the first place, I'm not going to go back and give them the satisfaction of me crawling back and saying, 'Can I come home?'
>
> (Kate)

Kate resisted the temptation to return home and instead contacted a friend who offered her a bed for the night. From there she moved between friends' houses, following the party, crashing wherever she found herself. Most of her friends were in the same scene, living from party to party. 'I had lots of friends who were living out of home down there. It's like a whole group of us.' Although she was too proud to ask her parents if she could return home, Kate remained in constant contact with them and happily accepted their offers of material support:

> My parents came up every week with shopping bags of food, because Cindy's mum was struggling with money and I ended up getting kicked out because of the phone bill. But I never used the phone, 'cause I had no one to call, apart from my parents, 'cause I lost all contact with my friends. The only people I called were my parents, but they had all these mobile phone calls and so they blamed me. . . . And all this stuff went missing – they blamed me.
>
> (Kate)

Christie also couch surfed once she left home and ended up staying seven months in a friend's shared house. The house was 'a really, really old Victorian house. Like there were plaster chunks falling out of the wall and the carpet just looked gross . . . it was just a big, cold house.' All the other residents were studying and receiving Austudy, the federal government's student allowance, but Christie spent each night sleeping on a 'really old and uncomfortable' couch because she wasn't paying rent – 'I didn't have any money.' By the time of her interview, she was again living in shared accommodation, but this time as a paying member of the household.

More than the others, Lucy's trajectory most closely fits the in and out of home category. Always ambivalent about leaving her mother, fearing for her mother's mental health and well-being, her first departure from home was into foster care:

> It felt really, really, really bad. I felt terrible. I just felt so depressed. You know, I wanted to leave, but I didn't want to leave because I always felt responsible for my mum. Because I always had to like do stuff for her when she was drunk, because she couldn't look after herself half the time.
>
> (Lucy)

Having finally made the break, Lucy was disappointed by her foster home arrangement, living with a single mother who had a young baby: 'I only stayed there for two months. I didn't really like it that much. I suppose it had a lot to do with her, because I didn't like her that much . . . she didn't really have a sense of humour. She was insensitive and she left me to do most of the housework.'

After this failed experiment, Lucy returned home. Once again, the move was accompanied by a deep ambivalence:

> I was writing in my diary stuff like, 'Oh, how could you be so stupid? Like, if you go back home, she's just going to start drinking and then you're gonna like break down,' and all that. But after that I went home anyway and . . . it was okay for a couple of weeks, like about a month, and then she got drunk again. 'Oh,' I thought. 'How stupid are you?' I just got really angry at myself. I'm like, 'I can't believe I came back home to this!'
>
> (Lucy)

As Lucy had predicted, the stress of living with her mother again took a heavy toll on her own mental health. Within two months she had attempted suicide and then spent five weeks in a psychiatric unit. Released from the unit, she returned home for a brief period in which she again became critically depressed. Readmitted to the unit and again discharged, she was this time placed in the care of her uncle and aunt:

> My uncle came and picked me up. I was meant to stay with him for a couple of days but they wanted me to stay there for longer. . . . They said I could stay there for a couple of days and I took some stuff from home and after that practically never went back for a long time.
>
> (Lucy)

Lucy enjoyed living with her uncle and aunt and made new friends in the town where they lived. However, her mental state remained fragile and she continued to self-harm. This became a source of great tension, particularly for her aunt who, Lucy claimed, 'always wanted me to go home'. After one self-harming episode, the uncle drove Lucy back to her mother's house, reassuring her that he would collect her again in a couple of days. Instead, three days later he rang Lucy's mother to explain that Lucy could no longer live with them:

> My uncle rang my mum up and said, 'We can't deal with this, you know. We can't have her in our house doing that while we've got our son, you know, he's only six.' I think they were afraid that if I ever just lost the plot and like went completely crazy or something. Or if I ever tried to kill myself and their son saw it. They were afraid that he would see me like

that. Then they said, 'We love you dearly, but we can't have you in our house doing that.'

(Lucy)

Taking refuge

Like Lucy, Lauren's departure from home involved a stay in a psychiatric hospital. Once discharged, she returned home for a month but her continued heavy marijuana use caused conflict with her mother and resulted in her being asked to leave. Rather than couch surf at friends' places or stay with relatives, Lauren found temporary accommodation at a refuge:

> The refuge was a big space, but it was good. Like, they'd made it purely out of brick because apparently in the last house people had kicked in walls and put holes and stuff so they said, 'Pure brick.' . . . It was really ugly and really awkward to be in because it wasn't nice to look at, but it was all right, we got along.
>
> (Lauren)

From the refuge, Lauren gained a place in a supervised house. Unfortunately, she had a 'major conflict' with one of the other residents which ended with them both being forced to leave. Lauren then found accommodation in a different refuge, but within six weeks she was again asked to leave. 'One of the workers decided she wanted me to leave. I don't know if it was my fault or not. I didn't think I'd broken any of the house rules, but I didn't argue with her.'

Throughout this period Lauren's parents had remained in contact with her and for a time they and their daughter attended family counselling together. While the old issues and tensions remained unresolved, the fact that both parties had continued to communicate with each other meant that when Lauren found herself expelled from another accommodation service she at least felt able to ask her parents if she could return home. Faced with living on the streets, Lauren rang her mum and explained, '"They gave me 48 hours to leave. Can I come home? I've tried every refuge in Melbourne and everything." And she said, "Yes." And we wrote up a contract; my conditions for them, their conditions for me.'

After being told to leave his mother's house, Tim spent the first night at his girlfriend's place and then couch surfed at a friend's house. 'I went and stayed there for a couple of months, sleeping on the couch. But that didn't work out. Sleeping on the couch wasn't very nice, and they'd try and have people over and there's someone on the couch. So I went to a refuge.' Tim had a low opinion of refuges. He found them to be 'a laugh', partly because of their residents and partly because of their rules and regulations. He saw himself as very different from most other refuge residents, who he described as 'complete bloody dickheads . . . nut-jobs, like the CIA's out to get them'. He had similar disdain for the restrictions some refuges imposed on their residents:

> Like some refuges will kick you out at ten o'clock in the morning and let
> you back in at six o'clock, and I think that's stupid. Like they break your
> balls to go and find somewhere to live. They pressure you to find a job or
> something like that, tell you everyday, 'Go here, go to some service and
> talk to them about . . . what's it called? . . . Government Housing.' Which
> was a load of crap. I've been on their waiting list for about 12 months.
>
> (Tim)

Unlike many in the using the system pathway, Tim's admission to a refuge did not signal the end of his itinerant lifestyle; rather it was merely one among many forms of insecure accommodation in which he temporarily resided. Tim also spent time living on the streets. 'I moved around a lot. Got to know my way around a bit. I've seen the lovely things in St Kilda [a suburb renowned for street prostitution]. I lived there for about two months. Just sleeping on the street. . . . I've seen a lot of Melbourne.'

At the time of the interview, Tim was living in a shared house with friends. The house was close to a train station, had a TV and a comfortable couch, and he paid $50 a week from his youth allowance for his own room. Although this arrangement suited him, he saw it as just another move; in no sense did he think of it as being stable and ongoing. Anticipating his past pattern he said, 'I'll stay until I'm told to go.'

Damon too stayed with mates in the week immediately following his forced departure from home. He then spent a fortnight at his aunt's house before finding accommodation in a refuge. Unlike Tim, he appreciated the services provided by the refuge, particularly the fact that the workers there taught him how to cook. The refuge supervisor told him he could stay there for a month and this provided Damon with enough stability to continue working. This was what he most wanted:

> Just a roof over my head so that I could keep going to work, because at
> that point in time if I didn't have my job I would've had nothing, no

income, nothing. So that was my main focus, to make sure that I was able
to get to work everyday. It gave me that little bit of leeway. I could relax.
That, like, guaranteed me four weeks with a roof over my head. I had four
weeks to look for a new house, so that took a lot of stress off.

(Damon)

In that time, a friend of a friend offered Damon a room in his flat. At
first, this arrangement seemed to work well. When not at work,
Damon kept to himself, staying in his room. 'I was in there smoking,
so I just stayed in there. I didn't want to bother anyone, didn't want
the smell of it to go throughout the house, so I pretty much just kept
my door shut and just stayed to myself, listened to my music.' Despite
maintaining this low profile, one day 'out of nowhere' Damon's
flatmate began to argue with him, picking a fight. Before he knew
what was happening, Damon was being strangled, 'whipped with all
kinds of shit'. Even worse in Damon's mind, his flatmate smashed his
acoustic guitar. 'He just threw it on the ground, broke the back off it,
and I just thought, "I don't need this in my life. I'm trying to sort my
own shit out."' Despite this bad experience of shared accommodation, at the time of his interview Damon was again living in a shared
house.

Education and employment

While not as committed to education as those in the using the system
pathway, nonetheless all six young people in the in and out of home
pathway remained in some form of schooling for most of the 18
months of the study. At the time of their interviews, Lucy, Kate and
Lauren were all enrolled in and attempting to attend secondary
school. Lucy changed schools when she moved to her uncle and aunt's
house and by the time of the final interview had returned to her old
school to undertake Year 12. After becoming homeless, Kate missed
the whole of Year 9. Knowing that she 'couldn't get anywhere on a
Year 8 pass' she was keen to return to school for Year 10. Once there,
she felt out of place. 'Now, back at school, I feel like an outcast. I feel
like no one's in the same boat as me. . . . I'm finding it hard to
manage the workload because I'm not turning up regularly.' Lauren
dropped out of school after her stay in the psychiatric hospital but
decided to return to her studies while she was living in the refuge.

Christie finished Year 12 during the course of the study and by the
final interview was enrolled in an Arts degree, studying criminology
and psychology. Recently though she had deferred her place because

she needed to earn more money. Both Tim and Damon were enrolled in vocational courses at technical and further education (TAFE) colleges. For Damon the TAFE course was a component of his cabinetmaking apprenticeship work, which, as we saw earlier, he greatly valued.

In fact, of the six only Damon had stable, ongoing employment. Lucy and Kate had no employment throughout the 18 months of the study, Tim had part-time work when the study began but not during the 18 months, and Lauren worked in various part-time jobs. Christie was employed part-time in a supermarket, but had also worked as a tabletop dancer, a form of employment she despised but was repeatedly drawn to for its financial rewards:

> Well, the very first time I went there it was just depressing, you know, I wasn't as heavy as I am now, but I still didn't have a very good body image and a lot of people there were just disgusting old men. It was bad, like, you know, you'd sit there and be friendly and flirt and convince them to go into the back room for a dance, but it was basically begging. I can remember some of their eyes and just dirty old men. Just gross. . . . I was still young and had hopes for my future and these were all people that were, you know, I don't know, 50 or 60, just still unemployed drunks, horrible people and I just, I couldn't find anything to relate to them about, to talk about. It was just kind of sad. . . . I pulled a muscle or something and it just started getting depressing, so I stopped going. I didn't want to do it. I told myself I was never going to do it again 'cause it was just gross and demeaning.
>
> (Christie)

Despite making this pledge to herself, during the interview Christie admitted that in her current financial situation ('I've got a car to repay and I've got credit cards that have to be repaid') she was contemplating returning to this more lucrative form of work.

Violence

Consistent with the comparative lack of violence in their family lives, most of the young people in this pathway were neither regular perpetrators nor victims of violence once they became homeless. As we have already seen, the one exception to this was Damon. The violent rage that led to Damon's mother taking out an intervention order against him was not an isolated incident. Damon had a short temper and fancied himself as a fighter. 'If someone's looking for a fight, I'm more than happy to, because, once again, I know exactly what I'm doing. Unfortunately I've been taught how to fight, which makes me a bit cocky as well.' His aggressive attitude, his temper and his occasional dealing in drugs meant that, once homeless, Damon was regularly involved in violent episodes:

> I can't really say it's never been my fault, but it's always – the thing with it is, if someone wants to fight me I'm more than happy to have to defend myself and I know exactly what to do to get out of a situation unhurt. But no one will ever fight me one-on-one. It's always been four people against me. Like I've had people come up to me in the street – I don't even know them – four people, and they start beating me up. The majority of the time I'll run, but if it's just one person then I'll fight.
>
> (Damon)

While the others in this pathway did not speak of experiencing physical violence once they were homeless, the patterns of conflict and violent arguments that often typified their home lives were generally repeated in their new accommodation arrangements. Kate's falling out with her friend's mother, Lauren's expulsion from a refuge and a medium-term accommodation unit, and Tim's itinerant existence, in which he merely waited to be told to leave his current dwelling, all attest to the ongoing presence of conflict in their lives.

Mental illness

Given the extent and seriousness of the mental illnesses experienced by most of these young people prior to them becoming homeless, it is not surprising that their mental health problems remained or worsened after that event. Like those in the on the streets pathway, these young people either had pre-existing mental health issues or developed them in reaction to becoming homeless. Also like the street-based young people, and in contrast to those in the using the system pathway, the mental illnesses affecting these six were exacerbated by their continued heavy use of drugs and/or alcohol after they became homeless.

As noted earlier, Lucy and Lauren both had periods in psychiatric hospitals which, in a sense, signalled the beginning of their homelessness. Lucy remained depressed and continued to attempt suicide and self-harmed during her times away from home. These expressions of her mental anguish caused her uncle and aunt to ask her to leave their home and led to her returning to her mother's house. Still there at the time of the interview, Lucy's psychological state remained highly unstable:

> I could say that I'm more depressed than I ever was. I suppose because I know a lot more about my family and what's going on. . . . You find out more about your family truths and it sort of opens all these doors. Sometimes it shuts all these windows. Sometimes it shuts both windows and doors and you feel trapped. . . . Sometimes you just feel like you want to die. That's just me.
>
> (Lucy)

While conceding that she wasn't 'doing so well at the moment', Lucy continued trying to manage her depression, employing her own forms of therapy. 'Mostly I draw. I think drawing always reflects my thinking. . . . Drawing helps me get it out, like writing. Writing in my diary, that's part of me as well.' Unfortunately though, her depression remained acute. Combined with her mother's own mental illness and alcoholism, this makes it difficult to believe that her return to home represented a resolution of the issues that led to her leaving it in the first place.

In Lauren's case, her psychiatric care and the family counselling had positive effects on her depression. Her parents' desire to improve their relationship with her was crucial to the mother/daughter reconciliation that occurred at Lauren's eighteenth birthday party. Having not spoken to her parents for six weeks, Lauren received a call from her mother asking if she could see her on her birthday. Lauren invited her mother to a party at the supervised house where she was staying:

> We cried, we talked, we cried more. It was kind of good, because she didn't hold anything back. She just said, 'I'm so sorry.' And I said I was sorry and it was really good at the time because I was so used to her holding how she felt back from me and she didn't. So I didn't hold anything back either. I was expecting to have a really crap day, but I had a really good day. And then Mum and I built up a relationship.
>
> (Lauren)

This breakthrough conversation prepared the way for Lauren's return home. As with Lucy, some of the underlying issues that originally led to Lauren becoming homeless remained unresolved so that by the time of the interview she admitted, 'There's been a little bit of conflict recently, so I've been staying with friends on and off.' Even so, her general outlook had been transformed by the experience of being homeless:

> I'm actually really glad it all happened. I mean, I don't think I'd be the person I am now if it hadn't. I don't think I'd be as motivated to enjoy my life. . . . Like, it was such an experience and I think with everything I've gone through, it's made me a better person, especially going into the hospital, 'cause you just realize what everyone else is going through.
>
> (Lauren)

Since leaving home, Christie's depression increasingly centred on her poor body image. She regularly felt depressed and occasionally would have panic attacks and would watch television, binge eat and then purge herself afterwards. 'I kind of feel better 'cause I've had the food, but then I just feel guilty and ashamed and then my stomach just hurts 'cause I've eaten too much.' For a time after she became homeless, Christie saw a psychologist once every three weeks. 'I was a lot more emotionally messed up and just depressed and paranoid and angry.' When she felt she had made little or no progress she eventually stopped seeing her psychologist. By the time of the interview, Christie felt her psychological state had improved slightly:

> I think I've become more independent, I don't know if I like it much though. I mean, I don't have as many friends, I don't do stuff as often with them, and I just spend a lot of time by myself. But it's okay. I think I'm happier. I'm not, you know – I don't know if I'd call myself happy though.
>
> (Christie)

Once homeless, Damon also abandoned any formal therapeutic attempt to remedy his anger and depression. 'I've been made to go to counselling, but I refuse to anymore because they say the exact same thing as the last counsellor, and I know exactly what they're gonna say to everything I say.' At the time of the interview he was 'treating' his mental health issues with a combination of music and self-medication in the form of marijuana:

> If I've had a really bad day and I'm really angry, I channel my energy into my bass. When I play my bass, all my energy, all my anger is just focused on playing the bass and I usually play really well. . . . And, like, if I've had a really bad day at work and it's just giving me the shits really bad, I generally get something to smoke.
>
> (Damon)

Health

For Lauren, Christie, Kate and Tim, poor mental health was accompanied by more general ill health. When Lauren returned to live with her parents, her mother, noticing a bulge below her daughter's abdomen, thought she was pregnant. 'So she took me to the doctors and I had a cyst in my uterus that was 11 centimetres.' The cyst was benign but after the operation to remove it Lauren was told that she would not be able to have children. 'It didn't really affect me at the time. I mean, since then I've gotten upset over it and cried and I've got mad. I've hurt myself, and just all the normal crap, but I can deal with it. I know I've got other options, so I'll get to it when I get to it.'

Soon after becoming homeless, Christie was diagnosed as suffering from the sleeping disorder narcolepsy. The sense of overwhelming tiredness that afflicted her had an enormous impact on her social life. Whereas once she had regularly gone out drinking and dancing four nights a week, after the onset of the narcolepsy she could no longer cope with late nights. 'But now I – you know, I couldn't even have one late night. You know, even if I was doing nothing the next day I'd still be tired all the next day and it just wouldn't be worth it.'

As with some in the using the system pathway, Kate blamed her constant poor physical health on her diet and lifestyle. Plagued by colds and other viruses, she said, 'I'm actually getting sick a lot. I think that's because I don't eat regularly and I'm not sleeping enough. . . . My immune system is very low and I'm constantly getting sick.' While not talking of its negative health effects Tim, too, spoke about his depleted diet:

> I don't eat. I haven't had anything to eat in the last three days. I just don't get hungry. Maybe that's my way of dealing with things. Like I'll eat chocolate here and there or a little bit of this or a little bit of that, but nothing regular. That's why I'm so bloody skinny. . . . Some days I can't be bothered getting up off the couch to go and get something to eat. I'm very lazy.
>
> (Tim)

While not suffering from a sexually transmitted infection, Hepatitis C or HIV, Tim was concerned about contracting these diseases and regularly had himself tested for them. Although he had never used needles, he believed he was at risk because 'of places that I've stayed, they haven't been very healthy' and because he often had unprotected sex.[2]

Drugs and alcohol

The mental and general health of the six young people comprising the in and out of home pathway was negatively affected by their continued use of drugs and/or alcohol. With the exceptions of Christie (who said her only experiences of drugs were her prescribed medications for narcolepsy and migraines and some experiments with marijuana) and Lucy, the rest in this pathway continued their use of drugs and/or alcohol once they became homeless. Significantly, at the time of their interviews, Tim, Damon and Kate had given up or drastically reduced their use of drugs.

Lauren stopped smoking marijuana during her six-week stay in the psychiatric hospital but resumed once discharged. It is unclear from her interview whether a reduction or quitting of this habit was made a precondition of her return home in the contract she drew up with her parents. Given the conflict it caused prior to her leaving, this seems a likely possibility.

Tim was a polydrug user before he left home ('I've done speed, I've done coke, I've done pills, I've done marijuana, but that's about it') and maintained the same pattern of use once he was homeless. 'Like I'd get up in the morning and I was doing labouring work or something, and I'd have a pill in the morning to keep me going. So it became a bit serious. Yeah, but I loved the effects of it – you feel good.' Tim felt in control of his drug use, though he did admit to nearly overdosing on a couple of occasions. 'I've had too much, and you feel really nauseated and everything. You get hot and cold spells, and as soon as that starts happening you know you're in trouble, so you just drink orange juice or eat oranges 'cause it completely counters the effects.' When he felt close to becoming addicted, Tim altered his behaviour. 'I just said, "Nah, that's it. Stop that." And I did. That was it, but like I still use speed and pills.'

As with Tim, Damon saw his drug use as something he had under control, something he was experimenting with. His drug of choice was marijuana but he also used ice, speed and ecstasy.

> And with the drugs that I do take, mainly they are experimental. If I do like them a lot then I might keep going for a bit, always knowing that it's never gonna be a long-term thing. Yeah, it's mainly because I am so experimental and I do like the feeling I get. If I just turn around and if it's offered to me, I'll take it. A lot of the time I won't go out looking for it.
>
> (Damon)

By the time of his interview, Damon had reduced his drug use. The primary reason for this reduction was financial. 'I probably spent 30 grand on it I'd say in the last three years. And that's all the money I've earned through my apprenticeship. I've got nothing to show for it, only a couple of guitars.' Having reduced his marijuana use, Damon discovered he was drinking 'a hell of a lot more. I've noticed it's either one or the other I can go without, but I generally prefer to either be stoned or at least have a couple of beers in me every night.'

More than anyone else in this pathway, Kate dramatically increased her drug use after she left home. Her heavy use of marijuana had been a key source of tension with her parents, but once free of the constraints they had placed on her behaviour it became the primary focus of her daily life. While couch surfing at a friend's place, Kate met Matt, who she described as 'the biggest pot smoker I have ever met'. They started going out and before long Kate moved into his house:

> I was getting the youth allowance. We used to put our money together and get that much marijuana it was to the point where I felt stoned when I was straight. We were chewing through that much money, just spending it on dope. It was just insane. It was to the point where I was afraid to get on to busy trains. I was missing trains 'cause I was just that paranoid. . . . I couldn't remember stuff 'cause I was that drug-fucked.
>
> (Kate)

After she broke up with Matt, Kate significantly reduced her marijuana use. 'I still smoked and got more stoned because I wasn't smoking so much, and I really hated it. Absolutely hated it. Then I would cut down more, cut down more, cut down more.' By the time of her interview, she had stopped smoking dope altogether:

> I feel so much better. And so many people say that I've changed. Instead of me just sitting there giving the one word answer, like, 'Yes', 'No', 'I don't know', 'Maybe', now I'm talking. I'm remembering. . . . I couldn't remember what I did that day; no exaggeration. Don't even ask me what I did yesterday! I wouldn't be able to remember. I mean, my memory's still affected, but it's a lot better.
>
> (Kate)

Engagement with services

Apart from accommodation services, more young people in the in and out of home pathway were higher service users than those in the using the system pathway. As we have already seen, both Tim and Lucy had long histories with the Department of Human Services (DHS) and brief, unsuccessful stays in foster care homes. It was, however, the prevalence and severity of the mental illnesses suffered by those in the in and out of home pathway that demanded their greater use of services, particularly health-related ones. All six sought assistance for practical matters such as income support and employment, and Lauren and Lucy received extensive support from mental health services. Lucy had an ongoing connection with a dedicated young people's mental health service. 'It's a really good service, I think. I think it helps me out a lot, 'cause the counsellor I'm seeing I've seen before and she's really nice.'

Tim was even more enthusiastic about the services available to homeless young people. 'Homeless services are great. They're the best; they're the best thing!' Talking about one particular centralized service for homeless young people, he said:

> That's good because it's got a heap of services mixed into one. Like it's got doctors, lawyers, Centrelink – everything you need day-to-day. They've got food there in the afternoon. They've got everything: social workers, computers . . . I used to go in everyday, so I got to know the people there, but I don't spend much time there now. But like if I've got nowhere to stay, I'll go in there everyday and just bum around for something to do, 'cause I'm bored.
>
> (Tim)

Christie found that most forms of government assistance were not available to her because her parents had informed DHS that she was welcome to return home. Tim had a similar experience.

> DHS spoke to my mum and my mum was like, 'Yeah, I'd be happy to have him back.'
> 'So, Tim, why aren't you going back there?'
> 'My mum's a bitch; she'll kick me out again.'
> 'Oh, that's not what she's saying, she seems very cooperative on the phone to us.' They rang her up and they couldn't see any problem; they can't be bothered with me. They've got bloody 800 cases a week to look after . . . It's a lot of work, so if they've got a parent saying 'Yeah, I'll have him back', then they don't care, they say, 'Well, go back to her.'
>
> (Tim)

The underlying commitment to their children of most of the parents in this pathway meant that the government categorized them differently from most of the young people we have described previously.

In many cases, the families of these young people remained willing and able to support them if they resolved key issues in their lives, more often than not their drug use. In a policy climate dominated by a notion of mutual obligation, this parental commitment seemingly absolved the state of its responsibility to provide these young people with a safety net. Interestingly, Lauren and Kate both affirmed that they were better off than those who lacked family support. Lauren said:

> I just saw myself as nowhere. Like, I wasn't homeless, because I thought no matter how bad it got, I always had an option and there's always a choice I could make. I just thought, well, there were so many people that do actually live on the streets and I've got it pretty good here, so . . .
>
> (Lauren)

Echoing these sentiments, Kate explained why she did not access more services:

> It wasn't a decision not to go to services . . . I suppose if I was on the street for a while . . . but there was always my parents' place that I could go back to. So I didn't see the point of going to that degree to get somewhere to stay, and food and stuff. I did always have my parents. It was just me being stubborn.
>
> (Kate)

Relationships

Family

Despite the fact that four of the six young people in this pathway were told by their parents to leave the family home, these same parents had an ongoing commitment to their children and this generally had a positive effect on the young people's experiences of homelessness and their accommodation outcomes. Superficially, it might be thought that a parent evicting his or her child from home reflects the worst kind of breakdown in parent/child relations. However, as we observed with the using the system pathway in which five of the seven young people left home of their own accord, a young person fleeing the family home often signals a desperate and abusive family situation. In some cases in the in and out of home pathway where the young person was told to leave, this command was given at a time of crisis and intolerable family stress (Kate and Lauren). In other instances it was issued as a last resort once the parent(s) had exhausted all other strategies for managing their child's erratic behaviour (Tim and Damon). In all four of these cases, the parents attempted to remain in contact after the young person left home and, at least in Lauren and Kate's cases, were willing to negotiate their return. In fact, it was when the young people left voluntarily (Lucy and Christie) that parents were least able or willing to maintain a relationship with them.

Kate believed that the time she spent living away from her parents was crucial to her discovering a more positive direction for her life. 'I think the time apart from my parents I needed . . . I shouldn't have gone about it that way, but I reckon that time apart, just that space that we had, was a good change. It also had a lot of bad effects as well, and then when I moved back home, it kind of started again, in a way.' By the time of the interview, she had decided that her relationship with her parents worked best when the contact was brief but regular. 'I need to take my parents in small doses . . . I just don't wanna live there all the time at the moment. . . . At the moment I'm maintaining contact . . . if I talk to them over the phone we get along great, but if I go home it's a whole different story.' Kate's analysis of the family dynamic was that her mother, the reasonable one, was forced to play a mediating role between Kate and her father, 'the stubborn ones'. As this suggests, leaving home acted as a circuit breaker in Kate's conflict with her parents and accorded her a distance from which she could reflect on her own behaviour as well as theirs and could begin to navigate a different, healthier relationship with them into the future.

Lauren too thought of her experience of being homeless as something positive, something that made her into the person she had become which, unlike her earlier self, was someone she quite liked. She also thought that the rupture of her leaving home ultimately had a good effect on her mother and their relationship. 'I think Mum grew a lot as well, she learnt that, you know, all I wanted was for her to open up and tell me how she was feeling and so I knew what I was doing wrong.' Her father was apparently little changed by events. 'Dad hasn't really changed. He's learnt to deal with situations now when people get angry. I don't know if he learned anything. He's still the same.' Speaking of her relationship with her mother, Lauren said, 'We bonded so well afterwards. I mean, we've drifted apart a little bit now, but that's because she's a bit overprotective, because she's my mum, and all that stuff. I'm liking living with them.'

In contrast to Kate and Lauren, Lucy felt she was little affected by her time away from home, though since returning she found an improvement in her mother's outlook and behaviour:

I'm pretty much the same person. My mum, she's a bit more happier now. Yeah, she's happier. She's not really depressed that much because she's like got her fiancé, which is really good. She's less strict; she's more easygoing now. She doesn't yell as much. I don't know, we just get along better. She seems in a better mood.

(Lucy)

Even less had changed in Christie's family relations. At the time of the interview, the only encouraging sign was that on several occasions Christie had spoken to her father on the phone and had found that she was able to 'tell him things'. Her mother's response to this was one of jealousy ('So he's your favourite!') and she and Christie continued to fight and argue whenever they were in each other's company.

After Damon's mother took out an intervention order on him, he 'told her straight out that I'd never speak to her again and that any chance of a relationship was gone'. His mother ignored this threat and made numerous overtures to him after he left home. When his mobile phone broke, his mother bought him a new one so that she could maintain contact with him. Reneging on his pledge not to see her, accompanying her to the shop, Damon also accepted her offer of a television, DVD player and a PlayStation. This act of generosity had the desired reconciliatory effect. 'So she bought that for me and that's when we started getting on a bit – our relationship strengthened.' Surprisingly, it was an intervention by his absent father that ultimately brokered Damon's return home:

My dad called me and said, 'All right, I've spoken to your mother and I've talked her into it, you can stay with her. But you just have to respect her and do anything she says. Don't take any drugs while you're there and just clean yourself up.' And then I went back there for a month and it just got – our relationship just strengthened each day.

(Damon)

Despite his pivotal role in Damon's reconciliation with his mother, his father remained a great disappointment to his son:

I just didn't want to have anything to do with him 'cause he kept making promises he never kept. He never sent me birthday presents but he always sent my brother and my sister birthday presents, and I have no idea why. But I just said, 'Nup, got something against me, fine, I just don't speak to you anymore.'

(Damon)

Of the six, Tim's relationships with his parents remained the most intractable. His blunt assessment of them was, 'They're dickheads.' Despite their efforts to keep in touch with him, Tim had little time for his father and seemingly none for his mother. 'Like, my dad like contacts me. My mum tried to contact me ages and ages ago and I just told her to fuck herself, 'cause I didn't want to speak to her.'

Friends

Given that most of the young people in this pathway relied on the hospitality of friends once they became homeless, it is surprising to discover that, in general, they are more socially isolated than those in either the on the streets or using the system pathways.

The fatigue that accompanied Christie's narcolepsy isolated her socially. No longer able to spend her nights partying, she found that her circle of friends rapidly contracted. Also, couch surfing for so long at her friend's shared house had a detrimental effect on what had been her closest relationship. Of her friend, Christie said, 'She just felt really, really crowded and it was making her very irritated. . . . ever since moving, everything seems kind of more shallow. We haven't really, you know, had a long deep and meaningful or connected over anything.' Christie's self-described loneliness was relieved only by her close friendship with Joe who she used to see a few times a week. However, now due to their different work schedules and the geographical distance between them she saw him only once every three weeks.

Lucy felt similarly isolated and she too had only one good friend with whom she felt a genuine connection:

> I don't really have many friends. . . . But I met Sarah at the start of the year, on the first day of school, and we've been inseparable ever since. That's pretty good. We're pretty close. We have this sick sense of humour. It's just weird. I don't know, we think the most stupid things are really funny.
>
> (Lucy)

An incident at a birthday party prior to Damon becoming homeless led him to realize that the people he thought were his friends were in fact not. The legacy of this betrayal was that he now found it hard to trust people. 'I haven't really made many friends since then; just pretty much kept to myself.' He had some acquaintances, people he was happy to catch up with, but 'not people I can trust to do things for me, people I can trust to say things to'. Reinforced by his mother's decision to take out an intervention order on him, Damon's sense of betrayal ran deep and had left him wary of self-disclosure and the vulnerability that intimacy brings. Having insight into this, he put it succinctly when he said, 'There's not really that many people that are important to me 'cause I find it very hard to trust people.'

Tim lacked intimate trusting relationships too, but it was not a lack that he lamented. On the contrary, he enjoyed casual sexual encounters and partying with friends. 'I've been going out with people my own age, friends from TAFE [technical and further education], getting pretty drunk at the beach, a park, wherever – doing the teenage thing.'

For Lauren and Kate, friendship and intimate relationships played central roles in their pathways through homelessness. While at the time of her interview Lauren was once again based at her parents' house, she continued to stay with friends when tensions at home demanded it. Usually she would stay with Simon. 'He's gay, but we have a fantastic relationship, which is quite disturbing at times. But, you know, we just get along really well. We always have things to talk about. We both like to laugh.' She also had a boyfriend living in Sydney and whenever he was in Melbourne they would stay together and go out and enjoy themselves.

Just as Kate's relationship with Matt resulted in her dramatically increasing her dependence on marijuana, her later relationship with Kane was pivotal in her giving it up:

> When I met Kane, he just said 'Nuh' every time someone offered him a bong. Then I'd be stoned and he wouldn't be and I'm like, 'I don't like this.' He helped me in that way of not saying 'don't smoke,' but just him saying no kind of influenced me.
>
> (Kate)

As with Kayla and Jamie in the on the streets pathway, this positive relationship had had a transformative effect on Kate's life, enabling her to alter some of her most self-destructive behaviours and to envisage a better, healthier future for herself. As was true for Kayla and Jamie, Kate's self-esteem radically improved because she suddenly felt understood and cared for, had found someone she could trust:

> Kane and I don't have one issue that we can't talk about with each other. . . . Whatever I'm doing, I'm comfortable no matter what with Kane. I talk about anything and everything with him, really. . . . At the moment he has actually made me a lot happier and even my mum was saying the other

day that this is probably the happiest she's seen me in a long, long time. And that's Kane's doing.

(Kate)

Professionals

Despite the fact that only half of these young people accessed accommodation services, the friendliness of certain service workers still marked positive points on the journey through homelessness taken by three of the people in this pathway. Damon found the workers in the hostel he stayed in to be extremely helpful and supportive. 'They were willing to explain anything to you, how to cook and just anything you needed. If you asked, they were more than willing to help.' This reflected Lauren's experience in the first refuge in which she stayed. 'The people were really nice. I got along really well with my worker.'

As we have already seen, Lucy had a positive relationship with her current counsellor, but she also spoke fondly of one of her past youth workers. 'She was really, really nice. She helped me a lot. Yeah, she used to take me places and like we'd have a milkshake or coffee or something.' As with some of the more vulnerable young people in other pathways, these small affirmations and demonstrations of support were enormously important in shoring up Lucy's fragile sense of self.

Positive futures?

In contrast to the majority of young people in the on the streets and using the system pathways, the six in this pathway were less clear about their ambitions and more uncertain as to what their futures might hold. When asked about his future Tim simply said, 'I don't even know what I'm doing tomorrow.' Lauren's attitude to the future was more philosophical, less goal orientated than that of most of her peers. Her experiences of being homeless, of being hospitalized for mental illness as well as for the removal of an ovarian cyst had made her determined to enjoy life for what it had to offer. From this new, hard-won perspective, to plan for the future would be to betray dissatisfaction with the present. Hence, her 'theory' was 'just to have fun and try to forget about things and enjoy time with other people'.

Kate too lacked any definite career-type aspirations. While trying to commit to finishing secondary school, she admitted, 'It's really hard to be motivated and to want to go to school and get my VCE [vocational certificate of education] when you don't know why you're doing it. I mean, I have no idea what I want to do. No idea at all.' On another level, Kate had a clear idea of what she wanted for herself into the future. Revealing remarkable insight and self-knowledge, she said:

> I'm just reliant on other people's company to make me happy. I just think I need to spend more time by myself and get through that, so I'm more self-reliant. I see myself as not spending as much time with Kane. I need to start being more alone, hopefully living more at home and seeing Kane occasionally, rather than living at Kane's and seeing my parents occasionally. Yeah, I just need to get stationed at home and that would make it a hell of a lot easier to go to school every day. Kind of get into a routine; have a more permanent place to stay.
>
> (Kate)

Damon's ambitions were more dreamlike and revolved around his passion for music. Projecting into the future, he saw himself playing in his current band, but it being 'a lot bigger – touring worldwide'. While this might have been his fantasy, he did have more attainable goals for his band. 'Just practise every rehearsal we have. Just get our stuff together, make sure we've got our list and then as soon as we've got our list we'll be able to start getting into clubs.'

Interestingly, Christie and Lucy, two of the more isolated and vulnerable young people in this pathway, had the most thought-through and strategic visions for their futures. In terms of future relationships, Christie described her ideal partner as 'someone who's ambitious. You know, works hard and has goals and works hard towards them.' Given this, it was not surprising that her aspirations were ambitious and closely calculated:

> I need to do about six years all up. I need to get honours and get my Masters to be a psychologist – that's what I'm gonna be. After this year, what I'll do is, I'll work full time in the big three-month holiday at the end of each year. It depends on where I work, you know, I'll probably still need to work part time, but that should be enough to get me through the year.
>
> (Christie)

Similarly, in spite of her recurrent depression, or perhaps in defence against it, Lucy possessed a detailed blueprint for her future:

> I have my future planned. Well, not all of it! I chose my subjects for next year to coincide with my career, which is nursing. I'm pretty sure I'll pass

with flying colours. I'm looking to finishing Year 12 and then doing a year at TAFE [technical and further education] to get my nursing degree. I'm pretty excited. I really can't wait until TAFE. I just wanna like start now and go for it! But I've got a couple of years to go yet.

(Lucy)

Conclusion

For some in this pathway (Lauren, Kate and Damon), being forced to leave home acted as a circuit breaker in the family conflicts and crises that led to that event. This eventually resulted in an improvement to the parent/child relationship, and with that the possibility of the young person returning home. However, others (Christie and Tim) remained more or less estranged from their families though they had managed to house themselves in shared, privately rented accommodation. Ironically, Lucy, one of the two who left home voluntarily, had been forced to return home without there being a significant improvement in her relationship with her mother.

What separates the young people in this pathway from those in the on the streets and the using the system pathways is that at the time of their final interviews they had either returned to their family homes or had secured another source of private accommodation. On an accommodation measure of homelessness, this placed them in a stronger position than their street-based and service-based counterparts. However, the unresolved mental health and drug use issues prevalent among the young people in this pathway means that in terms of stability they were less settled and, we argue, in some sense more homeless than most of those in the using the system pathway.

When a young person who has experienced homelessness has secure, ongoing and stable accommodation and has in some way resolved the conflicts and issues that led to their homelessness, their pathway through homelessness might be thought of as having moved beyond that pivotal, often traumatic experience. The stories of those who have followed that pathway, the majority of those we interviewed, are told in the next chapter.

8 Going home

> I went out with a chick that lived at the refuge one night and I came home and she stayed out and the next day a fella rang up and said, 'Oh, she died last night.' And it was like, 'Oh my God!' It was just crazy. And then I moved back to Geelong with my adoptive parents, 'cause I just wanted to go, 'Oh, fuck this, I've had enough.'
>
> (Emma)

The defining characteristic of the young people in this pathway was that their period of homelessness was comparatively brief. Hence their experiences of homelessness were less varied than those in the other pathways. Another significant point of contrast between the experiences of the young people in the going home pathway and most of those in the other three pathways was that over half maintained positive contact with a member of their family or extended family. This provided them with support during their period of homelessness and also increased the likelihood of them being accommodated within the wider family in the future.

Accommodation

Only two of the young people in this pathway had lived either on the street or in squats, while six of the 22 had not accessed any service-based accommodation. In accord with the shorter duration of their experiences of homelessness, the young people in this pathway moved, on average, only two or three times in the 18 months between leaving home and their interview. However, the accommodation experiences of five in the pathway did not conform to this general pattern. Instead, their pathways through homelessness were complex and convoluted and involved ten or more moves, mostly couch surfing at friends' or relatives' places, and with minimal use of refuges or supervised houses. Even so, at the time of the interview they had all been stably accommodated for at least six months.

Seven of the 22 young people accessed both refuges and medium-term accommodation, another four used refuges only and five accessed only medium-term accommodation services. Of those who used medium-term accommodation, most moved through to stable rental accommodation or back to friends' places or to their family home. None of the 22 had repeated stays in crisis or medium-term accommodation.

The accommodation experiences of our five featured young people broadly mirror those of the pathway. One, Phoebe, did not access any accommodation services. After leaving her uncle and aunt's house she moved in with her boyfriend, then they travelled to Brisbane together. Their lifestyle in Brisbane was transient, focused as it was primarily on the acquisition and consumption of marijuana. After several months Phoebe began to miss Melbourne and briefly returned there without her boyfriend. During that time she attempted but failed to access crisis accommodation. 'But when I came to Melbourne and looked for somewhere to live, there was nowhere 'cause the waiting list was too long. There were too many people that needed some-where. . . . You'd probably have to wait a few days.' Instead of doing that, Phoebe returned to Brisbane and her boyfriend.

In contrast, Tom's accommodation experience was, in its vulner-ability, more akin to those of his street-based and service-based counterparts. Having left his stepfather's house, he turned to his friends for support:

> I went and stayed at a mate's place for three days. So that was all right. I just went to school and I had no problems. I went and got the rest of my stuff. . . . Then I stayed with one other mate for a night, and that was it. . . . My mates didn't really help. I told 'em the situation and they're just like, they didn't want to know about it, basically. They just put me up for the night and that was that.
>
> (Tom)

Feeling like he 'had to basically help myself, because no one else would', Tom did this by seeking professional advice from his school counsellor. She provided him with the number of a youth support services:

> So I gave them a call and went down and saw them and they found me places to live. They were very helpful and good; easy to talk to. I went

there like at ten o'clock at night, so they couldn't find me something right
there and then. So they did that the next day. They found me a motel . . .
After that, they found me a refuge. There was six people there. It was
pretty good. I mean, it was a two-storey place, you know, fairly nice and
neat and clean and all that.

(Tom)

Tom was then placed in transitional housing and from there he
arranged to move in with his grandmother and his uncle. 'The usual
three-bedroom place . . . except my grandma's got a lot of clutter. I
basically spend all the time in my room. . . . Basically, I get home
from work, put my bag down, go lie on the bed, turn the TV on, and
that's it.'

When Suzie's father told her to leave he was also effectively evicting
Suzie's friend, who had left her own parents' house a few weeks earlier
and had been staying with Suzie and her father. The young women
rented a flat together. The problem was they barely had enough
money to cover the rent. 'Centrelink fucked me around and didn't pay
me for the first six weeks and then didn't back pay me. . . . Like all I
had was what my nanna gave me – my nanna put it in my bank
account, the amount of rent I needed every month, plus 20 dollars
every week.' Even with her grandmother's support, without receiving
her youth allowance Suzie's private rental arrangement was
unsustainable. Hence she and her friend applied for transitional
housing. 'I was living off bread and rice and pasta and then I got –
my Centrelink payment started the day before I moved into the
transitional housing, which is really good. So from then, like, my rent
was a lot cheaper; 15 dollars a week.'

When the lease on Suzie's transitional house was coming up for
renewal, her boyfriend said '"Move in with me," and I'm thinking,
"Yeah, you're joking," and he's going, "No, I'm serious. Move in
with me." So I did.' By the time of her interview, Suzie had been
living with her boyfriend for seven months. She was in no doubt that
her move away from home had been for the best:

I'm so happy that I moved out of home. Like I could not stand living with
my dad, like even if someone paid me a million dollars a week to live with
him, I wouldn't. . . . I wouldn't put up with it again. And I like being
independent. I like doing what I want when I want, going out when I want,
coming home four days later if I want.

(Suzie)

Similar to Ben in the on the streets pathway, who found the stric-
tures of supervised housing an affront to his desire for independence,

Nick was shocked that, having been forced to leave the rule-dominated environment governed by his father, he found himself subjected to new 'curfews and chores' at a refuge. Thus, when he described it as being 'kind of like home' he was not being complimentary. Nick was like Ben in another way too, in that at least initially he saw himself as quite different from those around him:

> I didn't see myself as homeless, you know, 'cause I had a roof over my head. You know, I had a bed to sleep in, there was food in the cupboard. You know, like, I wasn't homeless even – just because I wasn't living at my home. It just didn't really mean shit to me, you know. It just means I was living at a different place. Except there was people, other people living there and it had a name. You know, it's a refuge. So what? You know, I needed somewhere to stay.
>
> (Nick)

Despite not appreciating its rules and regulations, Nick stayed at the refuge longer than was officially allowed. 'Well the longest like you could stay, right, was six weeks and I was there for like, aw, I was there for seven weeks and then I went to detox for ten days and I come back and I was there for another four and a half weeks. And then I got kicked out.' Interestingly, it wasn't until he left the refuge that Nick began to think of himself as homeless. 'Yeah, like, not while I was living in the refuge, like when I was living around with mates, that was when I saw myself as homeless, because I was jumping from house to house, mate to mate. So I did not have a stable place to live.'

As with many in the going home pathway, in hindsight Nick thought of this period of homelessness as something positive. Being forced to look after himself gave him a new appreciation of his parents, so that when he moved back in with them he brought with him a more cooperative attitude:

> Yeah, it's been bad, but it's, it's been good, you know. Like, it changed me for the better, you know. I had to learn it the hard way. Like I had to get an idea, you know – I now know what, what it's about, you know, out there, like, when you're living by yourself and you have to fend for yourself. I know what it's all about now. So, yeah, I'm just gonna stay at home as long as I can, you know. I'm gonna be, you know, be like associating with my parents as much as I can, you know.
>
> (Nick)

Emma too remained in a refuge for the maximum time permitted. Having been kicked out of her mother's house, she knew that her grandparents would welcome her back, but a combination of pride and concern stopped her from returning to them. Pride, because when she left them she was confident she could make her way in the world on her own, without their support. And concern because 'I'd put them under so much stress as it was, you know, like with all of the shit' and she did not want to add to their burden. The refuge provided Emma with the time and space with which to resolve her dilemma:

> That first day in the refuge I felt shattered. I sort of didn't know who I was and like, um, I, I don't know, I sort of – I felt stuffed like, I knew I couldn't go back to my biological mother, but I wouldn't wanna . . . So I sort of felt really, really stuffed. That's why I stayed there for like a month and a half, two months. But in the end I just thought, 'Fuck it', and my pride didn't get in the way of me going back.
>
> (Emma)

Relationships

Relationships were pivotal to the abilities of the young people in this pathway to move through homelessness and into stable accommodation. We have seen the importance of the interventions of loving partners in restoring a sense of self-worth in the cases of Kayla and Jamie in the on the streets pathway and the efforts of workers to find service-based accommodation for some of those in the using the system pathway. We have also seen the potential for family reconciliation made possible by ongoing parental contact in the in and out of home pathway; for those in the going home pathway, ongoing positive relationships with at least one of family, partners and/or workers featured in their pathways out of homelessness.

The 22 young people in this pathway can be categorized according to which of these three types of relationship was most important to their transition through homelessness. The first of these clusters comprised the five most transient young people who, in describing their pathways out of homelessness, emphasized the importance of their relationships with members of their extended family rather than their limited stays in refuges or transitional housing programmes. It was the care, the emotional and material support of their relatives, that proved crucial in enabling these young people to again secure stable accommodation.

A second cluster, comprising almost one-third of the young people, followed a classic transitional pathway through the youth accommodation service system. From home, they went (sometimes via a very brief stay with a friend) to a refuge and from there, directly to medium-term accommodation and on to stable housing. These young people stressed how significant their relationships with service workers had been in their pathways out of homelessness. While they acknowledged the importance of the material support they received through services, it was the emotional support given by individual workers that figured most for them. Encouragement and affirmation from these workers fostered their self-confidence and self-belief, enabling them to take the necessary steps to exit homelessness.

Those in the third and largest cluster, representing half of the young people in this pathway, emphasized their relationship with a boyfriend or girlfriend when describing their pathway out of homelessness. Often, as with Suzie, the existence of the boyfriend or girlfriend was a key source of tension in the family conflict that precipitated them leaving home. In this way, the partner can be seen as both a cause and a cure of the young person's homelessness. When these young people left home, they initially stayed at a friend's house (often their boyfriend's or girlfriend's parents' house) and from there secured stable accommodation, typically a private rental property with their partner. Several of them had brief stays in an accommodation service between couch surfing at friends' houses and finding their own rental property. These young people did not usually identify themselves as homeless or as service users and tended to emphasize their desire and capacity to be independent. All were employed and/or in schooling at the time of their interview and most came from close families with whom they retained positive relationships over the longer term.

Family

The experiences of our five featured young people cover all clusters. Tom's experience exemplifies those for whom familial relationships were of primary importance. While he received limited support from his friends and from youth and accommodation services, it was his ongoing relationship with his grandmother that finally resulted in him regaining stable accommodation. It was also to grandparents that Emma turned when her time at the refuge finally expired. It was their generosity and willingness to take her back even after she had left them to live with her mother against their advice that put an end to her homelessness and again provided her with a stable place to live, a home. Emma acknowledged her debt to them. 'Like my adoptive parents, my grandparents, they're grouse. Like, you know, they're always there for me. . . . I mean, they've helped me out of so much shit.'

For Nick, as with some in the in and out of home pathway, leaving home operated as a circuit breaker in his familial relationships. Nick had always got along well with his mum who he considered 'a legend', the 'nicest lady', and this positive relationship endured once he left home and made his return easier. In the interim, his time away from home gave him a new perspective on and appreciation for his parents. 'Now I'm getting older and like I've started to realize that they're not gonna be around like for all my life, you know. So I've gotta, like, be nice to them and like don't get them worked up. You know, 'cause they – I've like put them through a fair bit of stress.' This change in attitude resulted in a change in behaviour for both Nick and his parents and better communication and mutual understanding:

> Like we're talking more like, you know, we talk. My parents never used to talk to me normal, like, with manners and that kind of thing. You know, so they're getting better with that, you know. So I'm respecting them more. So I've had to tell 'em, 'Don't talk to me like I'm some sort of dog or something. You know, I'm a human and I need to be spoken to civil.' You know, 'cause in the past it's, like, got me mental. . . . They're getting better, you know. They've realized that that's the way I am and if they want the house to be happy, that's the way it has to be. Like the way I should speak to my olds, you know, the way they should be treated, you know, like with respect and, you know, manners.
>
> (Nick)

His improved relations with his parents meant that by the time of the interview Nick's view of his family life had been transformed from the one he had held when his father had ordered him to leave the family home. 'Most of the people I know either live with their mum or their dad or they live with both their parents, and they don't live very well, you know, so I'm aware of that kind of thing and like I'm – I reckon I'm just lucky.'

Suzie's nan materially supported her after she left home and Suzie also maintained a strong bond with one of her uncles. 'Me and him have always been very close. Like he could ring me up and he'll go, "Oh, I can't talk for long, because like I'm on my way out and I just rang up to see how you were," and like, we'll be on the phone for three hours.' These gestures of support helped keep Suzie connected to her family while she was homeless. In another sense, much like Nick, the move from home had a positive effect on Suzie's relationship with her father, though in her case it did not result in a return to his home:

> He was never comfortable with me, we always fought and it was much better me moving out. And, um, so me moving out actually made me and

him actually talk without fighting these days. . . . It's so much better now because we can get along. . . . He accepted it after I moved out of home. Him and my boyfriend actually became very good friends.

(Suzie)

With the day-to-day conflict removed from their relationship, Suzie and her father found new ways to support each other and developed a renewed affection for each other. Suzie now visited her dad once a week, on Saturdays. And for his part, he has found ways to affirm and materially support her new life. For example, when he realized that Suzie needed a washing machine he gave her his quite new model and bought himself a replacement.

As we have seen, Phoebe's departure from her uncle and aunt's house represented a conscious reorientation of her life away from her extended family and towards her friends (see pp. 69–70). While her family relationships were not pivotal in her regaining stable accommodation, there is a sense in the interview that, to the degree that she had succeeded in her quest to become reconciled with the trauma of her past, her renewed contact with her mother was an important part of the process. Suffering from severe schizophrenia, Phoebe's mother was living in a women's refuge. Since returning to Melbourne from Queensland, Phoebe visited her 'all the time'. 'I have to relate myself to my mother, to – in order to grow up. It's been a really hard concept, just thinking, "How am I like her?" And I don't want to be like her. But I have to admit to myself that I am slightly like her, but not necessarily in a bad way.' Ever since her grandmother's death, Phoebe has felt that 'it's been just me and my mum getting closer'. In terms of her uncle and aunt, Phoebe had not seen them much since settling back in Melbourne 'because I feel ashamed of what I've done . . . I feel ashamed that I left all of a sudden and 'cause I was on drugs and stuff'.

Professionals

While it was Emma's grandparents who provided her with stable accommodation once she decided to return to them, it was a worker in the refuge in which she was staying who encouraged her to make this and other positive decisions:

She sort of felt like a big sister, in a way. Like, you know, I'd sort of tell her how I was feeling and she'd – I don't know, she'd just tell me, you know, 'Emma, you're not like that. Okay, you've done this, you've done that, but are you doing it now? Are you trying to still do it now or are you trying to stop doing it?' . . . I'd hang around with her and, I don't know, we'd just get into these deep and meaningful conversations and, I don't know, it was just, it was just a really good place to be.

(Emma)

This kind of positive intervention by a service worker in the life of a young person experiencing homelessness is typical of the accounts given by those in the second cluster in the going home pathway. Interestingly, in general, these relationships were not valued by the young people for their strategic or practical outcomes but rather for their affirming, friendship-like qualities.

Even when a young person's relationship with a service worker is not instrumental in them gaining stable accommodation, it can help improve their self-esteem and self-confidence. As we saw with Craig and Jamie, two of the most vulnerable and isolated young people in the on the streets pathway, the everyday conduct and conversations of service workers, their small demonstrations of care and concern, can have large and lasting impacts on the lives of young people experiencing homelessness. In the going home pathway, Phoebe said of the women she encountered in a Job Network office, 'They give me so much confidence. They all say, "Oh, you look nice, your hair looks nice." But, yeah, they're really good.'

Partners

Of the five, Suzie's relationship with her boyfriend Jawad best illustrates the experiences of those in the third and largest cluster within the going home pathway. As we have seen, the subject of her boyfriend figured prominently in the fights with her father that led to Suzie leaving home (see p. 72). And then it was Jawad who offered her stable accommodation when her period of transitional housing was due to expire. At the time of the interview, Suzie and Jawad were living in a shared house with another male tenant. The household functioned well largely because of the stability of Suzie and Jawad's relationship. 'Well, me and him, we see each other every day and we've never had a fight in seven months.' This social and emotional stability also had a positive impact on Suzie's mental health:

Well, Jawad has been a big help in my life, because I used – like my anxiety was really, really bad, being in a house where I didn't feel comfortable. Then when I moved, I was very uncomfortable to start off with, but the two guys made me feel extremely comfortable, made me feel at home. Since then my anxiety has improved a lot.

(Suzie)

It might be said that, according to most definitions, Suzie and Jawad and their housemate had succeeded in creating a home for themselves.

While Tom did not move in with his girlfriend Sally, and it was his grandmother who provided him with a secure residence, it was the care and concern of Sally that helped him to emotionally move beyond his sense of being homeless:

> If I feel upset about anything, two years ago I wouldn't have let anyone know about it; I'd just let it build up inside, 'cause I thought that no one wanted to know about it. With my girlfriend, with Sally, it's different. Now I'm learning that if I'm upset I can let her know, because she'll help me through it. And I'm learning that not everyone doesn't want to know about my problems . . . I thought that the whole family didn't want to know. My grandma, my mum, brothers and sisters – no one wanted to know, that's what I thought. So now I'm learning that . . . people will help me through it, and Sal is the best person that helps me through my problems.

(Tom)

Tom's relationship with Sally had a transformative effect on his life. Just as leaving his stepfather's house and his proxy-parent responsibilities resulted in his discovery of newfound freedoms (see pp. 70–72), so his relationship with Sally introduced him to new possibilities in terms of intimacy and connection:

> Communication is something I've never done in my life, because I've had no one to communicate to. So all my life I've just kept to myself, had no one to talk to, no one to express my feelings to or anything. So I've been learning to do that with Sally, because she's there for me, she will be there for me and she's an important person in my life.

(Tom)

Perhaps unsurprisingly given the way his relationship with his step-father soured, having now experienced a positive relationship with Sally, Tom saw 'love, trust, believing in each other, and communication' as the ingredients of a good relationship.

Phoebe had the same boyfriend throughout the study. 'I'm still with the same man, which is probably the only thing that is really the same.' But unlike in Suzie's and Tom's cases where their partners in some ways rescued them from their homelessness, in Phoebe's case her boyfriend seemed almost incidental to her pathway through home-lessness. This was because for Phoebe becoming homeless was part of a larger personal odyssey about her own identity and could only really be resolved by her. As we have seen with the positive influences of service workers and her reconciliation with her ill mother, others did impact on her pathway, though it would be hard to argue that they in fact altered its course. However, Phoebe's boyfriend did provide her with emotional support and love which she described as 'under-standing and caring' and, in a sense, they travelled the pathway together. At the time of her interview, Phoebe and her boyfriend were living back in Melbourne and had made a home for themselves:

> At the moment I live in an apartment on the first floor, and you walk into the lounge room and we've got the TV, the VCR, we've got a couple of couches, couple of chairs and we've got, you know, a pretty cool atmo-sphere. . . . So it's a typical house and we've got two bedrooms, one bedroom has the rabbits and one's got the double bed where I sleep with my boyfriend and a bathroom and a kitchen. I worked hard to get that, actually, 'cause it – I've been in so many places. Yeah, it does feel like home.
>
> (Phoebe)

Emma had been with her boyfriend for two years but he was a 'druggie' too and when she was trying to kick her habit 'he chose the drugs over me'. After moving back to her grandparents' house, she began seeing another man and eventually she moved in with him and one of his friends, into a shared house in a regional town in eastern Victoria. Emma wasn't convinced that this house was a home:

> The one thing I don't like about the house – because I've moved in and there's already two guys living there, it's their house, it's got nothing representing me in it. It's like, I don't have a spot that I like to sit with all my beautiful things and you know sort of – it's just a place where I sort of stay. It's not very – I don't know, warm to be in and comfortable. Like they love it, they think it's just wonderful 'cause it's got all their crap in it.
>
> (Emma)

On the one hand, romantic or sexual relationships had little impact on Nick's pathway through and out of homelessness. 'The longest I've been with someone was three months. You know, that's the longest. I've always sort of – a month or a month and a half, three weeks, like that.' On the other hand, if our study had been extended for another two months such a relationship may have appeared crucial to Nick's story, for within that timeframe he was due to become a father. Interestingly, when he contemplated his impending parenthood he expressed conventional notions of home and family life and his role in both:

> Like we're doing the right thing, you know. Like being there, you know, like, mum and dad; but we're not together. Yeah, but we, we get along. . . . Well, we'll be living together. She can – she gets Commission or, um, Ministry of Housing or something, and, um, so we'll be doing the right thing. You know, hopefully it's around like our area. So, yeah.
>
> (Nick)

Engagement with services

Although all the young people in this pathway sought some practical assistance from services (such as income support, health, legal and employment), the majority did so only briefly and five of the 22 stated that they had only accessed accommodation and support services once they had exhausted all other options. They cited a range of reasons for their resistance to services, including a desire for independence, non-identification with other service users, and feelings of diminished self-worth when accessing such services. In contrast, another seven in the pathway (all of them female) reported using multiple and diverse services and three of these continued this pattern of use throughout the period of their homelessness and beyond. Even more so than those in the using the system pathway, these young people were able to clearly identify, seek out, obtain and persist with the help that they needed, whether it be with accommodation, employment or other support services.

Tom was impressed with the help he received from a support service dedicated to young people and the urgency with which it found him emergency accommodation. Phoebe was similarly glowing in her praise for the services offered ('rent assistance, bond assistance, food assistance and like money assistance') by another non-government organization (NGO). 'They're really good . . . they'll go out of their way, like, she even bought me a uniform and stuff for work.' She contrasted this with the atmosphere and attitude she encountered in the government service, Centrelink. 'It isn't anyone's favourite place, but it's never been that friendly. . . . It's fantastic, but it's like everyone there has to do their job, there's no – there's nothing else to it . . . that's their job, you know.'

Emma was more scathing about the treatment she received from the 'job network people'. 'They look at you like you're a shitty person 'cause you don't have a job or something. They sort of treat you like a fool and things like that, you know. I just feel like saying, "Do you think I'm as dumb as dog shit?"' She acknowledged however that not all the workers were like that. 'And others are like, "Yeah, grouse, come in. Oh, I've got something that would suit you just fine", you know.'

Suzie was one of the few in this pathway who, at the insistence of her support worker, sought professional help for a mental illness. The counselling she received, however, was largely unsuccessful due in part, she admitted, to her lack of cooperation. 'Whenever I went to the counsellor, I wouldn't talk and I felt very uncomfortable.'

In contrast, Nick was someone who continued to seek help from a service even after it had performed its function, in his case finding him work:

> Oh, I still go to JPET [Job Placement, Employment and Training], 'cause like if I need something, or I need to find out something, you know, well, I get what I ask for. You know, if I need to go there and ask 'em, 'How do I do this? or How do I do that?,' you know, and if they know, they'll tell me. . . . They've helped me a bit. Like, um, just to help me think, think about life in a different way.
>
> (Nick)

Health

As with most of the young people in the three pathways already described, those in the going home pathway commonly complained of poor general health. Typically they associated this with their experiences of homelessness, particularly with their poor diets and, in some cases, their use of drugs. Tom explained how when he was homeless his lack of money impacted on his diet:

> There was a time when I was . . . living in transitional housing by myself and there were times there, in fact all the time there, where I would eat a chicken and make it last a week. Have a loaf of bread, a bit of butter, some vegemite, cheese, milk in the fridge and the chicken, and I'd have sandwiches. Then I'd go out and get coke and chips and have them for dinners, for lunches and breakfasts. There was a time in which my eating went sort of right down, past the drain, sort of down into the storm waters.
>
> (Tom)

Since moving in with his grandmother and uncle, Tom's diet had improved. 'Now, though, I'm eating properly, as in having proper dinners.'

Nick told a similar story about the toll his lifestyle was having on his health, admitting it had 'pretty much stuffed my body up'. Again, diet was a key issue. Although lamenting his lack of fitness, Nick saw his smoking as a positive; he believed it kept him skinny despite his heavy consumption of junk food. 'If I didn't start smoking seven years ago, I'd be like so fat the way I eat now. You know, I'd be huge.' Emma too was concerned about her diet and her general state of well-being. 'Oh, I feel like I'm about 30 or 40 in my body. Like, it sort of feels really old and worn out inside. Like, um, I don't know, I don't feel very healthy. Like, um, I really need to start doing something and eating healthier food.'

Suzie's main general health problem related to her asthma, which she kept under control with the use of a preventer and she made no mention of her diet. In contrast, for Phoebe healthy eating had become an important focus. Describing herself as a 'real health freak', someone for whom health issues were 'always on my mind', she still struggled to maintain a balanced diet when in the company of her friends. 'All the junk food – it's like something I have to deal with because a lot of people eat junk food and it's very bad for you, but you still do it, and it's not that bad to do it every now and then, but 'cause people eat it every day, that disturbs me.' More disturbing though was Phoebe's contraction of a sexually transmitted infection. When it was first diagnosed she 'burst into tears'. 'It was absolutely horrible, like, dreadful. It was the worst thing that I've ever felt in my whole life, and I thought it would never stop and I got really upset. That's why I came back to Melbourne.' Over time things had improved and by the interview she felt that it was 'pretty much sorted out'.

Drugs and alcohol

Of the 11 young people in this pathway who reported having periods of problematic drug and alcohol use, most had reduced their use by the end of the study and no longer considered it problematic. Generally, they did this without assistance from dedicated drug and alcohol services. This was true of the three of our five who in the early stages of the study described their drug use as problematic.

Phoebe reached a point where she became tired of the numbness that had originally attracted her to marijuana. She wanted to feel again, to think clearly and to confront her past traumas. By the time of her interview she had not smoked dope for six months. The effects of this abstinence were far-reaching and difficult:

> I've had to deal with stuff I've numbed for so long. . . . Not smoking, um, I just – I think differently. Like, I haven't really seen my friends as much lately, so I've been thinking about what changes I could productively make to, like to make the person I am now happy. Like back then there were things I could do to make myself happy. I'd always smoke marijuana, go to friends' houses and smoke marijuana and like that sort of stuff. That was my social life sort of then. And now it's like, well, I can't do that, I can't base my life on that, so what things can I do to, you know, productively to be happy? And that's why I'd – I've just been thinking a lot lately. And that's what I wasn't doing. I was thinking, but in more of a detailed manner to the situation I was in. But whereas now it's like everything all together.
>
> (Phoebe)

Drawing a link between her poor health and her drug use, Emma said, 'I sort of feel lucky that I'm still even on this earth to feel sick.' Having stopped using heroin and speed during the course of the study ('I still smoke a bit of pot here and there'), she felt fortunate to have survived her addiction:

> Just 'cause of all the drug use and stuff I did, like, I'm surprised I never OD'd [overdosed]. Like, in the end I'd use like seven grams a day to myself. Just over the top. Like I'm surprised I never died and, you know, and now that I am here and I'm alive and I'm off the drugs and, you know, my life's a lot more positive and better; it's worth living.
>
> (Emma)

Having realized that she had done some 'pretty crazy things' in the past few years, Emma decided to 'sort of straighten out' and 'be normal', stop 'doing illegal things'. The success or otherwise of this attempt to redirect her life lay, she knew, in whether or not she could beat her addictions to heroin and speed. Seemingly, by the time we interviewed her, she had, without professional assistance, succeeded in withdrawing from both drugs. 'I've gotten off of it, stayed off of it and just never want to go back there.'

Twelve months after he became homeless, Nick realized that his heavy use of marijuana, speed and inhalants was seriously damaging his health and his mental capacity:

> I made that mistake, you know . . . started smoking, man, you know. It's not good for ya, you know. I'd, I'd be twice as smart as I am, I'd be so much healthier or have a better body, you know, like, it's not good. . . . Like, I can't – I have trouble putting words into sentences and like, speaking and maths, you know. 'Cause I, I was really good at maths some time ago, and I, I done – I was doing good at school, but then drugs took over.
>
> (Nick)

His physical and mental deterioration caused Nick to take stock and to reduce his drug use. 'I just cut down because I was just going on the skids . . . You know, so I decided to cut down and just, I dunno, just do some little things for myself.'

Mental illness

As their problematic drug use declined over the period of the study, so too for most young people in this pathway did their mental health problems. Nearly all the young people in the going home pathway who suffered from a mental illness prior to leaving home reported that their condition had improved or had totally resolved by the time of their interview. Again, these changes were typically achieved without professional assistance or support.

Nick did not cite his depression as a contributing factor in leaving home, but once he became homeless, once he left the refuge and was couch surfing and he began to see himself as being homeless, his condition worsened. Such reactive depression was common among those in this pathway who suffered from mental illness. At his lowest point during this period, Nick self-harmed. However, as his circumstances improved so too did his sense of self and his depression. Since his return home and his reduced drug intake, Nick's mental state had stabilized and he had not self-harmed again. 'I'm – I feel better about myself. Like, I'm getting my self-esteem back up, and, you know, like I'm caring more and, yeah, just having a good life at the moment.'

As we have seen, Suzie's anxiety actually improved once she left home and was greatly aided by the emotional stability and support provided by her boyfriend and her other housemate. According to Suzie, this positive development occurred despite rather than because of her seeing a counsellor who she said 'was more dim-witted than me'. There is a sense that these gains in Suzie's mental health are provisional, that the underlying disposition that contributed to the conflict with her father and ultimately to her being forced from home remained. Even though she declared that her anxiety has 'just got better in the last few months'. She also admitted, 'I get a bit of anxiety when I don't have my mobile phone near me. When I can't see it I get very paranoid as well.'

Violence

In keeping with the lack of violence experienced by the young people in this pathway before they left home, few reported experiencing violence once they became homeless. As Emma was the only one of our five to experience violence in the family home, so too she was the only one to mention a violent episode during her period of homelessness, although she seemed to think it was more comic than violent. 'We got a little bit drunk, all of us, and, um, me and my boyfriend ended up having a bit of a blue about some shit – I can't even remember, it was just crap – and I ended up punching a window, like smashing it. Yeah, I've got a bit of a temper at times.'

Education and employment

At the time of their interviews, only three of the 22 young people in this pathway were neither employed nor studying. Of the remaining 19, the majority were either at secondary school, technical and further education (TAFE) college, or in an apprenticeship. While some of them dropped out of school for a time during the period of their homelessness, it was a distinctive feature of those in this pathway that most remained in employment, either full- or part-time, throughout that period. Those in work at the time of their interview were employed in low paid and/or unskilled jobs.

Having recently moved to a new town, Emma was one of the three who was neither studying nor working. Before the move she had had a succession of part-time and casual waitressing jobs and was looking for similar work in her new location:

> Like I'd like to get a job where I'd only have to work like half a day, 'cause I've always been really interested in, um – like I'm not very good at making clothes, but I'd like to try. But I was doing like beaded detail on 'em, like I've got stacks of glass beads at home – just doing really nice little flowers and stuff with beads. If I could, I'd probably try and get into that a bit more and just, yeah, spend me day crapping round doing that sort of stuff.
>
> (Emma)

Suzie was still at school, doing two Year 12 subjects, at the time of her interview. She was working towards completing secondary school in order to be eligible to enrol in a vocational diploma. Despite her light workload and the motivation of knowing what she wanted to do next, Suzie was a reluctant student. 'Well most days I don't start school 'til 1.30. But Monday morning is horrible. Monday, I'm there from 10.30 in the morning 'til 3.30 in the afternoon. I just talk all through class and don't really pay much attention.'

Employed in a supermarket, Phoebe said she was 'working a hell of a lot'. By her own assessment she had done well in her final years of secondary school and was now dissatisfied with the lack of stimulation in her job. Apart from her interaction with regular customers, the boredom of the job was alleviated only by the friendliness of her colleagues:

> If you don't have friends where you're working, you just get completely miserable. . . . We can't be just like machines all the time, we have to have social status in the workplace as well, otherwise it's just ridiculous. Even if you're only a check-out operator, even if you're just a cleaner or something, it's still important.
>
> (Phoebe)

Unlike Phoebe, Nick's job was new and he was enthusiastic about it. It made him feel better about himself now that he was working, 'not bludging so much'. The job was in fact a traineeship to become a diesel mechanic and represented something like the realization of a dream for him:

> Oh yeah, like, I've wanted to be a mechanic for a while, but it's just like no, no employer would give me a go. Like I had no experience at all with cars or trucks or whatever, you know. Like, no experience at all, you know, so I'm happy I found – got in contact with this employer and he's given me a go, 'cause he, he likes to teach people that don't know very much. He's a good guy and that's it.
>
> (Nick)

Tom was still at school when he became homeless but soon after he secured an apprenticeship. Regardless of his accommodation circumstances, throughout the rest of the research period he worked hard at his job, 'waking up at 5.00 to get to work by 7.30'. Tom enjoyed the challenges of the job and also its intrinsic rewards:

> In the building industry, and with tiling especially, you tile the room with good tiles, good equipment and everything, then you can actually stand back and look at the room, look at the work, and you feel good about it 'cause you've actually done something. And you appreciate what you've done.
>
> (Tom)

Positive futures

In contrast to the young people in the in and out of home pathway, and even more so than those in both the on the streets and using the system pathways, these young people had well-defined goals regarding their futures which provided them with personal direction and purpose and they were sustained by having a strong sense of their own agency. Many were highly motivated too and believed themselves capable of forging positive futures that would involve well-paid jobs, travel and stable housing. As we have already seen, the support of services workers, parents and partners was crucial to them maintaining this fundamental self-belief, even during this period of personal crisis.

Of our five exemplars, Suzie's clearly defined vision of her future most closely reflects the general attitude of the larger group. Despite her reluctant attitude to her secondary school studies, Suzie was determined to complete Year 12 over the coming two years so that she could then undertake a diploma in hairdressing. She considered this only a stepping stone towards her ultimate career goal:

> I'm hoping that within five years I would've done my 12-month diploma in hairdressing and started my course in architecture, doing hairdressing part time. I've always been interested in designing houses and stuff. I've always wanted to do that, but I want to do architecture with interior design at the same time, so I don't have to hire someone to do the interior design, I can do it myself.
>
> (Suzie)

While she was very definite about the course she wanted her career to take, Suzie was much less sure about the future of her relationship with her boyfriend. 'Oh, I'm not even sure – I don't try and think that far ahead with the relationship. Day by day.'

Phoebe's thoughts about the future were less defined than Suzie's and were borne of frustration with her current employment in the supermarket. As a result of her boredom, Phoebe had decided to return to study the following year. While looking forward to the prospect of greater intellectual stimulation, she also feared that her past drug use had 'fried my brain a bit'. 'I've been getting really insecure about how able I will be to do well at it. Like, because I've been so lazy with my brain, my brain's sort of half asleep all the time.' Again, it was frustration that, in a flippant way, made her think she might become a supermarket manager. 'I mean, it's not that hard to organize a supermarket, and they can't even get that right! It annoys me. I think I want to be the manager one day.' Phoebe also talked about pursuing her passions in the future. 'I'd like to be doing art work, making music, playing my clarinet, like all that sort of stuff. I have a clarinet; it's actually hocked at the moment. It's in hock, but it's only 45 dollars left to take off.'

For Emma, her projected future was envisaged against the backdrop of her past. The one thing she was certain of was that she did not want her future to be dominated by drugs the way her past had been. Considering herself a survivor, she wanted to make the most of what she now thought of as bonus time:

> I just realized how much time I wasted and like – yeah, it was good and I loved it, and the drugs were all right and all that sort of stuff, but I've sort of realized now there's so much more to life. Like, I want to get into a sort of job one day, like as a career where, you know, I'll help young people, like youths with drug problems and things like that.
>
> (Emma)

Nick believed his future would be defined by his determination to complete the traineeship he had recently commenced and an apprenticeship after that. 'So I'll do four years of training but after that I'm thinking of going to TAFE and doing like a management course or something.' Beyond 'the practical things . . . my education, like work and financials', Nick was not thinking too far into the future. 'Like I, I don't plan ahead, 'cause, you know, I could wake up dead tomorrow, you know, and then I'd be in shit because I have – I'm having a kid next month.' In terms of his prospective fatherhood, Nick and the child's mother had begun to do some planning; they had 'started talking about what we have to do, and what we have to get and like'.

Even more than Nick, Tom thought the course of his future direction was set by his apprenticeship. Tiling, he hoped, would become his trade and would provide him with employment long into the future. 'I'd actually like to make a career of it once I get my apprenticeship.' Another of his passions was the music he made as a drummer and guitarist in a rock band. Unlike some of his fellow band members who wanted the band to 'become big now', Tom had other priorities, first among them his apprenticeship. 'I don't know, it's just I don't want to become big right now, you know. I've got better things to do than try to become big in a band. The reason I started up a band was because I just wanted to have some fun.'

Conclusion

When compared with the other young people in the study, those in the going home pathway had moved through a (relatively brief) period of homelessness into a secure and sustainable form of accommodation. As we have seen, this stability was both aided by and reflective of an emotional stability provided by positive, ongoing relationships with various family members and/or a partner. Often individual service workers had helped these young people by emotionally supporting and encouraging them as much as they had through any practical assistance they may have provided. This greater stability was also fostered by a relative lack of personal and/or parental recurrent mental illness and/or problematic drug use.

It is especially noteworthy that the minority who suffered from a mental illness and/or self-identified as having a problematic drug or alcohol habit minimized or largely resolved these issues during the course of the research. Typically they did this without direct assistance from dedicated mental health or drug and alcohol services. For example, Phoebe's ability to first reduce, then cease her use of marijuana represents a crucial difference in her experience of and transition through homelessness in comparison with that of Ben from the on the streets pathway. While both these young people made initial choices for their drug habits and against the forms of familial support offered to them, Phoebe, who had a far more traumatic past, reached a point where she no longer wanted to be numbed by the effects of marijuana and chose to give it up. This decision enabled her to reorient and reprioritize her life around other goals, one of which was the securing of stable accommodation. In contrast, Ben continued to define his independence as his ability to prioritize his drug use over all else so that this one choice, repeatedly made, created its own necessity and left him, as he admitted, 'enslaved to the evil herb'.

The ability of the young people in the going home pathway to exercise their agency and to make choices directed towards more positive futures for themselves is what enabled them to transition through homelessness back into stable accommodation. While the young people in the using the system pathway made similar positive choices, the difference was the support that those in the going home pathway received from family members and partners, their interdependence with others. This support not only gave them the confidence and sense of self-worth to make such decisions, but it also guided them in that direction and often ultimately provided them with the material assistance they required. A good example of this is the way Suzie's nan gave her financial assistance and her boyfriend cared for her and eventually offered her stable accommodation.

Taken together, the experiences of the young people in this pathway suggest that in order to successfully move through a period of homelessness a young person needs the support of a family member and/or a caring partner, as well as social services that provide both practical assistance and some level of personal encouragement. With these support structures in place, these young people are often able to address and sometimes resolve the issues that led to them leaving home and, in time, make choices that create positive and sustainable futures for themselves.

9 Conclusion
Interdependence not independence

So if there's any advice I could give to anyone, it's don't shit on your family. That's it.

(Barry)

The preceding four chapters provide detailed descriptions of young people's experiences and understandings of homelessness and, where applicable, of their movement beyond it. In this concluding chapter we ask how these subjective accounts and interpretations can further our own understanding of the phenomenon of youth homelessness. We also outline the possible implications of our findings for future policy directions and service practice, particularly as they relate to a notion of interdependence. But first we provide a brief summary of key elements of the four pathways we created.

Pathways summary

Members of the on the streets pathway had the most problematic journeys. Their disengagement from education and sustainable employment left them disconnected and likely to remain marginalized, if not homeless. Those in the using the system pathway were, for the most part, highly motivated to complete education and forge lives independent of their families. Their connection with services enabled them to access support in times of personal, financial or accommodation crisis. Young people in the in and out of home pathway often fled highly stressed families that nevertheless remained supportive over time. Many continued to have ongoing mental health and drug and alcohol issues and tenuous connections to education, employment and accommodation.

Finally, the going home pathway was characterized by fewer personal and familial problems. Most had experienced only a short period of homelessness and had straightforward accommodation pathways, with their parents typically maintaining a connection and the young people often returning home. Supportive partners and/or positive relationships with workers and continuing engagement in education and employment assisted the process of them regaining stability.

There were commonalties in experience amongst those young people who were stably accommodated, irrespective of accommodation type – whether service-based or private accommodation. Young people in these two groups had less severe and more reactive mental health problems which reduced over time. In contrast to those in unstable accommodation, most did not report mental health problems at the time of the interview. Also, very few had problems with drug and alcohol use, unlike those in the unstable accommodation pathways, many of whom were still engaging in polydrug use. Generally, young people in the stable accommodation pathways did not report parental mental health issues or drug and alcohol dependence. They also shared similar accommodation pathways once homeless. For example, they had few moves compared to those in the unstable pathways and those who engaged with homelessness services were more likely to have had a seamless accommodation trajectory from refuge to medium-term accommodation. There were two notable differences between young people in the two stable accommodation pathways. Members of the going home pathway were more likely to leave home in order to move towards independent living. Those in the using the system pathway were more likely to be moving away from familial conflict or parental rejection. While violence was cited as a reason for leaving home by more than half of those in the latter, young people in the former did not report parental violence. It was also the case that those who were unstably accommodated, whether between home and other places or simply on the street, shared a similar drug and alcohol use and mental health profile as well as a similar history of engagement with homelessness accommodation services.

Across the pathways

How then can we make sense of young people's experiences within and across these homelessness pathways? The following discussion ranges across all four pathways to reflect on how the experiences of homelessness of these young people can be understood in terms of some of the issues raised in Chapter 2. As such, our considerations are focused through the following lenses: structural and individual factors; transitions; relationships; and policies and services. As the discussion in Chapter 2 reveals, we employ these categories fully aware of their limitations and interpenetrations, and also, in part, to further contest their ability to explicate the experiences of young people who are, or have been, homeless.

Social and individual factors

Consistent with Beck's (1992) individualization thesis and Giddens's (1990, 1991) notion that people in modernity treat their lives as reflexive biographical projects – that 'we are not what we are, but what we make of ourselves' (1991: 75) – most young people in our study represented their experiences of homelessness in highly individualized terms.

Individual factors

As one might expect, the young people who left home to seek greater freedom and independence were the ones most likely to interpret their experiences as outworkings of their own agency. Having made that crucial choice, they typically saw the circumstances that flowed from it as pliable, subject to their own will and actions. The most extreme example of this attitude was Ben, in the on the streets pathway. Believing he and his mates had exercised choice by 'dropping out', Ben was convinced that he could reverse this decision whenever he wished, could return to the middle-class life he had rejected in favour of his partying lifestyle. Interestingly, in drawing a distinction between himself and his mates who had chosen homelessness and others who were homeless by necessity, Ben at one point does so via structural considerations, i.e. he and his type are not from 'poor families', but then at another defines the difference in terms of personal characteristics, i.e. he and his mates have 'brains', while other homeless young people are 'morons' and 'useless people'.

Many of the young people who left home due to persistent, ongoing family conflict also interpreted their experiences of homelessness primarily in terms of individual agency. In the using the system pathway, Fahra's and Maree's successful, planned and premeditated flights from abusive homes framed their experiences of homelessness. While tacitly acknowledging a structural constraint in the neglected physical state of the supervised accommodation offered to her, Fahra's response to this situation was primarily individualistic. Although she could reflect on the impact of this depressing setting on others, the action she took was to paint her own room. From an early age, Fahra learnt that if she did not like something it was up to her to change it. 'I make up my own decisions. . . . when I was seven I knew I was on my own.' Similarly, Maree's solution to the social unease she experienced in her shared, service-provided accommodation was to create a 'comfort zone' in her own room and to regularly escape to the State Library, where she could better concentrate on her studies. In terms of Giddens's understanding of the modern self, Fahra and Maree are exemplars of young people living in difficult circumstances, yet successfully operating within the discourse of 'reflexively organised life planning' (1991: 5). Faced with numerous individualized risks (e.g. drug abuse, mental illness, unemployment, violence, etc.),[1] they had, with careful planning and enormous determination and self-discipline, steered courses towards long-term education, employment and relationship goals.

The degree to which most young people in our study viewed their lives as relatively free of social constraints, as being susceptible to their agency, was demonstrated in their typically positive projections regarding the future. Some who came from more chaotic and abusive family situations than both Fahra and Maree and had, to that point in their lives, been far less successful than them in managing 'risks' and making positive choices, nonetheless had equally ambitious, often detailed, visions of what their futures would hold. One of the most poignant examples of this optimism came from Lucy, in the in and out of home pathway. Despite her mother's alcoholism and her own repeated suicide attempts and unresolved housing situation, Lucy was eager to finish secondary school so that she could attend a technical and further education (TAFE) course for a year and then enrol in a nursing degree. Interestingly, her recent past and present predicaments did not deter her from believing this future was hers for the choosing.

In contrast, others in the study such as Kayla and Jamie (on the streets), Victor (using the system) and Lauren and Kate (in and out of home), felt so battered by their experiences of homelessness that the present was a matter of survival, the future something only dimly envisaged. Even so, they generally understood their hardships to be the results of personal choices (e.g. drug use) or afflictions (e.g. mental illness), rather than as manifestations of social phenomena.

Considered collectively, our data attest to the capacities of young people to make strategic decisions that have positive impacts on their lives. This is most clearly demonstrated through four of the stories told in the using the system pathway (see Chapter 6). Although they continued to feel homeless, Fahra, Maree, José and Adam all managed to access housing and other services that assisted them in achieving their educational goals. During this period, they also all remained in part-time employment and forged or maintained important friendships. Significantly, all of this was achieved without the support of their families. However, the limits of this individualized, reflexively planned mode of experiencing and enacting upon homelessness are also underscored by the stories of those like Kayla (on the streets) and Victor (using the system) who, for social or individual level reasons, were less able positively to alter their circumstances through their own agency and action.

As mentioned above, two crucial factors impacting on the pathways and accommodation outcomes for these young people were drug and alcohol use and mental illness. Although both can be considered sociologically, as responses to or symptoms of post-traditional, modern life, the young people perceived them as solely individual matters: the former as largely a matter of choice; the latter as a disposition or affliction. In recognition of this fact, we have placed the following general observations regarding drug and alcohol use and mental illness on the individual side of what we acknowledge is a porous divide between social and individual factors.

Drug and alcohol use

Drug and alcohol use alone were not predictive of accommodation, education and employment outcomes for these young people. As we have noted elsewhere (Mallet *et al.*, 2003, 2005), few young people became homeless as a direct consequence of their own drug and alcohol use and most of those who did, tired of, or became bored with, the associated lifestyle and subsequently reduced and/or gave up problematic drug use over time (Keys *et al.*, 2006). Even so, it is noteworthy that a feature of the two most stable pathways (using the system and going home) was that they contained less young people with histories of problematic drug or alcohol use. This is unsurprising given that stability was a key criterion in our assessment of their accommodation outcomes, because, as the stories of the young people attest, heavy drug or alcohol use typically causes financial stress and has negative impacts on general and mental health.

The young people who continued to have problematic drug use tended to be polydrug users. Often they would give up one drug only to replace it with another. Most of these people had abusive or chaotic family backgrounds and/or had personal mental health problems. While they usually expressed a strong desire to change their patterns of drug use, the issues that prompted it remained unresolved. Perhaps, then, it is unrealistic to expect young people to give up a practice which seems either to ameliorate the effects of their mental illness or helps them forget or repress the trauma of their early lives.

Mental illness

While a minority of the young people suffered from clinical mental illness, many reported depression and/or anxiety that seemed to be a reaction to their life circumstances. When combined with drug and alcohol use, this severely affected their capacity to initiate and maintain positive changes in their lives, engage with services and establish sustainable futures. Over time it was evident that with social support, stable accommodation, family reconciliation, and income stability these reactive mental health issues were resolved. Often those with clinical depression and/or eating disorders and psychosis had difficulties maintaining stable accommodation, employment and education. This was especially true of those from highly chaotic, troubled backgrounds. Others though had obtained stable home- or service-based accommodation after 18 months and seemed to be managing their mental health problems. A number of factors were associated with this, including good help-seeking behaviour, positive experiences of mental health services, and ongoing social connections with family, partners and/or friends.

Social factors

The young people rarely described their experiences in social and/or structural terms, beyond acknowledging the assistance that they received from service providers. Even their criticisms of certain services were usually focused on the attitudes and behaviours of individual workers rather than organizational structures or systems (see Phoebe, p. 148). Where one might have expected them to blame society or express resentment towards those better off than themselves, this was almost never the case. Any sense of blame was directed inwardly, at themselves, for poor choices or behaviour, and/or at their families, usually their parents, though in a few cases also siblings. This then suggests the degree to which these young people experienced the world according to the neoliberal notions of self identified by Beck and Giddens. In this way, their sense of self and their understanding of society echoed those of the young people in a study of school leavers in south London who saw 'themselves as individuals in a meritocratic setting, not as classed or gendered members of an unequal society' (Ball *et al.*, 2000: 4).

There were, however, a few exceptions, the most notable being Jamie (on the streets). Where some young people made a point of distancing themselves from others experiencing homelessness, defining their identity against them, as being different from them (see Ben, pp. 48, 79; Toby, p. 103; Tim, p. 122; Nick, p. 143), Jamie identified with homeless people, seeing himself as part of a loose collective of people with similar problems and interests. For him, the identities of homeless people were defined and limited by everyone else, everyone who had more money, power and opportunities than they did. 'We're on your doorstep and you see straight past us' (p. 78). In Jamie's analysis, social inequalities and prejudices worked against people like him affecting lasting, meaningful change in their lives. As such, he believed there needed to be social, structural change to improve the plight of homeless people. 'I'd like to see an organization that would give homeless people work . . . the same day we get employment is the same day we don't have time to cause mischief' (p. 87).

Despite the fact that, apart from Jamie, the young people did not relate their experiences of homelessness to social level factors, taken together their accounts of those experiences nonetheless reveal how social phenomena affected their pathways into and through homelessness and ultimately their accommodation outcomes. By analysing these accounts across all four pathways we made the following findings.

Age

The age that young people leave home is an important factor in their pathways through homelessness. Most quantitative research, including that component of *Project i*, report poorer outcomes in relation to accommodation, education and employment among those who leave home aged 15 or younger. However, our qualitative research demonstrated that age was not entirely predictive of accommodation outcomes. A combination of factors, including family background, personal mental health, drug and alcohol use, connection with family, partners, social networks and accommodation type all mitigated the impact of age on accommodation outcomes. For example, the very young who moved early into supportive supervised accommodation continued their education, engaged in employment and expressed optimism about their futures. However, others who came from highly abusive and chaotic families remained on the streets.

Another noteworthy aspect of age is how, with the passing of time, many young people altered their understandings of the causes and circumstances of their home leaving. This reflexive process often resulted in them taking more responsibility for their role in the family conflict that precipitated their departure, and also in them developing a capacity to see the situation from their parents' perspectives. In some cases these insights were crucial to enabling family reconciliation.

Gender

Three obvious differences were observed with regard to gender. First, young women and young men engaged differently with services. While both sought practical assistance (e.g. accommodation, income support, employment, etc.), young women were much more likely to seek assistance for family and mental health issues. Second, parental disapproval of partners and an associated desire on the part of the young person for greater autonomy and independence were relatively common reasons given for young women leaving home. This was not the case for young men. Third, although equal numbers of young men and women were in stable accommodation at the 18-month interview, young men were more likely to be living back in the family home. In contrast, young women were more likely to be living in private rental with their boyfriend or in their boyfriend's family home. It is not clear why young women were less likely to return to the family home or why young men were not being accommodated by their girlfriends' families. What is apparent though is that boyfriends were often involved in young women's pathways into and/or out of homelessness. The implications of this finding for service providers is that they need to engage with the desires of young women to live with their partners, understanding that this is often both a trigger for, but also a potential solution to, their homelessness.

Ethnicity

With the exception of a small group of young people who were born overseas, most young people in our sample were from Anglo-Celtic family backgrounds. It is therefore difficult to say anything conclusive about the impact of ethnicity on young people's homelessness pathways. However, as we have seen, those young people born overseas did share common homelessness pathways and outcomes. All reported intense family conflict over cultural expectations of their behaviour and described feeling emotionally disconnected from parents. These first-generation immigrants had only limited, if any, extended family and lacked wider community connections. As a result, when their family life became intolerable they were forced to rely on services. All were highly motivated to continue their education and engage in employment, and to establish careers and homes independent of their families. The success of these young people in accessing services and creating stability for themselves led us to ponder if there was some particular quality to cross-cultural conflict that was damaging enough for these young people to want to leave home and not return, but not so damaging as to derail them from achieving their conventional aspirations. Whatever the case, we note that none of the young people with culturally and linguistically diverse (CALD) backgrounds returned to live at the family home during the course of our research.

Family breakdown

Two-thirds of the young people were living in single-parent households prior to leaving home. It was evident that family breakdown, whether it occurred in early childhood or in adolescence, had multiple effects depending, in part, on whether or not parents repartnered. Most of those in single-parent households were living with their mothers. These young people frequently described stressful households with significant conflict around independence, rejection of parental authority, poverty or financial hardship and/or violence. At times this was associated with parental substance abuse. Young people in these families often left home in their early teens and over time, with experience and maturity, gained insight into their own contribution to the difficulties of single parenting. Those young people whose parents formed relationships with new partners often reported feelings of displacement as well as problems negotiating the role and authority of the step-parent. Several factors impacted on this, notably, the length and intensity of the step-parenting relationship, the living arrangements, as well as the step-parent's relationship style. There were a couple of exceptions, wherein the step-parent acted as a mediator in the conflict between the biological parent and the young person. Generally, though, the presence of a step-parent made family reconciliation and a return to the family home far less likely.

Socio-economic disadvantage

Young people from materially impoverished backgrounds were more likely also to have experienced chaotic and abusive family lives, and their parents to have had drug and alcohol and mental health issues. As such, they were also more likely to have been in foster care and to have had a long and often unhappy association with government services. The trauma of these young people's pasts often found expression in their own drug and alcohol abuse and in serious mental illness.

Among homeless young people, those reporting this constellation of socio-economic disadvantage constitute the most vulnerable of the vulnerable. With no family support and a chaotic family life, returning home was not an option for them. Hence, it was unsurprising that these young people had the worst accommodation outcomes in the study. By necessity, through isolation and disenchantment with services, some of these young people were the most fiercely independent. Interestingly, though, this individualism did not mean that they were well served by policies and services predicated on individual rational choice theory. Rather, their disadvantage, their past traumas and current drug and mental illness issues, combined with their disengagement from education, made the task of them discerning their own best interests all the more difficult. In this way, their very independence, their eschewing of available services and supports, worked against them gaining assistance in finding and maintaining stable accommodation and merely reinforced their social disadvantage.

Transitions or a 'new adulthood'

The young people we interviewed, whatever their social reality, continued to uphold conventional notions of and hopes for their transitions into adulthood.[2] Most desired skilled, well-paid employment, a house, a partner and children. The fact that in many cases this envisioned future bore little or no relation to their current circumstances, and that there was no clear path between the two, affirms the symbolic importance that such transitions retain, while also underlining the sense that they represent a model that no longer reflects young people's lived reality. In other words, these traditional aspirations operate as ideals that for many can never be attained.

While these conventional future projections demonstrate the hold that the Baby Boomer transition model continues to have on young people, the examples of life planning exhibited by many in the using the system and going home pathways affirm Wyn and Woodman's

(2006) notion of a 'new adulthood'. They posit a 'new adulthood' defined not by a linear sequence of markers (such as school completion, marriage, parenthood), but rather by emphases on responsibility and choice, personal relationships and balance in life (p. 507). Drawn from and directed towards a general youth population, the third of these emphases, balance in life, is less relevant to a marginal population such as homeless young people, beyond the fact that attaining stable accommodation is undoubtedly a prerequisite for a balanced life. The personal relationships of the young people in our study will be discussed in detail in the following section, but suffice to say that the importance of them, not only to the young people's accommodation outcomes but also to their well-being and senses of self-worth, strongly supports the emphasis given to them by Wyn and Woodman.

The notion that responsibility and choice are now central to young people's experiences of adulthood fits neatly with the previously discussed theoretical assertions of Beck (1992) and Giddens (1990, 1991). Wyn and Woodman claim that 'young people have embraced the idea of building a life and are quite positive about their own possibilities' (2006: 508). As we have seen, this is a reasonably accurate description of the likes of Farah, Maree and Adam (using the system) and Tom and Suzie (going home), all of whom had indeed embraced the challenge of taking responsibility for and actively planning to create positive futures for themselves.

For a young person experiencing homelessness, key to this planning and building process is an ability to access services that facilitate the attainment of their goals. The fact that these goals remained traditional transition markers (i.e. home ownership, ongoing, skilled employment, parenthood, etc.) suggests that while Wyn and Woodman consider the post-1970 generation to be 'under pressure to become' (2006: 508), these young people still aspire to become home owners, parents and secure employees. Roberts (2007) claims that most contemporary young people do in fact 'reach adult destinations, meaning here that they marry, become parents, and achieve employment that will support an adult lifestyle' and that disorderly school-to-work transitions are 'usually the symptoms of disadvantage' (p. 265). Although our findings support this latter claim, we would argue that while young people still aspire to the statuses of stable employment, home ownership, etc., these statuses no longer define adulthood. In other words, young people think of themselves as adults, and are legally treated as such, long before they attain some or all of these statuses. Hence, for them, early adulthood is defined by the process of 'becoming' rather than any sense of arrival, and is typified by constant change and choice. This, we would suggest, is particularly true for young people who exit home earlier or in difficult circumstances.

Whether viewed as part of a transition process or as part of an 'emerging adulthood' experienced as process (Arnett, 2004), education, employment and accommodation remain crucial factors in the lives of young people, particularly those who have experienced homelessness. Examining the stories across all four pathways, we made the following observations regarding these three factors.

Education

The majority of the young people (25 of 40) remained in some form of education (secondary school, TAFE or university) throughout the 18 months of the study. While eight completed Year 12 either immediately prior to or during that period, another eight had dropped out of school prior to the study and 11 more did so during it. Although very few young people nominated issues to do with education as a reason for leaving home, their dropping out of school often coincided with this occurrence. Some who left school later returned or enrolled in vocational training courses. Five of those enrolled in a secondary school or TAFE college admitted to being disengaged with their education, that they were unsure how it related to their present or future lives and therefore found regular attendance difficult to maintain. All five either suffered from severe depression and/or had a history of problematic drug use. Regular attendance was, however, a more general problem, with almost half of those who attended school doing so less often after they became homeless. This though contrasted with the almost 20 per cent whose school attendance increased once they left home.

Employment

Over half of the young people (23 of 40) had intermittent employment during the research period. Eight of these gained employment during the course of the study. Another eight maintained employment throughout, while nine others were unemployed for the two years. Only three of those in employment worked full-time, with two having secured apprenticeships and another, a traineeship. In keeping with studies into the employment patterns of disadvantaged youth (Ball *et al.*, 2000; Byrne, 1999; MacDonald and Marsh, 2001; MacDonald *et al.*, 2005), the vast majority of young people in our study were employed in unskilled and insecure casual or part-time positions, predominantly in the service sector, in cafés, restaurants and night-clubs. As such, most changed jobs a number of times during the 18 months, though with no sense that their employment situation had improved. Rather, these jobs led only to more unskilled jobs with similar low pay and insecurity. Without further education and quali-fications, the young people seemed destined to remain in these 'poor work' (Byrne, 1999: 69) forms of employment.

Despite the low levels of pay and security offered by such jobs, the young people who possessed them experienced more stable housing outcomes, whether in the form of a return to the family home, or in shared rental or service-based accommodation. The most vulnerable young people, those in the most unstable housing situations, were neither engaged in education nor employment and training by the end of the study period. It is worth noting that this was more often the case for females than males.

Accommodation

At the start of our project, irrespective of age and gender, the most common forms of accommodation for the 40 young people was in a refuge or with friends, with a small percentage living in medium-term accommodation. For both young women and men, refuges were an important initial source of accommodation. By the time of the final interviews, only eight of the 40 young people were living in crisis, medium-term or other service-based accommodation. The majority were living with family or friends or had their own private accom-modation. Roughly a third of the 40 spent some time over the research period living back in their family home. It is also noteworthy that extended family members provided accommodation for a sig-nificant number of the participants, especially among the young men. So too did the parents of partners, though this arrangement was exclusively favoured by female participants.

Relationships

In terms of accommodation outcomes, no other single factor was more important than the nature of the young people's relationships with family and friends. It is perhaps unsurprising that emotional stability and support had a strong and direct positive effect on the young people's capacities either to return to the family home or to create a sense of home of their own.

Families

It might be said that family conflict causes youth homelessness. Certainly it was the common factor in all the cases in our study. However, as we have seen, this term covers a wide range of scenarios, including young people rebelling against stable, caring family environments; tensions over cross-cultural expectations; fights regarding boyfriends; reactions to external crises; shifts in family configurations; parental neglect; and domestic violence and systematic abuse. Hence, the family-level 'causes' of youth homelessness are diverse and complex and are entangled with both individual and social factors.

In our research, the nature of the family conflict that led to a young person's departure from home was predictive of the severity and duration of their homelessness, as well as of their ability to return home in the future. As already discussed, family configuration (i.e. blended) influenced the likelihood of reconciliation. Ethnic background, or at least the presence of cross-cultural conflict, also impacted negatively on young people returning to the family home. Similarly, young people from chaotic, neglectful and/or abusive families were more likely to remain in unstable accommodation and were highly unlikely to return home. In cases where parental drug and alcohol abuse and/or severe, ongoing mental illness were significant factors in a young person leaving home, they rarely returned. The notable exception being Lucy (in and out of home) who, after a failed attempt at foster care and a more successful time spent living with her uncle and aunt, was forced to return to live with her alcoholic mother. This, though, was not a reconciliation so much as an act of desperation, a last resort (see p. 120).

In contrast, when the family conflict arose from an external crisis and/or the parental mental illness was reactive and impermanent (see Lauren's, Kate's and Christie's cases in Chapter 7), the young people often reconciled with their parents and sometimes returned home once the crisis had passed and the parents' equilibrium had been restored.

Violence

Violence, particularly of the systematic and/or malicious kind, was another threshold factor in terms of accommodation outcomes and the possibility of returning home. In no instance where this occurred did a young person return home or even desire to return home. Three of the five street-based young people had been subjected to repeated domestic violence and, as we have seen (pp. 81–82), this pattern was repeated in their experiences of homelessness, with Jamie and Craig becoming perpetrators, and Kayla remaining a victim of male physical abuse. The fear and anger produced by this early and repeated exposure to violence seemed largely responsible for the deep-seated instability and isolation of these young people; their betrayal as children making it impossible for them to know who they could trust. In contrast, 16 of the 22 young people in the going home pathway had never experienced domestic violence, and the six that had depicted such incidents as isolated, reactive outbursts. Despite past conflicts, for these young people, the family home continued to represent security, a place where they would be safe, where the people around them could essentially be trusted.

Trust

Issues of trust and security, along with those of risk and danger, are central to Giddens's conception of modernity (1991: 19). As risk has increasingly been privatized, so too has trust. Hence, we have learned not to place too much trust for our well-being in social institutions such as governments and non-government organizations (NGOs). There-fore, the trust between child and parent has become even more crucial. Giddens argues that such trust 'can be seen as a sort of emotional inoculation against existential anxieties' (p. 39). In addition, he claims that the establishment of trust is 'the condition of the elaboration of self-identity just as much as it is of the identity of other persons and objects' (pp. 41–42). A knowledge and experience of trust is vital to the modern self as biographical reflexive project; to our capacities to form stable identities and to balance opportunity with risk. It is therefore unsurprising that when a young person's trust is betrayed or when they have never known it, they struggle to create positive futures for themselves. Certainly this was borne out in our study.

Reconciliation

In cases where the type of family conflict had not caused an irrepar-able rift between the parents and the young person – a fundamental loss of trust – reconciliation and/or return to the family home became possible when both parties maintained contact. Although Kimberley (on the streets) remained extremely vulnerable and had no intention of returning home, her mother's willingness to pay for reverse charge phone calls meant they were in regular contact. Having gained her freedom, Kimberley had come to appreciate her mother's love and concern, and acknowledged her own poor behaviour in spurning it during her time at home. The fact that she remained in contact with her mother meant she still had her support, someone she could trust and turn to if, as seemed likely, her chaotic, itinerant lifestyle ended in crisis.

In terms of the young people who did return home, their parents typically made overtures of practical and emotional support, often offering and/or seeking forgiveness for past conflicts (see Kate, Lauren and Damon in Chapter 7 and Emma and Nick in Chapter 8). Some also accessed family counselling services to try to facilitate reconciliation. In other cases, it was members of the extended family that provided the necessary support, acting as surrogates for parents who, through their own neediness or neglect, had lost their child's trust (see Lucy in Chapter 7 and Tom, Phoebe and Emma in Chapter 8). Regardless of other individual and social level factors affecting their lives, the young people who remained connected or reconnected with their (extended) families had a level of support that was reflected in their typically better accommodation outcomes.

Friends/partners

The other main source of practical and emotional support for the young people came from their friends, particularly their partners. At the time of leaving home, this avenue of support was often seen as oppositional, or at least alternative, to familial support. The vast majority of young people in our study spent their first night after becoming homeless at a friend's place. For many, this period of couch surfing was quite prolonged. While for Ben (on the streets), his group of 'dropped-out' mates operated as a surrogate family, many of the young people became increasingly isolated in their homelessness, the most extreme cases being Craig (on the streets) and Victor (using the system). As we have seen though, in the course of the research, even some of the most isolated young people entered into new relationships that radically altered their senses of self-worth, if not their accommodation outcomes (see Kayla and Jamie in Chapter 5 and Tom in Chapter 8). In reference to Giddens's emphasis on trust, Kayla's and Jamie's new loving relationships allowed them to experience trust for the first time. This had a transformative effect on their self-identities and their senses of security (see pp. 91–92). For Tom, his relationship with Sally restored the trust he once had with his stepfather (see p. 149). Slowly, he was learning to trust again, to believe that 'not everyone doesn't want to know about my problems'.[3]

More typically, such relationships were longer standing and pre-existed the research period. Often for young women, their relationship with a boyfriend was the focal point of the family conflict that forced them from home. As already noted though, these relationships were also frequently responsible for the young women finding or making a new home. For example, eight of the 22 young people in the going home pathway (all of them female) established stable accommodation with a partner. Of these, three moved in with their boyfriend's family.

Being able to depend on someone for emotional and practical support, either a family member or a loving partner, was a pivotal factor determining how the young people in our study experienced homelessness and, in many cases, how they emerged from it.

Policies and services

The young people's accounts of their pathways into and through homelessness do not include reflections upon current youth homelessness policies, rather they are reflective of them. With the already noted exception of Jamie (on the streets), their narratives reveal the extent to which they had imbibed a neoliberal notion of individualism.[4] Generally, they perceived their predicament to be the result of their own and their families' poor choices, afflictions and short-comings. Their prescribed solutions to these situations were similarly individually focused, concentrating on their own schooling, drug use, employment and housing. Hence, these young people almost totally lacked what C. Wright Mills famously called the 'sociological imagination', in which private troubles are understood as interpenetrated by social issues (1959: 8). For these young people, their troubles remained their own. At most, they saw them as outworkings of family issues. This highly individualized view of the self is reflected in and reflective of the social discourses that it implicitly denies; generally, in neoliberal, rational choice theory, and specifically in the stated aims of government policies directed at assisting homeless young people.

Supported Accommodation Assistance Program (SAAP)

Independence

In Australia, the state and federal governments' key policy and service response to homelessness is the Supported Accommodation Assistance Program (SAAP), which funds homelessness assistance, with the goal of helping people who are homeless 'achieve the maximum possible degree of self-reliance and independence through the provision of support and supported accommodation' (Australian Commonwealth Government Accommodation Assistance Act, 1994).

For the purposes of SAAP, young people are defined as those above the minimum school leaving age of 15 and younger than the age of 25. The SAAP funds a range of services for young people who by choice, force, coercion or mutual agreement become homeless. These services include congregate and cluster model refuge accommodation, transitional accommodation and support, case management services, short-term financial assistance, family reconciliation, links to employment, and education and training initiatives. While there is a diverse range of youth-specific services, many young people are assisted by adult and cross-target services.

Knowingly or not, SAAP's emphasis on independence and self-reliance posits a neoliberal notion of the individual. It implies that to regain his or her social equilibrium, a homeless person must gain or regain his or her independence, become autonomous. However, as the evidence presented in Chapter 2 attests (pp. 32–35), Australian young people remain financially and emotionally dependent on their family, especially parents, until their early twenties (de Vaus, 2004; Schneider, 2000). Given this, how appropriate, feasible and/or desirable is it to have 'maximum possible' independence and self-reliance as a key aim in a policy designed to assist young people experiencing homelessness?

For all its denigration of the collective, and its emphasis on individual choice and autonomy, the reality is that social policies inspired by neoliberal principles are invariably predicated on the smooth functioning of the smallest social institution – the family (in all its contemporary constellations).[5] So while young people increasingly view their lives as reflexive projects governed by choice and agency (Giddens, 1991), paradoxically, they do so while being increasingly dependent upon their parents for financial and accommodation support. The rhetoric of individualism obscures the fact that in practice the efficacy of individual agency is often based on familial resources. Hence, patent inequality is papered over and communal effort (i.e. the collective effort of the family) is misrepresented as that solely of the individual. This raises the question: If young people from well-resourced, supportive families are remaining dependent on the collective efforts of their families while they complete tertiary studies and establish themselves in careers, why should disadvantaged young people experiencing homelessness be encouraged to rapidly become independent and self-reliant?

Family links

Interestingly, another of SAAP's explicit goals is to 're-establish family links where appropriate'. While this does not necessarily contradict the aim of enabling self-reliance, these two goals would be in tension if the re-establishment of family links entailed a young person becoming dependent on family support. Perhaps, though, the inference in SAAP's aims is, in this instance, neoliberal in the pragmatic sense that dependence upon family is acceptable, but not upon the state. What though of the many young people who become homeless because they are fleeing abuse and neglect, the cases where re-establishing family links would definitely not be 'appropriate'? As we have seen with Jamie, Kayla and Craig in the on the streets pathway, these are often the most vulnerable homeless young people. Why then should we expect this most disadvantaged youth population to successfully develop and enact positive 'life plans' (Giddens, 1991: 85) without a substitute for the material and emotional support that their more fortunate peers are receiving from their families?

Services

The young people in *Project i* reported mixed experiences of homelessness services. Some were positive (see Adam, pp. 102–103; Tom, pp. 141–142), others pragmatic (see Fahra and Maree, p. 103; Damon, pp. 122–123), and others still were highly critical (see Ben, p. 79). One young person, Tim, was extremely positive about a particular service hub dedicated to helping homeless young people (p. 131), and equally negative about the rules and regulations he encountered in refuges (p. 122).

Most positive comments regarding services were, however, reserved for individual workers who had been particularly helpful and/or, more typically, had befriended the young person. These demonstrations of concern and friendship bolstered the young people's self-esteem and sometimes remained symbolically important to them long after the association had ended. In contrast, in the using the system pathway we observed the risks involved in service workers trying to negotiate a young person's return to the family home when such a return was considered inappropriate by the young person. Just as a service worker can play an important positive role in a vulnerable young person's life by extending and receiving trust, so too can they have a negative effect when that trust is perceived to have been betrayed.

While, naturally enough, the young people did not refer directly to the theoretical policy underpinnings of these services, their experiences of them should nonetheless be understood in the historical context of how SAAP-funded programmes and services have attempted to reconcile its dual goals of enabling self-reliance and of re-establishing family links in its dealings with homeless young people.[6]

Until relatively recently, such services clearly prioritized independence and resolving crisis over re-establishing family links. This priority is reflected in both past and current policy, service models and workers' practices. Since the late 1970s and early 1980s, following the collapse of the youth labour market, economic recession and increased family breakdown, the principal frontline response to youth homelessness has been crisis accommodation. Youth refuges, from their inception in Australia in 1979 under the Commonwealth-funded Youth Service Scheme (YSS) and later in the mid-1980s under the joint Commonwealth/state-funded SAAP scheme, were envisaged as a temporary form of accommodation for young people in crisis (Crane and Brannock, 1996). Refuges were the principal intervention aimed, at least in part, at resolving what was understood as homeless young people's primary and immediate crisis, namely a need for shelter. Employment and income support were also recognized as important related issues for this population, but these issues fell beyond the policy parameters of SAAP.

Throughout the 1980s and 1990s, SAAP-funded refuges sought to fulfil another of SAAP's key goals, to 'resolve crisis', in specific and limited ways. In practice, they defined a homeless young person's crisis simply as 'homelessness' and sought its resolution through the provision of safe, stable accommodation. To this end, SAAP workers aimed to assist young people to live independently. They did this in the main by supporting their efforts to access limited medium-term accommodation options and/or public housing through the Youth Housing Program, and/or directing them to employment/education programmes and/or income support. Where necessary and possible, young people were also referred to individually focused specialist services for drug and alcohol, mental health, and legal support.

Overlooked in this response, however, were alternative ways of understanding the nature of the crises precipitating young people's homelessness (e.g. relationships with family, friends, and/or institutions, poverty and neglect, the changing nature of family and adolescence, employment and education) and the range of possible solutions to these crises (such as family/couple counselling, respite care, extended family care/support, mentoring). Moreover, as Chesterman notes in the first evaluation report of SAAP, *Homes Away from Home* (1988), preventative responses and early intervention strategies for those at risk of homelessness were considered beyond the scope of SAAP.

This remains the case today, despite the proliferation of federal and state funded family- and school-based preventative programmes for those at risk of homelessness that followed in the wake of the Burdekin report, *Our Homeless Children* (1989), commissioned in the late 1980s by the Human and Rights and Equal Opportunity Commission, and the Morris report in the mid-1990s. Like SAAP, these programmes (e.g. parent/adolescent mediation, Reconnect, school-focused youth services) effectively cast homeless young people and those at risk of homelessness as distinctly different populations from their 'homed' adolescent peers, despite the general acknowledgement that homelessness is not an event, but rather a process. This approach is reinforced by the differing target ages of these programmes – 12 to 18 years for the preventative programmes and 15 to 25 years for SAAP services. Moreover, these preventive programmes cast the crises and their solutions differently. Where SAAP's diagnosis and cure is focused on the individual, those of the preventative programmes are focused on conflict and/or breakdown in relationships, typically between young people and their families and/ or with their schools.

Over the past five to ten years there has been a slight shift in emphasis in some Victorian SAAP services targeted at young people, particularly those co-located in generalist youth services. Following the lead taken by the preventative programmes, these services have focused more on SAAP's other key goal, the re-establishment of family links. This acknowledgement of the importance of family connection has been reflected in the casework practices of workers in refuges and medium-term accommodation units, and in the employment of dedicated individual/family counsellors in select refuges. In 2004 the Victorian Office of Housing funded a state-wide pilot project, Family Reconciliation and Mediation Program (FRMP), which aims, where possible, to assist homeless young people aged 15 to 25 to re-establish relationships with their families. While this project signals recognition of the importance of family reconciliation within youth homelessness policy and service delivery, this should not be mistaken for a complete change in policy direction, for we would argue that the development of young people's independence remains the dominant goal in SAAP and the Transitional Housing Movement. This, then, returns us to the issue of the appropriateness of this aim.

Interdependence

The young people in our study who had the most stable accommodation outcomes comprised the going home pathway. As previously discussed, 12 of these (and therefore over a quarter of the total number of interviewees) were, by the study's end, living back in the family home, with a member of their extended family or with their partner's family. In other words, their brief period of homelessness had been resolved through family reconciliation or surrogate family support.

While still considering themselves homeless, the young people in the using the system pathway had also secured stable accommodation and accessed other youth services that enabled them to maintain their education and part-time employment; in Giddens's terms, to actualize and reflexively adjust their 'life plans'. Most in this pathway could not conceive of returning to the family home. Hence they sought, and fortunately found, the kind of material support others receive from family, from government and NGO services. Our findings suggest that it was their ability to depend on these services that in fact enabled them to behave and to consider themselves (as others dependent on parental support do) as independent, reflexive young people, working hard to construct positive futures for themselves.

It is on the basis of these cases and the already discussed protracted financial dependence of young people on their families in the general population that we question policy goals like those of SAAP, which seek to maximize and expedite homeless young people's independence and self-reliance. We argue that such goals are misplaced, unrealistic and out of step with the reality of most young people's lives. While the majority of young people may conceive of themselves as autonomous agents, enacting choices in order to construct positive, self-directed futures, they generally do so with the financial and emotional support of their parents and wider family and social networks. SAAP-like policy goals confuse the perception for the lived reality, and then attempt to impose a more pure expression of neoliberalism on the most vulnerable population of young people.

The experiences expressed in the preceding chapters suggest that SAAP's goal of maximum self-reliance and independence sets homeless young people up for failure in the following four ways. First, it assumes that young people experiencing homelessness are somehow better placed than their home-based peers to achieve secure housing, ongoing education and employment without the financial safety net and emotional support provided by family, partners, and/or friends.

Second, contrary to the available evidence (AIHW, 2003; Council to Homeless Persons, 2004), it assumes that existing forms of service support (housing, income, education, employment, mental health) for this population are adequate. Third, in effect if not by design, it assumes that young people who leave home prematurely wish to sever ties with their families, especially if they leave in pursuit of greater freedom or adventure. Fourth, it effectively responds to all young people as if they are single, thereby discounting the importance of partners in some young people's lives.

In criticizing this policy emphasis we are not advocating a form of welfare dependence, nor are we necessarily attempting to alter young people's views of themselves as autonomous biographical projects by encouraging them to exercise a sociological imagination. Rather we are concerned that policies aimed at assisting disadvantaged young people reflect the reality of how young people in the general population live, which, despite their neoliberal, highly individualized conceptions of self, remains social. While contemporary young people may not prioritize collective identities based on class, gender, religion, political affiliation, ethnicity, etc., their individualism remains embedded in, and often materially supported by, familial and social networks. Therefore, we claim that homelessness service delivery and the related mental health, juvenile justice, and drug and alcohol sectors should aim to encourage homeless young people's sense of interdependence on family, partners, friends and the service sector where necessary. In the Victorian context, the homelessness service sector should follow the lead of the homelessness preventative services (e.g. Reconnect, parent–adolescent mediation), and develop the capacity to work with family members, including parents, siblings and other relatives. The homelessness assistance sector should also take the lead in developing service models and practices with young people's partners and friends. Where contact with family is unrealistic and undesirable, we recommend that the sector fosters young people's long-term connection with other significant adults, including mentors and service providers.

In her review of research and policies regarding the transitions of vulnerable youths, Collins (2001) suggests that others in the field, at least in the USA, have drawn similar conclusions (see Maluccio *et al.*, 1990):

> Some scholars question the ideological underpinnings of 'independent living,' suggesting that a more appropriate concept is 'interdependent living;' too much focus on independent living conveys inappropriate expectations of adolescents, emphasizes

social isolation, negate a need for connectedness, and places the burden of preparation on adolescents.

(Collins, 2001: 278)

Our proposed shift towards the encouragement of interdependence in the homelessness sector is in sympathy with broader policy initiatives regarding social inclusion and 'Third Way' notions of equality of opportunity and mutual obligation (Giddens, 1998). Around the time that our research was conducted, the policy context in the state of Victoria was dramatically altered by the state government's release of two policy documents which recast social disadvantage and responses to it in terms of social inclusion and exclusion and community renewal. This new policy direction acknowledged that a sense of connection with and belonging to community, including family and friends, is fundamental to people's long-term health and well-being. While this broadly affirms our position, our use of the term 'interdependence' rather than 'connectedness' or 'belonging' signals our intention to emphasize the needs of homeless young people for ongoing material and financial support, over and above the emotional support they would derive from a sense of connectedness and belonging. Where this cannot be provided by family and friends, we would argue that it should be provided by service providers on behalf of governments.

Summary

Whether interpreted according to individual or structural factors, or more appropriately through a theoretical matrix that incorporates both, the young people's experiences of homelessness expressed in our research strongly indicate that their accommodation outcomes are considerably more stable when they can depend on either family and friends or homelessness services for material support. In addition, when this material interdependence is reinforced by relationships of mutual trust, when vulnerable young people value and feel valued by others, they are more able to join their home-based peers in constituting 'themselves as individuals: to plan, understand, design themselves as individuals' (Beck, in Giddens, 1998: 36). The challenge for policymakers is to design youth homelessness services that acknowledge and effectively respond to the paradox that, for young people to project their individualism on to successful and sustainable futures, they continue to require material and emotional support from social and/or service networks.

Notes

2 Youth homelessness in context

1 However, self-reported reasons for leaving home are often confused and conflated with causes of homelessness (Beer *et al.*, 2003; Crane and Brannock, 1996; Fopp, 1993).
2 Though it must be noted that this was not a common problem with the 40 young people interviewed for this research.
3 We use this term here, following Crane and Brannock (1996: 16), rather than 'leaving home', to emphasize the phenomenon of home leaving rather than young people's agency or action in the phenomenon. Clearly some young people choose to leave home; others are forced to leave or are removed through circumstances beyond their control.

7 In and out of home

1 This, then, points to the limitations of both longitudinal social research and the heuristic value of the pathways metaphor in life writing. For regardless of the length of the span of longitudinal research, it must, by definition, artificially frame its subjects' experiences in time. While experiences that occurred prior to the study can be incorporated into it as personal history, creating a sense of contingent, narrative coherence to that point, what occurs after the study has ceased must necessarily remain undocumented. In terms of understanding individual lives, the timing of the timeframe of such research is vital. For people such as Maree and Fahra in the using the system pathway, the timeframe of our study seems to have captured crucial turning points in their lives. Their decisive breaks from abusive family homes, their securing of stable, supported accommodation, their lack of dependence on drugs and alcohol and their dedication to work and study all occurred or became evident in the course of our research. While these developments in Maree's and Fahra's lives do not enhance our capacity to predict what might happen to them in the future, they do suggest that some of the issues in their past, many of which led to them becoming homeless, have been decisively addressed, if not resolved. This though was not the case for the young people in the in and out of home pathway.

2 It is worth noting that he became aware of these diseases and the means by which they were contracted by reading pamphlets and posters displayed in a homelessness service dedicated to assisting young people.

9 Conclusion

1 Like Bessant (2002b), we acknowledge that Beck's and Giddens's uses of the concept of risk differ significantly from the way it is employed in youth policy settings. However, when the 'at risk' factors used in youth policy are seen to have been internalized by young people within a neoliberal, post-traditional paradigm, we believe the differences and convergences of these uses offer an insight into how vulnerable young people create and understand their identities in late (or radical) modernity.

2 Bottrell and Armstrong make a similar finding in their study of 'excluded' young people in the UK, when they write: 'On the one hand, there is evidence in the case studies of the desire for conventional pathways and rewards; on the other, there is recognition that alternative rewards are readily accessible in marginal pursuits, despite the risks' (2007: 364). In our study, key among these alternative rewards was the pleasure and release (at least in the short term) offered by drugs and alcohol.

3 For another example of the importance of trust, or its lack, in the lives of these young people, see Damon in Chapter 7, who said he did not know any 'people I can trust to do things for me, people I can trust to say things to' (pp. 135–136).

4 This is consistent with Clapham's point that 'discourses influence the shape of the interventions designed to "deal with" the problem of homelessness and that consuming the services can mean accepting the implicit discourse' (2003: 125).

5 See the (in)famous comments of Margaret Thatcher, one of the late twentieth century's key neoliberal socio-economic reformers: 'I think we've been through a period where too many people have been given to understand that if they have a problem, it's the government's job to cope with it. "I have a problem, I'll get a grant." "I'm homeless, the government must house me." They're casting their problem on society. And, you know, there is no such thing as society. There are individual men and women, and there are families. And no government can do anything except through people, and people must look to themselves first. It's our duty to look after ourselves and then, also to look after our neighbour. People have got the entitlements too much in mind, without the obligations. There's no such thing as entitlement, unless someone has first met an obligation' (Margaret Thatcher, quoted in *Women's Own* magazine, 31 October 1987).

6 Clapham asserts that 'the identification and elucidation of appropriate discourses is a vital part of the [homelessness] research task. It is then necessary to relate them to the "perceptive world" of key actors in a personal biography in order to relate the personal and the structural' (2003: 124).

References

Anderson, I. (2003). Synthesizing homelessness research: Trends, lessons and prospects. *Journal of Community & Applied Social Psychology, 13,* 197–205.

Anderson, I. and Christian, J. (2003). Causes of homelessness in the UK: A dynamic analysis. *Journal of Community & Applied Social Psychology, 13,* 105–118.

Anderson, I. and Tulloch, D. (2000). *Pathways through homelessness: A review of the research evidence.* Edinburgh: Scottish Homes.

Arias, P. (1962). *Centuries of childhood.* London: Jonathan Cape.

Arnett, J. J. (1997). Young people's conceptions of the transition to adulthood. *Youth & Society, 29*(1), 3–23.

Arnett, J.J. (2004). *Emerging adulthood: The winding road from the late teens through the twenties.* New York: Oxford University Press.

Arnett, J.J. (2006). The case for emerging adulthood in Europe: A response to Brunner. *Journal of Youth Studies, 9*(1), 111–123.

Australian Institute of Health and Welfare (AIHW, 2003). *Homeless people in SAAP: SAAP National Data Collection (NDCA) Annual Report 2002–03.* Canberra: AIHW. Cat. No, HOU91.

Bailey, S.L., Camlin, C.S. and Ennett, S.T. (1998). Substance use and risky behavior among homeless and runaway youth. *Journal of Adolescent Health, 23,* 378–388.

Ball, S., Maguire, M. and Macrae, S. (2000). *Choice, pathways and transitions post-16.* London: Routledge Falmer.

Baron, S.W. (1999). Street youths and substance use. *Youth and Society, 31,* 3–26.

Beck, U. (1992). *Risk society: Towards a new modernity.* London: Sage. (First published in German in 1986.)

Beck, U. and Beck-Gernsheim, E. (1995). *The normal chaos of love.* Cambridge: Polity Press.

Beck, U. and Beck-Gernsheim, E. (2002). *Individualization: Institutionalized individualism and its social and political consequences.* London: Sage.

Beer, A., Delfabbro, P., Oakley, S., Verity, F., Natalier, K., Packer, J. and

Bass, A. (2003). *Meeting the needs of young people in rural areas.* Melbourne: Australian Housing and Urban Research Institute.

Bender, K., Thompson, S.J., McManus, H., Lantry J. and Flynn P.M. (2007). Capacity for survival: Exploring strengths of homeless street youth. *Child and Youth Care Forum, 36*(1), 25–42.

Bessant, J. (1999). 'Deregulating poverty': Liberal-national coalition government policies and young people. *Australian Journal of Social Issues, 34*(1), 1–14.

Bessant, J. (2000). From sociology of deviance to sociology of risk: Youth homelessness and the problem of empiricism. *Journal of Criminal Justice, 29*(1), 31–43.

Bessant, J. (2002a). Generative metaphor, problem setting in policy and the discovery of youth at risk. *Youth & Policy, 77,* 33–46.

Bessant, J. (2002b). Risk and nostalgia: The problem of education and youth unemployment in Australia – A case study. *Journal of Education and Work, 15*(1), 31–51.

Bessant, J. Sercombe, H. and Watts, R. (1998). *Youth studies: An Australian perspective.* Sydney: Longman.

Bessant, J., Hill, R. and Watts, R. (2003). *Discovering risk: Social research and policy making.* New York: Peter Lang.

Bottrell, D. and Armstrong, D. (2007). Changes and exchanges in marginal youth transitions. *Journal of Youth Studies, 10*(3), 353–371.

Brandon, P.D. (2004). Identifying the diversity of children's living arrangements: A research note. *Journal of Sociology, 40*(2), 179–192.

Brynner, J. (2001). British youth transitions in comparative perspective. *Journal of Youth Studies, 4*(1), 5–23.

Buck, N. and Scott, J. (1993). She's leaving home: But why? An analysis of young people leaving the parental home. *Journal of Marriage and the Family, 55*(4), 863–874.

Burdekin, B. (1989). *Our homeless children.* Canberra: Australian Government Publication Service.

Byrne, D. (1999). *Social exclusion.* Milton Keynes: Open University Press.

Chamberlain, C. and MacKenzie, D. (1992). Understanding contemporary homelessness: Issues of definition and meaning. *Australian Journal of Social Issues, 27*(4), 274–297.

Chamberlain, C. and MacKenzie, D. (1997). *Youth homelessness: Towards early intervention and prevention.* Victoria: Commonwealth–State Youth Coordination Committee.

Chamberlain, C. and Mackenzie, D. (1998). *Youth homelessness: Early intervention and prevention.* Erskineville, NSW: Australian Centre for Equity through Education.

Chamberlain, C. and MacKenzie, D. (2002). *Youth homelessness 2001.* Melbourne: Salvation Army.

Chamberlain, C. and MacKenzie, D. (2004). *Youth homelessness: Four policy proposals.* Melbourne: Australian Housing and Urban Research Institute.

Chamberlain, C. and MacKenzie, D. (2006). Homeless careers: A framework for intervention. *Australian Social Work*, *59*(2), 198–212.

Chamberlain, C. and MacKenzie, D. (2008). *Counting the homeless 2006.* Canberra: Australian Bureau of Statistics.

Chesterman, C. (1988). *Homes away from home.* Sydney: Department of Community Services and Health.

Clapham, D. (2002). Housing pathways: A postmodern analytical framework. *Housing, Theory and Society*, *19*, 57–68.

Clapham, D. (2003). Pathways approaches to homelessness research. *Journal of Community & Applied Social Psychology*, *13*, 119–127.

Clark, C. and Rich, R. (2003). Outcomes of homeless adults with mental illness in a housing program and in case management only. *Psychiatric Services*, *54*, 78–83.

Clark, W.A.V., Deurloo, M.C. and Dieleman, F.M. (2003). Housing careers in the United States, 1968–93: Modelling the sequencing of housing states. *Urban Studies*, *1*, 143–160.

Cohen, P. and Ainley, P. (2000). In the country of the blind? Youth studies and cultural studies in Britain, *Journal of Youth Studies*, *3*(1), 79–95.

Coles, B. (1995). *Youth and social policy: Youth citizenship and young careers.* London: Routledge.

Collins, M. E. (2001). Transition to adulthood for vulnerable youths: A review of research and implications for policy. *Social Service Review*, *75*(2), 271–291.

Council to Homeless Persons (2004). New direction in program and service delivery. *Parity*, June.

Crane, P. and Brannock, J. (1996). *Homelessness among young people in Australia: Early intervention and prevention. Report to the National Youth Affairs Research Scheme.* Hobart, Tasmania: National Clearing House for Youth Studies.

de Man, A., Dolan, D., Pelletier, R. and Reid, C. (1993). Adolescent run-aways: Familial and personal correlates. *Social Behavior and Personality*, *21*, 163–168.

Després, C., (1991). The meaning of home: Literature review and directions for future research and theoretical development. *Journal of Architectural and Planning Research*, *8*(2), 96–115.

de Vaus, D. (2004). *Diversity and change in Australian families: Statistical profiles.* Melbourne: Australian Institute of Family Studies.

Dryfoos, J. (1990). *Adolescents at risk: Prevalence and prevention.* New York: Oxford University Press.

Dwyer, P. and Wyn, J. (2001). *Youth, education and risk: Facing the future.* London: Routledge.

Ellis, B. (1996). Leaving the nest, not! How young people with parental support are living at home longer. *Youth Studies Australia*, *15*(1), 34–36.

Ennett, S.T., Federman, B., Bailey, S.L, Ringwalt, C.L. and Hubbard, M.L.

(1999). HIV-risk behaviors associated with homelessness characteristics in youth. *Journal of Adolescent Health, 25,* 344–353.

Fine, B. (2001). *Social capital versus social theory: Political economy and social science at the turn of the millennium.* London: Routledge.

Fitzpatrick, S. (1999). *Young homeless people.* Basingstoke: Macmillan.

Fitzpatrick, S., Kemp, P. and Klinker, S. (2000). *Single homelessness: An overview of research in Britain.* Bristol: The Policy Press.

Flatau, P., James, I., Watson, R., Wood, G. and Hendershott, P. (2007). Leaving the parental home in Australia over the generations: Evidence from the Household Income and Labour Dynamics in Australia (Hilda) Survey. *Journal of Population Research, 24*(1), 51–71.

Fopp, R. (1993). The dilemmas of youth homelessness. In H. Skyes (ed.), *Youth homelessness: Courage and hope.* Melbourne: Melbourne University Press.

Giddens, A. (1984). *The constitution of society: Outline of the theory of structure.* Cambridge: Polity Press.

Giddens, A. (1990). *The consequences of modernity.* Stanford, CA: Stanford University Press.

Giddens, A. (1991). *Modernity and self-identity: Self and society in the late modern age.* Cambridge: Polity Press.

Giddens, A. (1992). *The transformation of intimacy: Sexuality, love and eroticism in modern societies.* Cambridge: Polity Press.

Giddens, A. (1998). *The third way: The renewal of social democracy.* Cambridge: Polity Press.

Hartley, R. (1990). The never-empty nest, *Family Matters, 26,* 22–26.

Hill, R. and Bessant, J. (1999). Spaced-out? Young people's agency, resistance and public space. *Urban Policy and Research, 17*(1), 41–49.

Horrocks, C. (2002). Using life course theory to explore the social and developmental pathways of young people leaving care. *Journal of Youth Studies, 5*(3), 325–336.

Hutson, S. and Liddiard, M. (1994). *Youth homelessness: The construction of a social issue.* Basingstoke: Macmillan.

Hyde, J. (2005). From home to street: Understanding young people's transitions into homelessness. *Journal of Adolescence, 28*(2), 171–183.

Johnson, G. (2006). On the move: A longitudinal study of pathways in and out of homelessness. Unpublished doctoral thesis.

Jones, G. (1993). *Young people in and out of the housing market.* Edinburgh: Centre for Educational Sociology, University of Scotland.

Jones, G. (1995). *Leaving home.* Buckingham: Open University Press.

Kelly, P. (2003). Growing up as risky business? Risks, surveillance and the institutionalized mistrust of youth. *Journal of Youth Studies, 6*(2), 165–179.

Kemp, P., Lynch, E. and MacKay, D. (2001). Structural trends in homelessness: A quantitative analysis. Edinburgh: Scottish Executive Central Research Unit.

Keys, D., Mallett, S. and Rosenthal, D. (2006). Giving up on drugs: Homeless young people and self-reported problematic drug use. *Contemporary Drug Problems*, *33*(1), 123–142.

Kilmartin, C. (2000). Young adult moves: Leaving home, returning home, relationships. *Family Matters*, *55*, 34–40.

Lanyon, A., Manicaross, M., Stimsson, B., Mackdacy, L. and Western, J.S. (1999). Support for the homeless in Australia. In S. Shaver and P. Saunders (eds), *Social policy for the 21st century: Justice and responsibility*. Sydney: Social Policy Research Centre, University of New South Wales.

MacDonald, R. and Marsh, J. (2001). Disconnected youth? *Journal of Youth Studies*, *4*(4), 373–391.

MacDonald, R., Mason, P., Shildrick, T., Webster, C., Johnston, L. and Ridley, L. (2001). Snakes and ladders: In defence of youth transition. *Sociological Research Online*, *5*(4). http://www.socresonline.org.uk/5/4/macdonald.html (accessed June 2008).

MacDonald, R., Shildrick, T., Webster, C. and Simpson, D. (2005). Growing up in poor neighbourhoods: The significance of class and place in the extended transitions of 'socially excluded' young adults. *Sociology*, *39*, 873–891.

MacKenzie, D. and Chamberlain, C. (2003). *Homeless career: Pathways in and out of homelessness. Report from the Counting the Homeless 2001 Project*. Melbourne: Swinburne and RMIT Universities.

McNaughton, C. (2005). *PATHE project final report – Crossing the continuum: Understanding routes out of homelessness and examining 'what works'*. Glasgow: Glasgow Simon Community.

Mallett, S. (2003). *Conceiving cultures: Reproducing people and places on Nuakata, Papua New Guinea*. Michigan: University of Michigan Press.

Mallett, S. (2004). Understanding home: Towards an interdisciplinary approach. *Sociological Review*, *52*(1), 63–89.

Mallett, S., Edwards, J., Keys, D., Myers, P. and Rosenthal, D. (2003). *Disrupting stereotypes: Young people, drug use and homelessness*. Melbourne: University of Melbourne.

Mallett, S., Rosenthal, D., Myers, P., Milburn, N. and Rotheram-Borus, M.-J. (2004). Practising homelessness: A typology approach to young people's daily routines. *Journal of Adolescence*, *27*, 337–349.

Mallett, S., Rosenthal, D. and Keys, D. (2005). Young people, drug use and family conflict: pathways into homelessness. *Journal of Adolescence*, *28*, 185–199.

Maluccio, A., Krieger, R. and Pine, B. (1990). *Preparing adolescents for life after foster care: The central role of foster parents*. Washington, DC: Child Welfare League of America.

Martijn, C. and Sharpe, L. (2006). Pathways to youth homelessness, *Social Science & Medicine*, *62*(1), 1–12.

May, J. (2000). Housing histories and homeless careers: A biographical approach. *Housing Studies*, *15*(4), 613–638.

Maycock, P., Corr, M.L. and O'Sullivan, E. (2008). *Young people's homeless pathways*. Dublin: The Homeless Agency.

Meert, H. and Bourgeois, M. (2005). Between rural and urban slums: A geography of pathways through homelessness. *Housing Studies*, *19*(1), 107–125.

Moore, D. (2002). Opening up the cul-de-sac of youth drug studies: A contribution to the construction of some alternative truths. *Contemporary Drug Problems*, *29*(1), 13–65.

Morgan, E. and Vincent, C. (1987). Youth housing needs: Housing questions? *Youth Studies and Abstracts*, *6*(4), 21–23.

Morris, A. (1995) *A report on aspects of youth homelessness*. Canberra: Australian Government Publication Service.

Neale, J. (1997). Homelessness and theory reconsidered. *Housing Studies*, *12*(1), 47–61.

Neil, C. and Fopp, R. (1992). *Homeless in Australia*. Melbourne: Australian Housing and Urban Research Institute.

Pears, J. and Noller, P. (1995). Youth homelessness: Abuse, gender, and the process of adjustment to life on the streets. *Australian Journal of Social Issues*, *30*, 405–424.

Powers, J.L., Jaklitsch, B. and Exkenrode, J. (1989). Behavioural characteristics of maltreatment among runaway and homeless youth. *Early Child Development and Care*, *42*, 127–139.

Quilgars, D., Johnsen, S. and Pleace, N. (2008). *Youth homelessness in the UK: A decade of progress?* York: Joseph Rowntree Foundation.

Rew, L., Taylor-Seehafer, M., Thomas, N.Y. and Yockey, R.D. (2001). Correlates of resilience in homeless adolescents. *Journal of Nursing Scholarship*, *33*, 33–40.

Ringwalt, C.L., Greene, J.M. and Robertson, M.J. (1998). Familial backgrounds and risk behaviors of youth with thrownaway experiences. *Journal of Adolescence*, *21*, 241–252.

Roberts, K. (1995). *Youth and employment in modern Britain*. Oxford: Oxford University Press.

Roberts, K. (2007). Youth transitions and generations: A response to Wyn and Woodman. *Journal of Youth Studies*, *10*(2), 263–269.

Robson, B. (1992). *Rough justice: A report on sexual assault, homelessness and the law*. Melbourne: North East Centre Against Sexual Assault.

Rosenthal, D., Mallett, S. and Myers, P. (2006). Why do homeless young people leave home? *Australian and New Zealand Journal of Public Health*, *30*(3), 281–285.

Rosenthal, D.A., Mallett, S., Milburn, M. and Rotheram-Borus, M. (2008). Drug use among homeless young people in Los Angeles and Melbourne. *Journal of Adolescent Health*, *43*(3), 296–305.

Rotheram-Borus, M.J., Mahler, K.A., Koopman, C. and Langabeer, K. (1996a). Sexual abuse history and associated multiple risk behavior in adolescent runaways. *American Journal of Orthopsychiatry*, *66*, 390–400.

Rotheram-Borus, M.J., Parra, M., Cantwell, C. and Gwadz, M. (1996b). *Handbook of adolescent health risk behaviour.* New York: Plenum Press.

Schneider, J. (1999). *The increasing financial dependency of young people on their parents: Discussion paper.* Sydney: Social Policy Research Centre.

Schneider, J. (2000). The increasing financial dependency of young people on their parents. *Journal of Youth Studies, 3*(1), 5–20.

Smith, J., Gilford, S. and O'Sullivan, A. (1998). *The family background of homeless young people.* London: Family Policy Centre.

Somerville, P. (1992). Homelessness and the meaning of home: Rooflessness and rootlessness? *International Journal of Urban and Regional Research, 16*(4), 529–539.

Somerville, P. (1997). The social construction of home. *Journal of Architectural and Planning Research, 14*(3), 226–245.

Stacey, J. (1990). *Brand new families: Stories of domestic upheaval in late-twentieth-century America.* New York: Basic Books.

Stacey, J. (1996). *In the name of the family: Rethinking family values in the postmodern age.* Boston: Beacon Press.

State Government Victoria (2001). *Growing Victoria together: Innovative state. caring communities.* http://www.dpc.vic.gov.au/CA256D800027B102/Lookup/GVTBooklet/$file/DPCbrochure.FA.pdf (accessed June 2008).

State Government Victoria (2005). *A fairer Victoria: Creating opportunity and addressing disadvantage.* http://www.dpc.vic.gov.au/CA256D800027B102/Lookup/SocialPolicyActionPlan/$file/fairer%20vic.pdf (accessed June 2008).

Symons, Y. and Smith, R. (1995). Noticed but not understood: Homeless youth at school. *Youth Studies Australia, 14*(1), 29–35.

Wardhaugh, J. (1999). The unaccommodated woman: Home, homelessness and identity. *Sociological Review, 47*(1), 91–109.

Weeks, J., Heaphy, B. and Donovan, C. (2001). *Same sex intimacies: Families of choice and other life experiments.* New York: Routledge.

Weiner, A. and Pollack, D. (1997). Urban runaway youth: Sex, drugs and HIV. In N.K. Philips and S.L.A. Straussner (eds), *Children in the urban environment: Linking social policy and clinical practice.* Springfield: Charles C Thomas.

Whitbeck, L.B. and Simons, R.L. (1993). A comparison of adaptive strategies and patterns of victimization among homeless adolescents and adults. *Violence and Victims, 8*, 135–152.

Whitbeck, L.B., Hoyt, D.R. and Ackley, K.A. (1997a). Abusive family backgrounds and later victimization among runaway and homeless adolescents. *Journal of Research on Adolescents, 7*, 375–392.

Whitbeck, L.B., Hoyt, D.R. and Ackley, K.A. (1997b). Families of homeless and runaway adolescents: A comparison of parent/caretaker and adolescent perspectives on parenting, family violence, and adolescent conduct. *Child Abuse and Neglect, 21*, 517–528.

White, N. R. (2002). 'Not under my roof!' Young people's experience of home. *Youth & Society, 34*(2), 214–231.

Williams, F. and Poppay, J. (1999). Balancing polarities: Developing a new framework for welfare research. In F. Williams, J. Poppay and A. Oakley (eds), *Welfare research: A critical review*. London: UCL Press.

Withers, G. and Batten, M. (1995). *Programs for at risk youth: A review of American, Canadian and British literature since 1984*. Melbourne: Australian Council for Education Research.

Wright Mills, C. (1959). *The sociological imagination*. New York: Oxford University Press.

Wyn, J. and Dwyer, P. (2000). New patterns of youth transition in education. *International Social Science Journal, 52*, 147–159.

Wyn, J. and White, R. (1997). *Rethinking youth*. Sydney: Allen and Unwin.

Wyn, J. and Woodman, D. (2006). Generation, youth and social change in Australia. *Journal of Youth Studies, 9*(5), 495–514.

Zerger, S., Strehlow, A. J. and Gundlapalli, A.V. (2008). Homeless young adults and behavioral health: An overview. *American Behavioral Scientist, 51*(6), 824–841.

Index